"How Come Boys Get
to Keep Their Noses?"

GENDER AND CULTURE

GENDER AND CULTURE

A SERIES OF COLUMBIA UNIVERSITY PRESS

Nancy K. Miller and Victoria Rosner, Series Editors
Carolyn G. Heilbrun (1926–2003) and Nancy K. Miller,
Founding Editors

In Dora's Case: Freud, Hysteria, Feminism
Edited by Charles Bernheimer and Claire Kahane

Breaking the Chain: Women, Theory, and French Realist Fiction
Naomi Schor

Between Men: English Literature and Male Homosocial Desire
Eve Kosofsky Sedgwick

Romantic Imprisonment: Women and Other Glorified Outcasts
Nina Auerbach

The Poetics of Gender
Edited by Nancy K. Miller

Reading Woman: Essays in Feminist Criticism
Mary Jacobus

Honey-Mad Women: Emancipatory Strategies in Women's Writing
Patricia Yaeger

Subject to Change: Reading Feminist Writing
Nancy K. Miller

Thinking Through the Body
Jane Gallop

For a complete list of titles in this series see page 275

Tahneer Oksman

"How Come Boys Get to Keep Their Noses?"

Women and Jewish American Identity
in Contemporary Graphic Memoirs

Columbia University Press
New York

Columbia University Press
Publishers Since 1893
New York   Chichester, West Sussex
cup.columbia.edu
Copyright © 2016 Columbia University Press
All rights reserved

Library of Congress Cataloging-in-Publication Data
Names: Oksman, Tahneer.
Title: "How come boys get to keep their noses?" : women and
Jewish American identity in contemporary graphic memoirs / Tahneer Oksman.
Description: New York : Columbia University Press, [2016] |
Series: Gender and culture | Includes bibliographical references and index.
Identifiers: LCCN 2015017794| ISBN 9780231172745 (cloth : alk. paper)
| ISBN 9780231172752 (pbk. : alk. paper) | ISBN 9780231540780 (e-book)
Subjects: LCSH: Graphic novels—History and criticism. | Jewish women in literature.
| Autobiography in literature. | Jews—United States—Identity. | American literature—
Women authors—History and criticism. | Comic books, strips, etc.—History and criticism.
| Women in literature.
Classification: LCC PN6714 .O38 2016 | DDC 741.5/973—dc23
LC record available at http://lccn.loc.gov/2015017794

Columbia University Press books are printed on permanent
and durable acid-free paper.

This book is printed on paper with recycled content.
Printed in the United States of America

c 10 9 8 7 6 5 4 3 2 1
p 10 9 8 7 6 5 4 3 2 1

Cover illustration: Lauren Weinstein
Author illustration, title page: Liana Finck
Book design: Lisa Hamm

References to websites (URLs) were accurate at the time of writing.
Neither the author nor Columbia University Press is responsible for URLs
that may have expired or changed since the manuscript was prepared.

For Jonathan

✿ ✿ ✿

Everyone, real or invented, deserves the open destiny of life.

—Grace Paley, "A Conversation with My Father"

*How do you know anything about your own history—most of all
the history of your subjectivity, and the part that
images have played in its construction?*

—Jo Spence, "The Walking Wounded?"

The Jewish mindset has driven me crazy my whole life.

—Vanessa Davis, "In search of the whole truth"

My own nose, which, surely, is, for all intents and purposes, myself?

—Nikolai Gogol, "The Nose"

I always start with the nose, that's all I know.

—Aline Kominsky Crumb, "Public Conversation"

Contents

Acknowledgments   xi

Introduction: "To Unaffiliate Jewishly"
1

1 *"My Independent Jewish Monster Temperament":
The Serial Selves of Aline Kominsky Crumb*
23

2 *"What Would Make Me the Most 'Myself'": Self-Creation and
Self-Exile in Vanessa Davis's Diary and Autobiographical Comics*
67

3 *"I Always Want to Know Everything True": Memory, Adolescence, and
Belonging in the Graphic Memoirs of Miss Lasko-Gross and Lauren Weinstein*
115

4 *"But you don't live here, so what's the dilemma?": Birthright and Accountability
in the Geographics of Sarah Glidden and Miriam Libicki*
167

*Conclusion—"Where are they now?": Translation and Renewal
in Liana Finck's A Bintel Brief*
221

Notes   231   Bibliography   247   Index   261

Color plates follow page   112

Contents

Acknowledgments

his book is the product of years of conversations and inter-
actions with colleagues and friends, and it was inspired by
countless works of scholarship, literature, and art, which I
have made every attempt to acknowledge throughout the text.
The project would not have been possible without the continued and unwavering support of Nancy K. Miller, who motivated me to write about what I loved
and offered her enthusiasm, encouragement, and incisive critique at every step.
There are no suitable words to express my gratitude. Hillary Chute provided me
with invaluable guidance, mentoring, and friendship and enthusiastically told me
from the beginning that if I wrote the book she would read it. I am thankful to her
for paving the way. My agent, Cecelia Cancellaro, believed in this project, helped
me shape it, and found it a home. I am delighted to be part of the Gender and
Culture series at Columbia University Press and thankful to its editors, Nancy and
Victoria Rosner. Also at CUP, thanks especially to Jennifer Crewe, Lisa Hamm,
Susan Pensak, and Kathryn Schell for their careful and discerning input, insights,
and attention to detail.

Many other colleagues and friends were patient enough to read through versions of my chapters, help me work out my ideas from the early to late stages of
writing, or just provide me with a precious support network. In addition to two
anonymous readers at CUP who gave me indispensable comments, I am thankful
to Laurel Harris, Seamus O'Malley, and Yevgenia Traps for feedback on various
chapters. Magda Maczynska and Jennifer Mitchell gave me last-minute advice on
the introduction. Nancy read through the whole manuscript and provided her
usual unparalleled feedback, and Hillary, Wayne Koestenbaum, and Sondra Perl

also read the full manuscript in its early stages and provided indispensible comments that helped shape it.

A number of cartoonists fielded my questions and offered me insights that have enriched the way I read and write about comics. I am thankful for inspiring conversations with Gabrielle Bell, Vanessa Davis, Sarah Glidden, Miriam Katin, Keren Katz, Miss Lasko-Gross, Miriam Libicki, Maurice Oksman, Anya Ulinich, and Lauren Weinstein. Liana Finck's way of seeing the world has transformed mine, and I delight in our new friendship.

I am appreciative of those who generously gave me permission to republish their artworks, including Gabrielle Bell, Vanessa Davis, Liana Finck, Sarah Glidden, Aline Kominsky Crumb, Miss Lasko-Gross, Miriam Libicki, Lauren Weinstein, and the folks at Drawn and Quarterly, Fantagraphics, HarperCollins, and MacMillan. In the final stages of the book, I was offered guidance from Michael Colvin, Sarah Lightman, and Kate Shaw, and I am thankful for their friendships. Lauren Weinstein expertly conceived of and created a cover image just for the book, and Liana Finck drew an author likeness under the condition, happily granted, of "free reign." I am in awe of both of these women's talents, imaginations, and generosity.

In addition to those mentioned above, many friends offered encouragement and countless acts of kindness over the course of the project; I am especially thankful to Michelle Andelman, Emily Dell, Esther Mandelheim Elliott, Heather Fabrikant, Emily Fink, Erika Heidecker, Agi Legutko, Kris W. Lohre, Molly Selzer Lorber, Mary Ellen Obias, Devon Powers, Melissa Sontag Broudo, and Jessica Wells-Cantiello. I was lucky to connect recently with Joyce Antler and Jeremy Dauber, and I am thankful for their counsel and friendship.

Many thanks to my former colleagues in the Writing Across the Curriculum Program at Brooklyn College, and particularly Ellen Belton, who has been both a colleague and role model, and Brendan O'Malley, friend and collaborator. Anne Lapidus Lerner and all those I met through the Hyman Mentoring Program have been encouraging of my research in its final stretches. My new colleagues and students at Marymount Manhattan College are a source of inspiration and enthusiasm, and I am especially thankful, in addition to those already mentioned, to Susan Behrens, Mark Bresnan, Cecilia Feilla, Nava Silton, and Laura Tropp. I am grateful for financial assistance from Marymount Manhattan College's Faculty Scholarship Award, made possible with the advocacy of Bradley Herling and the Committee on Faculty Leaves and Fellowships.

Acknowledgments

This project would not have been completed without the following additional institutional and individual backing: the Goldie and David Blanksteen Foundation, the Hadassah–Brandeis Institute, and the Jewish Studies Committee at New York University's Gallatin School of Individualized Study. Jay Barksdale at the New York Public Library offered me a space at the Wertheim Study, for which I am very appreciative. I am also grateful to the English Department at Rutgers University in New Brunswick for inviting me to teach a course on Graphic Storytelling in the spring of 2013, and I am thankful to my former students there and at NYU-Gallatin and Brooklyn College for many inspirational discussions.

A previous version of part of chapter 2 was published in *Studies in American Jewish Literature*, and a previous version of part of chapter 1 was published in *Studies in Comics*. I thank Ben Schreier and four anonymous readers for their very helpful comments. I have had the opportunity to write about what I love for various other outlets, and I am appreciative of Karen Rile and the folks at *Cleaver* for including me in their magazine, as well as *BookTrib*, the *Comics Alternative*, the *Forward*, *Jewish Book Council*, *Lilith*, and the *Los Angeles Review of Books*. Thanks to Al Filreis and the Kelly Writers House for existing.

My parents, Zipporah and Henry Oksman, and Jon's parents, Marc and Marcy Waldauer, continually provide me with unwavering love and guidance. Our families have been sources of love, and I am grateful for them.

Emily Berger, April Greene, Rosemary Joseph, Naomi Kramer, Linda M., Cecilia Martinez, and Alfreda San Juan offered me peace of mind as I set to work, and I will always be appreciative of that. Kudos to Unnameable Books and Bergen Street Comics, both thankfully within walking distance of my apartment, and my gratitude for all the great Brooklyn coffee shops that put up with me.

Zev and Liron, thank you for coming into my world.

Jon, what can I say? I couldn't have done it without you and I wouldn't have wanted to.

"How Come Boys Get
to Keep Their Noses?"

Introduction

"To Unaffiliate Jewishly"

In her 1989 comic, "Nose Job," Aline Kominsky Crumb describes a "disturbing epidemic" that took place in 1962 in the mostly Jewish Long Island community of her youth. Through her alter ego, The Bunch, she narrates her experience of watching all of her female peers as they showed up to high school with "new noses." Despite pressure from family and friends, The Bunch refuses this rite of passage and finds herself, years later, boasting, "So I managed to make it thru high school with my nose!!" (*Need More Love* 88). The Bunch's reluctance to conform within her actively assimilating Jewish community paradoxically sets her apart; she becomes an outsider because of her refusal to erase the bodily traces of that identity.

The story of how The Bunch keeps her nose unfolds in a series of bold panels exposing a variety of conflicted, raw, and often painful autobiographical representations. We see snapshots of a forty year old examining her body in the mirror, with some extreme close-ups as she pulls at this fold of skin and tugs at that one. We glimpse her high school experiences, and particularly moments when her difference surfaces plainly as the teenage girls around her acquire pug noses and heavy eye makeup. Makeshift balloons expressing spoken words and thoughts attributed to both "present" and past day The Bunches crowd these self-portraits, battling for space in densely scribbled, hand-drawn panels. In the span of three pages, twenty-five years of insecurity and pride, doubt and transparency are crammed into a characteristically bright, scratchy, and effusive mapping out of this alter ego's ever transforming sense of self and identity.

In form and content, Kominsky Crumb's comic depicts a politics of rebelliousness in relation to communal belonging that characterizes the works of a number of contemporary Jewish American women cartoonists. In her book on Jewish American literature and identity, Helene Meyers asserts that "if one can choose Jewish affiliation . . . then it becomes possible to unaffiliate Jewishly, either actively or through benign neglect" (3). The cartoonists that I consider, starting with Aline Kominsky Crumb and continuing with a younger generation of artists, including Vanessa Davis, Miss Lasko-Gross, Lauren Weinstein, Sarah Glidden, Miriam Libicki, and Liana Finck, are all interested in unaffiliating Jewishly. Rather than a simple negation, this process entails a complex negotiation, a dynamic that I term *dis-affiliation*. For these artists, actively identifying as generally secular Jewish women in postassimilated America begins with rejecting particular aspects and expressions of Jewish identity. It is a visual mapping practice based in rebellions and disorientations but nevertheless resulting in partial affiliations and identifications.

In late twentieth and twenty-first century America, the configuration of who and what is considered Jewish has become difficult to grasp, as neither religious participation nor communal cultural experiences, like immigration or institutionalized anti-Semitism, collectively mark the Jewish American experience or characterize its literature. The seven cartoonists I discuss here adopt notions of Jewish difference to establish an encompassing metaphor for Jewish American women's marginalized status within an already tenuously defined and situated community.[1] In their comics, by creating visual maps of their autobiographical selves, these artists manipulate signifiers of Jewish difference, through dis-affiliations, to form their own images and associations: not just of what they can look like, in costume, body, or posture, but also of who, in a broader, even ontological sense, they can claim to be. A neurotic twenty-something's musings on her relationship to Judaism, to family, to the men in her life, catalogued in a large, hard-covered compilation of loosely connected diary sketches and strikingly luminous, oversized color drawings. A child confessing to feeling panicked in Hebrew school and public school, episodes of humiliation and contemplation captured in resonant, expressive, and often brooding black-and-white images. A cynical American woman tracing her Birthright Israel trip in a two-hundred page travelogue, spinning unanswerable webs of questions articulated through meticulous, tightly designed watercolor panels. Although most of these cartoonists have moved on, at least somewhat, from The Bunch's fixation with the Jewish nose as a symbol for the marginalized female Jewish self, all of them continue, in their own ways, to reject conventional notions of what it means to claim and depict Jewish difference. Instead, they reconceptualize Jewish identity not only by rebelling against dominant modes of Jewish representation but also by creating new ways of asserting Jewish presence: inventive and provocative drawings of Jewish women's selves in space.

Because comics trades in space, in the potential to shape experience as a matter of perception, scale, and positioning, it is a medium well suited to the challenging task of envisioning a contiguous and relational sense of belonging and not belonging. Whatever the dominant aesthetic motif—whether toying with varying registers, modes, and designs or maintaining an even, sharply defined line and style over the course of a chronological narrative—what unites these cartoonists' works are their autobiographical depictions of orientation, disorientation, and reorientation. By this I mean the processes of navigating, over time, one's so-called identity in relation to other people, assorted places, and even differing versions of that self.

I use the term *postassimilated* to refer to the works of all the cartoonists that I dissect in order to show how this new metaphor of dis-affiliation is still very much tied to a larger history of Jewish American identity making. *Post* is not meant to imply that we are beyond certain experiences of assimilation, but rather that these new generations are still influenced, however indirectly, by the effects of assimilation experienced by those who came before them, even as they do not necessarily make those experiences central to their own narratives.[2] Assimilation is a metaphor, rather than a reality, for these artists, and they use it to describe their relationships to versions of identity and self-classifications that they can neither easily reject nor accept. As Harvey Pekar writes in his introduction to Kominsky Crumb's first collection of comics, *Love that Bunch*, published in 1990, "Aline's parents and most of her grandparents were born in the United States. Much of the old world heritage was lost to her" (iii). Pekar's introduction emphasizes the cultural moment that led to Kominsky Crumb's particular brand of dis-affiliatory sensibility, one that highlights a connection with a real-world past more so than those of the other cartoonists examined here. In Kominsky Crumb's comics, with her buzzing, richly detailed, and unconventional style and form, she points a critical eye at what she sees as a commercial and disconnected postwar generation. Nevertheless she maintains that that generation's concerns with consumption and acculturation persist as active influences in her life and work. For this reason, unlike the rest of the cartoonists discussed here, Kominsky Crumb's narratives are most invested in stereotypes: the historical moment that framed her childhood brought her closest to the struggles and effects of assimilation and upward mobility.[3] Her densely composed comics in many ways emphasize attempts to come to terms with a new version of Jewish being that is not reliant on either cleanly breaking from or connecting to past notions of Jewish identity. Nevertheless, Jewishness, for her, as for all these artists, is a process of self-discovery that always involves a collision between the past and present and both a recognition of and rebellion against the notion that, as Sander Gilman puts it, "[Jews] mirror within their own sense of selves the image of their own difference" (*The Jew's Body* 176). As the hyphen in *dis-affiliation* indicates, claiming Jewish identity means negotiating between inherited and invented structures, between rejections of, as well as attachments to, communal, individual, and historical notions of self and identity.

It is, in part, because of Jewish women's statuses as an often ignored, misrepresented, or underrepresented minority in an already misunderstood medium that they have perhaps felt freer to engage in what Hillary Chute has shown to be the "risk-taking self-representation" so frequently found in women's comics (*Graphic Women* 26). Jewish American women are just one of many groups of people whose work has often been underplayed or ignored in both academic and mainstream comics criticism. As Anne Elizabeth Moore points out in a 2014 review essay of Paul Gravett's *Comics Art*, a survey of comics culture from the last 150 years or so: "Any overview of comics will miss something, of course, because that is what overviews do. But the fact is that they all tend to leave out the same things: examples of work from the global South, work by women and people of color, work created primarily for communication purposes (which is usually created by folks in poverty), or work published in non-Western languages."[4] Responding to their historical absences from the dominant narratives of both Jewish American literature writ large, as well as that of North American comics, postwar Jewish American women cartoonists position themselves on the page through their often antiheroic alter egos. In drawing autobiographical comics featuring images that are meant to reflect particular, emphatically incomplete, and distorted versions of themselves and their experiences, these authors frame their graphic narratives by the contradictions and disjunctions inherent in the act of autobiography. Through their visual experiments, they paradoxically inscribe themselves into narratives they are working simultaneously to reject and revise; that is, they envision themselves inside and outside literal and figurative locations that have been designated for them, often by others, as "home."

Like other second-wave feminists with Jewish ties, Carolyn Heilbrun thoughtfully conveys secular Jewish American women's complicated relationships to their Jewish identities in her autobiographical ruminations at the beginning of *Reinventing Womanhood*.[5] She describes her mother's ambivalent relationship to her Jewish identity, how she would refer to "everything tasteless, in the sense of without savor" as "goyish," even as she carried a "horror of everything Jewish," working at a place that did not hire Jews and trying to persuade her husband (unsuccessfully) to change his Jewish-sounding name (61, 58). Heilbrun links that rejection of Jewish identification with her mother's sense of the traditional Jewish woman as passive and imprisoned, one meant to serve others. These kinds of negative associations—often based in traditional notions of religious Judaism—persist in some way for all secular American Jews, although perhaps especially for women. Many are often unwilling to publicly or unabashedly self-identify as Jews because of the political, social, economic, and cultural assumptions that come from claiming that identity. Even in a "postethnic" America, when it has become increasingly clear that one's Jewishness is not directly correlated with a particular geographical location, belief system, language, or set of practices, the questions remain: If you claim your secular Jewish identity, do you align yourself with or against a particular ideology or belief system? Are you connecting yourself with a larger Jewish body, composed, presumably, of others who act or think in some way like you? Are you automatically affiliating yourself with a legacy of Jewish American identity making and its representation in literature and the arts?[6] For the contemporary cartoonists explored here, the answer to these questions is a resounding *no*. As their comics reflect, Jewish identification *begins* with intraethnic difference, the very detail or details that separate one self-proclaimed Jew from another—not, as has been the norm in canonized Jewish American literary culture as well as traditional histories of Jewish American culture and identity, with the differences based in the oversimplified binary of Jew versus non-Jew.[7]

The partial and intraethnic dis-affiliations exemplified in Kominsky Crumb's comic, as well as in the works of the other cartoonists examined here, are intimately tied to the ways that Jewish American women experience and perceive themselves visually, practices that are ultimately connected to how others have portrayed them over time. In addition to seeing themselves through representations of Jewish women's bodies, so often distorted and manipulated by others, Jewish American women's visual identities have been mapped out in relation to particular places and spaces, perhaps most notably the kitchen and the home.[8]

As Joyce Antler notes of male writers idealizing their mothers in the early twentieth century, "The centrality of the kitchen to sons' remembrances of immigrant mothers was common" (*You Never Call!* 26). Consider, for example, the depiction of the mother in Henry Roth's *Call It Sleep*, a book first published in 1934 that Alfred Kazin refers to as "the most profound novel of Jewish life that I have ever read by an American" ("Introduction" ix). Roth's prototypical *yiddishe mama* is most recognizable laboring at home and especially in the kitchen, much like the mother-monster created by his literary progeny, the other Roth.[9] As the novel opens, the protagonist, young David Schearl, stands at the kitchen sink, thirsting for a cup of water, and his mother's presence is relayed through her invisibility or, more accurately, her interchangeability with a household cleaning object: "The unseen broom stopped to listen" (17). Schearl's childlike rendering of his mother as household object reflects the ways that many Jewish American male writers and cultural makers of the twentieth century have collectively represented the Jewish mother. The kitchen is the space where she has been objectified and molded into a stereotype.[10]

Even for the generation of postwar Jewish women artists and writers who rebelled and "talked back" to this patriarchal positioning of the Jewish woman in her tiny domestic space, the kitchen continued to be tied to the *other* Jewish women in their lives, the ones they were trying to define themselves against. Consider Vivian Gornick's 1987 memoir of a woman's battle for independence from her domineering Jewish mother, a text in which she too recognizes her mother as inseparable from the living spaces that she perpetually dominates: "The kitchen, the window, the alley. It was the atmosphere in which she was rooted, the background against which she stood outlined" (*Fierce Attachments* 15). For those writers who strongly identified as feminists, freedom and flight from the world of their mothers often meant relegating those mothers (and sisters and aunts and grandmothers) to the world of Jewish stereotype. Erica Jong's famous 1973 feminist novel of independence, *Fear of Flying*, for instance, includes a sister character, Randy, who represents everything the protagonist, Isadora Wing, most fears in life. She is a caricature of the domestic woman, a woman who, though she married "outside the faith"—a "Lebanese physicist at Berkeley"—has paradoxically *not* rebelled against the world of their mothers. Randy is characterized by her extreme mothering (she has nine children and is pregnant again at the time of the novel), and her inability to see the value in Isadora's desire to build a life outside the domestic sphere—a writer's life. She is everything Isadora fears most: a woman defined by "*Kinder, Küche,* and *Kirche*" (57). Indeed, despite Randy's postnuptial interest in Catholicism, she continues to epitomize the Jewish women that Isadora wants so much to move away from not only because of Randy's interest in the domestic, in motherhood, in organized religion but also because of her ignorance, her desire to claim her Jewish ties against all else. "I just get sick and tired of everyone bleeding about the poor Palestinians. Why don't you worry about us instead?" she snaps at Isadora after they pass a refugee camp in Beirut (321).

Erica Jong's depiction of Isadora's sister as the Palestinian-hating, overly domesticated Jewish woman—even in the face of this sister's chosen Catholic ties—pinpoints one of the dis-affiliations that are important to contemporary secular American Jews, including many of the cartoonists discussed in this project. Jong's caricature is an extreme response to the assumption that identifying as Jewish in contemporary North America is tantamount to being a Zionist and either supporting or ignoring/denying Palestinian oppression. This misleading connection has been especially troublesome for Jewish feminists—or, more precisely, women who self-identify as feminists and as Jews and who therefore find themselves at the margins of both communities.[11] In an effort to maintain the possibility of a communal secular Jewish American identity, many have turned to notions of collective ownership: of space, tradition, language, ideology, culture, and even sensibility—like humor. But conflating Jewishness with Zionism, much like conflating Jewish motherhood with the domestic, is an assumption that confines the Jewish body to particular spheres where it can then be "discovered." The Jewish woman's body in particular has often been restricted through suppositions of such national and domestic affiliations. She is presumed to feel most at home and in charge—most "in place"—in local spaces: her connection with others is limited to those she recognizes and encounters in her everyday life or those that, even though they are far away, are presumed to be most like her.

Over the past decade or so, a number of scholarly works have attempted to respond to such essentialist understandings of Jewish identity by turning to more inclusive models that engage, instead, in pluralistic "Jewish identities."[12] These revisionary configurations base contemporary understandings of Jewishness, and of identities more generally, in the postmodern project of recognizing the limitations of master narratives and categories. In other words, they acknowledge the vast discrepancies and contradictions contained in such categories as "Jewish" or "woman" and in the language and significations used to create such classifications. Antiessentialist models of Jewish identity are based, instead, in conceptions of Jewishness that recognize it as, in large part, a discursive process. Representing identity visually is a fitting and cogent scheme when we consider the multilayered dimensions of such process-oriented models. For instance, Stuart Charmé's antiessentialist treatise on Jewish identity catalogues two dimensions—the "diachronic" and the "synchronic"—that have been largely ignored in conventional models of Jewish identity, which are often based in the assumption that there is a shared and identifiable essential "core" among Jews. Unlike a static or crystallized notion of Jewish identity, Charmé's paradigm, which he describes as "spiral," recognizes that one's sense of being Jewish is affected by various, overlapping, and sometimes contradictory conceptions, which are often present in the same instance. As he explains, "'Synchronic diversity' refers to the multiple forms of Jewish *identities* that comprise 'the Jewish community (or communities)' at any particular moment in time. By 'diachronic diversity,' I mean the phenomenon of Jewish identity as a 'journey' over time, as a process that changes and unfolds in a variety of directions over the course of an individual lifetime, not to mention over the course of history in a broader sense" (119). Charmé's model is useful precisely because it does not take notions of Jewish identity *out* of time and space/place but instead focuses on a concept of identity that is framed in and through a relational, positional web. His model bridges the possibility of identity-as-invention with the definite historical and social contexts that orient such notions of identity.

This attention to direction, space, perspective, and place connects recent antiessentialist models of Jewish identity with issues that have loomed large in feminist notions of gender identity, beginning, perhaps, with Virginia Woolf's assertion in *Three Guineas*, her treatise against war, that "as a woman, I have no country" (129). Woolf's antipatriotic directive assumes a transnational connection among all women, who, in her view, at the very least have the common experience of being oppressed by men. Almost half a century after those words were first published in 1938, American-born poet and philosopher Adrienne Rich responded to Woolf in her now famous 1984 talk, "Notes Toward a Politics of Location," by asserting, "I am to speak these words in Europe, but I have been searching for them in the United States of America" (210).[13] Rich's acknowledgment challenges Woolf's notion of a kind of universal womanhood, a communal identity that is somehow meant to encompass the point of view of women everywhere. She advances the connection between space/place and identity; as she explains, "a place on the map is also a place in history within which as a woman, a Jew, a lesbian, a feminist

I am created and trying to create" (212). Like Charmé's spiraling model of Jewish being, Rich recognizes how intricately and indivisibly related are past and present notions of self, continually interacting in the textured space of the present.

Rich is but one in a lineage of women who have explored the importance of recognizing and claiming space and place as the keys to identification and articulation, to what French writer and poet Hélène Cixous calls "coming to writing" in a 1977 essay by that same name. Having been raised by a single mother following her Algerian father's premature death, Cixous feels herself an outsider, a wanderer with "false" identification papers. Labeling herself a "Jewoman" in part to indicate her sense of alienation based in not being tied to any particular place, she speculates, "Sometimes I think I began writing in order to make room for the wandering question that haunts my soul and hacks and saws at my body; to give it a place and time" (7). Writing, then, is Cixous's way of crafting an imaginary space from which she feels legitimated. Like Rich, she recognizes how her relationships to the spaces around her—in her case, her estrangements from places that have formed her narrative of citizenship and alienation—have shaped who she can imagine herself to be. And, for Cixous, as for Rich, this simultaneous sense of dislocation and possibility is tied to her Jewish sense of self.

Despite differing perceptions of the ways that their particular notions of "home" have molded their subjectivities, Woolf, Cixous, and Rich all recognize and claim real and/or imagined, communal and/or individual spaces as the keys to women's self-articulations. Women writers have often located themselves through writing, visually mapping their "politics of location," a politics that cements through an image-ing of those real and made-up spaces.[14] As Susan Stanford Friedman argues in *Mappings*, "feminism has moved to a concern with location—the geopolitics of identity within differing communal spaces of being and becoming" (3). Such a "locational feminism" is founded on what Friedman calls a "new geographics," one that "figures identity as a historically embedded site, a positionality, a location, a standpoint, a terrain, an intersection, a network, a crossroads of multiply situated knowledges" (19). Paradoxically, as Donna Haraway explains, "The only way to find a larger vision is to be somewhere in particular" (196). That particularity—one's present "location"—is built out of numerous synchronic and diachronic realities, out of a continual winding of many disconnected and sometimes contradictory notions of self. Like Charmé's spiral model of contemporary Jewish identity, this feminist geographics is based in the belief that in order to fully locate the self, one must be willing to relinquish notions of self grounded in the chronological, the hierarchical, and the durational in favor of those founded on the recursive, the episodic, and the elliptical.

The desire to represent the self in a way that captures the recursive and unsettled nature of "identity"—identity as process—is the basis of the works of the contemporary graphic memoirists I interpret here. Through their visual narratives, these cartoonists have joined a collective of women attending to space as a way of understanding the world and their relationships to it. Their works reflect how notions of space are inextricably tied to notions of time—how one's location is a matter not just of perspective in relation to others but also in terms of the changing self over time. A "sequential art" that maps time *as* space, the graphic memoir emphasizes the importance of both time and location as the keys to its unique brand of autobiographical storytelling.[15] As Chute asserts in the introduction to her groundbreaking 2010 work on women and comics, *Graphic Women*, "Against a valorization of absence and aporia, graphic narrative asserts the value of presence, however complex and contingent" (2). The autobiographical cartoonists that I consider in these chapters are always focused on "finding" themselves, on affirming their presences, by drawing themselves and their worlds both in the present and over time. These creators use comics to reorient their relationships to space, time, and identity as their geographics both respond to and reinvent the ways that Jewish American identity has been constructed. Each text that I examine powerfully reflects the feminist pursuit of challenging conventional notions of "space and scale" in order to collapse assumptions and expectations related to the invention, integration, and representation of identity (Pratt and Rosner 1).[16]

In a recent interview cartoonist Lauren Weinstein illuminated the connection between sequential narrative and ways of mapping identity. Describing the process of shifting gears from working as a painter to becoming a cartoonist, she explained, "I could paint anything but I just wasn't satisfied with any theme because it didn't get to the meat of anything for me" ("Thinking Panoramically" 187). Weinstein then recalled a moment that, looking back, revealed to her a cartooning impulse that had not yet been realized: "I distinctly remember making this one painting. I didn't know what it was, and then I divided it up into squares, and then I cut up those squares into smaller squares, and then I cut everything up into smaller and smaller squares, and then just threw it all away. I feel like that's a sign of someone who's a cartoonist and just hasn't figured it out yet." Weinstein's early act of artistic rebellion points to the formal potential of graphic narratives to confound the basic assumptions we maintain about our relationships to space. Graphic narratives make possible an opening up of perspectives, like that described in Weinstein's breakdown of her painting into smaller and smaller pieces. When a single perspective gets fragmented and consequently amplified, as in Antonioni's famous film, *Blow-Up*, the artist encounters new and unanticipated information in her work. For these autobiographical cartoonists, that information is primarily self-knowledge: of who she is and how she sees herself in relation to other people and the world around her, and of how those suppositions unravel once that perspective is shifted, once the scale system delineating her point of view changes. These cartoonists' autobiographical texts trade in the kind of "experiential space" that, as Griselda Pollock has argued of the works of impressionist women artists like Mary Cassatt and Berthe Morisot, reflect "a lived sense of social locatedness, mobility and visibility, in the social relations of seeing and being seen" (91, 93). Their works connect "space and social processes" (92), visually representing and integrating multiple and determined perspectives and experiences. By doing so, these graphic memoirs persistently resist the possibility of unification, of a formed and static sense of place or identity.

One work by Weinstein powerfully illustrates the potential, in comics, of mapping out and animating various planes of individual identity within the same potentially expansive space. In this richly detailed and colorful map (figure 0.1), which Weinstein dubbed "The Best We Can Hope For," the reader is witness as several narratives "unfold" for different characters in this scene in the park. Weinstein's map was initially printed on two facing pages, sized at roughly 8-by-13 inches total, in the art book *The Ganzfeld 7*, which also included a much larger poster-sized and fold-up version of the map in each publication. Readers could thus materially engage in a process of literal unfolding before or after they visually encountered the content presented on the map itself.[17] Within the image, a long, gray, unsteady walkway outlines the space in a kind of misshapen circle, with additional pathways connecting this central domain to other places off the page, places that the reader can then imagine on her own. Many comics scholars, including perhaps most famously Scott McCloud in *Understanding Comics*, have written about the unique properties of comics in terms of the reader's relationship to the text. They argue that, among other formal elements, the space between panels, also known as the gutter, invites the reader to participate in the making of the text.[18] Although Weinstein's map is a single panel, also known as a cartoon (as opposed to how McCloud, among others, characterizes comics as "a sequential art"), its architecture prompts a similar kind of work on the part of

0.1 Lauren Weinstein, "The Best We Can Hope For." Two-page map in the Ganzfeld 7, 2008, pp. 8–9.
Used by permission of Lauren Weinstein.

the reader, who must use her imagination to fill out the rest of the pathway as it extends off the page.[19] In addition to envisioning spaces not fully pictured—the crowded streets, houses, and buildings that presumably make up the remainder of this imaginary town and can be seen in small clusters atop the map—the reader must also fill in the gaps of time missing from this layered image: certain past and future events are not visible but alluded to in the picture itself. In this as well as other ways, the cartoon-map invites countless interpretations, visually emphasizing the fact that no individual perspective can ever be contained or fully reflected in any artwork. No world will ever fit on the page.

It is possible to distinguish four central figures on the map, although their paths do not unfold in a symmetrical or predictable way, and at times it is difficult to trace whether their figures are coming or going in the direction toward which they seem to have been moving all along. For example, a nonchalant woman in a yellow top, drawn in simple but distinct poses, her shadow carefully trailing her, "enters" the park from the top left corner of the panel. Her otherwise easy locatedness—she is a figure who is clearly walking *into* the park—is immediately thrown into question by her thought bubble. In it an old woman is pictured (herself, perhaps, in forty years?) with large glasses and arms folded, sulking in a bright pink bubble of space, a curiously cheerful background for such a melancholy image. Immediately, it becomes difficult to connect or trace the journey of this character, to match up how her mental and physical worlds intersect, as well as the ways that her life before and after the events pictured here have unfolded or will unfold. The reader might nevertheless try to follow this dynamic, thinking character, who soon finds herself a companion and frolics with him in the grass mere inches from where they initially met—perhaps even for the first time, though that question, too, remains unresolved. Soon, he is pulling her up out of the frosty green bushes, another curious gesture, and they can be traced crossing over a jungle gym, rolling down a slide together, and engaging in a series of joint acts. These come to the fore as the woman, alone once again, somersaults on the grass, emerges with a swollen, pregnant belly, labors as a crowd gathers around her, and finally releases a baby, dressed in red, who then rolls off on its own across the grass, its path crossing over her earlier somersaulting one.

The power of this visual stems from its resistance to relaying a cohesive narrative, both as a single narrative "map" and also as a series of smaller narratives within that encompassing framework. A map highlights the relationship between different elements in space. This map breaks down that possibility, disorienting its viewers and discarding any expected sense of proportion as cosmic red Frisbees fly into the air to take up an inordinate amount of space on the page and oversized lovers, mirroring their subjacent, tiny selves, lounge high up in trees. It collapses reader expectations about what it is supposed to represent, as the anticipated distance between symbol and real object extends well beyond any readable system of configuration. In other words, this is a map without a legend.

In place of narrative coherence, the map offers a way of understanding the act of looking, of seeing and being seen, as something tied, above all else, to one's place of perspective, or one's orientation. The spaces a person occupies in relation to others as well as in relation to past and future versions of herself is a determining factor in how she comes to see herself. In the image of the magnified couple sitting in the tree in the middle of the right part of the panel, for instance, the woman's face is tilted down toward the park, and in her disproportionately large size in comparison to other people on the map we recognize that her vantage point has changed the look of this scene for her. Viewing it from this decidedly unconventional perspective, she will inevitably "see" something that others are not necessarily seeing down below. In turn, we can speculate that even those individuals drawn to scale in relationship to one another experience this world differently based on their particular points on the map, their points in time and space. Location is the key to this complex and textured articulation of the relationship between subjectivity, time, and space.

This visualization of the "politics of location," so connected to contemporary feminist theory, is the subject of all the cartoonists explored here. Their works build on literary and artistic genealogies that emphasize the ways that women's viewpoints can offer engaged understandings of subjectivity as an "ongoing construction," one that is always related to vantage points inhabited and traversed, whether by necessity or choice (de Lauretis 159). Consider this excerpt from Grace Paley's 1974 short story "Faith in a Tree," a passage that verbally echoes the consideration of outlook and subjectivity built into Weinstein's map. In the short story, Paley's recurrent protagonist, Faith Darwin, is unhappily driven to immerse herself in domestic life, watching children play in the park instead of participating in what she calls "important conversation." Yet she transforms the scene by shifting her perspective, by disorienting herself: "But me, the creation of His soft second thought, I am sitting on the twelve-foot-high, strong, long arm of a sycamore, my feet swinging, and I can only see Kitty, a co-worker in the mother trade—a topnotch craftsman. She is below, leaning on my tree, rumpled in a black cotton skirt made of shroud remnants at about fourteen cents a yard. Another colleague, Anne Kraat, is close by on a hard park bench, gloomy, beautiful, waiting for her luck to change" (175–76). By hoisting herself up in a tree, Paley's Faith sees not the everyday scene that has, by virtue of its redundancy, undoubtedly worn itself down in her mind to its most basic components—children, parents (mostly mothers), toys, swings, grass. Instead, she sees Kitty as a "topnotch craftsman" and Anne as a woman with more on her mind than whether her child has skinned his knee. In other words, by looking at a familiar scene from a fresh point of view, the scale has shifted, and what Faith sees is almost new; the park and its occupants have gained a sense of significance in her eyes, of relevance. The figures in Weinstein's map have a similar effect on the reader. An everyday scene becomes a metanarrative about life, time, space, and change—or more accurately the complex relationship between all those elements as they converge in a single visual. What matters are not so much the story lines threaded before the reader's eyes, though they are certainly attention grabbing, but rather the vantage points inhabited, the relationships of parts to the whole.

Weinstein's map stands as a representative example of the potential for graphic narratives to relay how bound up individual experiences are to the individual's perspective and to her situatedness in relation to the self and others over time. The map communicates, too, the impossibility of tracing any single life path—of coming to terms with the various features and foundations of how we see ourselves and others, of the relationships that help define who we think we are. The reader might try to trace the woman in yellow and blue, her journey from a lone figure entering the park to an old woman with white hair sitting on a bench, playing with a dog or waving at her son, now high up in his own tree. But, in the end, any attempt to piece together the fragments of this life into a single, evolving, and coherent narrative will be frustrated.

This map also evidences the ways that so many women cartoonists have come to experiment with how stories are told, bringing innovative viewpoints to a world of comics that has for so long been dominated by masculine perspectives and reminding readers of the complex and sometimes invisible genealogies connected to all modes of storytelling. They offer inventive ways of seeing not just in the stories that they tell but also in the ways that they tell these stories. Through the innovative reworking of various genres—including visual memoirs, diaries, letters, travel narratives, and childhood and adolescent literatures—these comics deliberately violate long-held assumptions about what it means to tell a recognizable or traceable story. "Hybrid" autobiographical comics reflect antiessentialist notions of the self as constructed through a continual process that often involves rebelling against tradition and canon. All these works borrow from or refer to, often overtly, forms of everyday chronicling that are not often tied to the story of contemporary North American comics; like women's autobiographical works more generally, these practices are frequently devalued as transparent, narcissistic recordings of life rather than deliberate constructions.

A recent cartoon published by Gabrielle Bell on her Facebook page reflects this problem of canonicity, genealogy, and reception (figure 0.2). The cartoon was uploaded to Bell's Facebook page on September 30, 2014, without any comment from her, and within twenty-four hours it had been "shared" fifteen times and "liked" by over one hundred people, including a spate of cartoonists. The simple, almost childish black-and-white sketch, drawn in a style so markedly different from Bell's normally expert, delicate line, pictures three individuals, presumably the "critics," looming over a phallus-shaped, sculptured piece of artwork. Beneath them, their exclamations read, in scribbled handwriting: "Remarkable!" "profound!" "transcendent!" "important!" "Bold!" "powerful!" As those same critics gather around a sculpture shaped like a vagina, their expressions have dropped, with noses grown exaggeratedly more pointed. Beneath this parallel image, their

0.2 *Gabrielle Bell, "Female Art." Used by permission of Gabrielle Bell.*

reactions read: "derivative!" "insubstantial!" "self-indulgent!" "insignificant!" "diaristic!" "masturbatory!" Bell's satirical cartoon is a commentary on how strongly gender still shapes the way works of art are viewed and valued. Comics scholarship, like art and literary criticism more generally, needs to account for the assumptions so often made about artistic and literary forms and styles, the associations that markedly influence the way art, and art forms, get read in certain contexts. "Can I draw or not?" Lynda Barry's alter ego asks in her hybrid memoir and drawing manual, *Picture This* (41). "From the beginning of my time as a cartoonist people have said I can't draw or that my drawing is bad." Barry's book, which creatively weaves together memoir, collage, and instruction, is one of several recent groundbreaking texts proposing a transformative approach to art and drawing. Urging for a more nuanced and complex way of recognizing art practices as inevitably historicized, Barry powerfully ties the processes of creating art to the methods and perceptions that influence the artist in the creation of her artworks.[20]

The texts examined in this book all openly experiment with and rebel against gendered frameworks of audience expectation and perception or notions that, time and again, often overdetermine what kinds of artworks come to be considered masterful and worthy of attention and canonization. Each graphic narrative provocatively engages in formally reimagining innovative modes of self-representation and expression, recreating and highlighting nontraditional ways of sharing stories and depicting diverse perspectives and disrupting dominant notions of identity, self-representation, and artfulness. By playing with their readers' expectations of what comics and/or autobiography should look and sound like, these texts reinforce a sense of narrative conventions as imposing; they deflect clearly defined or essentialized notions of storytelling aesthetics and of self in order to reimagine what it means to have, and represent, life as possibility.

Zygmunt Bauman has written of "identity" as a concept that arises "whenever one is not sure of where one belongs" ("From Pilgrim to Tourist" 19). For Jewish American women constructing comics, the sense of being an outsider has been amplified by the ways the story of American comics has, for the past decade or so, been told as a story closely entwined with Jewish American acculturation—a narrative dominated by male figures. Scholars have argued that Jews established the superhero genre in particular in order to craft a space in which assimilation was not only possible, but could turn an "ordinary guy" into a superhero.[21] These discussions have virtually ignored women, most likely because of their limited involvement and visibility in earlier implementations of the medium, and particularly in the superhero and escapist traditions. But what many women cartoonists reveal, as is true also for many male cartoonists, is an interest in comics that stems from and is fed by sources often thought peripheral to the medium—the aforementioned diaries, letters, and visual memoirs, as well as photo albums, picture books, and even oral forms of storytelling. As Hillary Chute and Patrick Jagoda argue in their introduction to a recent special issue of *Critical Inquiry*, titled "Comics and Media," there is an often inaccurate and problematic notion of comics, not to mention other forms of representation, as an isolated medium. This presumption is, I would add, often gendered, and requires careful considerations of the ways peripheral forms and genres, like diaries or autobiographies more generally, are dismissed for their so-called feminine qualities. Such omissions reinforce isolationist approaches to literary and artistic genealogies.

Many Jewish women cartoonists have embraced an autobiographical and experimental approach to the medium partly to project their own fantasies and anxieties about what it means to be an outsider within one's assigned community or in relation to communal identities that the cartoonists, and many contemporary Jewish women more broadly, often reject. In addition, because American comics have often been reserved for representations of the fantastic and imaginary, as most easily recognized in the superhero comic, Jewish American women cartoonists are especially sensitive to this profound misrecognition. Their visages and characters remain woefully absent or misrepresented in the history of the superhero genre, not to mention other modes of Jewish American representation. In a sense, their autobiographical comics can be seen as a kind of antidote to that superheroic tradition, which presumes that only the all-powerful, assimilating male superhero and his counterparts, however much they are fantasies, deserve to be seen and heard. Reading these works in the context of a discussion of neglected or undervalued autobiographical modes and genres makes possible a recognition of the transmedial and transgenre nature of comics as a corrective to often exclusionary histories and discussions.

Each of the chapters that follows addresses cartoonists who present revisionary possibilities for what it means "to unaffiliate Jewishly" through a more particular, visualized process of dis-affiliation. I begin with the story of the self-proclaimed "great-grandmother" of women's autobiographical comics in chapter 1. Starting with her now famous 1972 comic, "Goldie: A Neurotic Woman," Aline Kominsky Crumb set the stage for women and men who would use the graphic medium to reveal their darkest secrets and explore their neuroses. Unlike the works of the later cartoonists, however, Kominsky Crumb's work is centered on the depiction and deconstruction of stereotypes. Ethnicity, sexuality, gender, nationality, religion, culture, and class: none of these categories has been off limits for the cartoonist who, at a 2012 comics conference, asserted: "I still feel very Jewish [though] at the same time, I hate it" ("Public Conversation" 128). Kominsky Crumb's comics subvert the idea that individuals are defined by stereotypes or notions of self collectively composed by others, even as she builds her narrative around such images and ideas. In the end her works offer the possibility that by recontextualizing and refiguring damaging group classifications, the artist offers new ways of imagining selfhood.

In chapter 2 I turn to Vanessa Davis, a cartoonist influenced by Kominsky Crumb's work who has nevertheless moved outside a direct fixation with the stereotyped Jewish and/or female body, and more generally with a pronounced attachment to the past. As Davis explained in a recent interview, "I'm not rejecting the existence of body image, but I'm also not concentrating on it" ("In Search" 181). Like the works of the other more recently debuted cartoonists explored here, Davis's comics shift the central focus of autobiographical reflection from an emphasis on the diachronic to the synchronic or the contradictory senses of self she experiences within the present over and above those that have affected her in the past. This shift reflects the distance she, like other younger artists, experiences from narratives of assimilation and integration that nevertheless continue, however peripherally, to inform her works. Incorporating diary comics into the fold of short narrative comics and one-page sketches, Davis's texts relay how framing, context, and perspective can undermine as well as reinforce a sense of place and belonging. In her 2010 graphic memoir, *Make Me a Woman*, as well as in her 2005 graphic journal, *Spaniel Rage*, her persona is consciously and dynamically shaped by the spaces she inhabits. Her works suggest how Jewishness can be reframed, primarily with respect to normative notions of identity as informed by one's relationship to place, one's notion of feeling "at home." In this way her comics, like those of her contemporaries, can be seen as furthering the project of visualized Jewish dis-affiliations as enacted in Aline Kominsky Crumb's comics.

Both published in 2006, Miss Lasko-Gross's *Escape from "Special"* and Lauren Weinstein's *Girl Stories*, which I turn to in chapter 3, are autobiographical narratives that revolve around questions of identity and notions of feeling like an outsider. These texts simultaneously fulfill and challenge expectations of what childhood and adolescent literatures should look and sound like. The focus on childhood and adolescence as the "present" in these memoirs sets up the liminal, or the in-between, as a helpful way of approaching self-representation and self-knowledge. These authors' personae relate to their past identities, especially as women and Jews, as figurations of the self at the threshold. By writing and drawing from the point of view of adolescence, these cartoonists demonstrate how to dis-affiliate by taking on an inherited point of view that nevertheless continually informs a present sense of self—the self composing the autobiography. Always in flux or between worlds, the experience of the adolescent self exemplifies the uneasy sense of dislocation alongside the desire to belong that all these cartoonists are interested in exploring.

In chapter 4 I turn to works by two authors that investigate Jewish women's relationships to Israel in the early twenty-first century. These texts deconstruct Israel both as a place and an idea. Sarah Glidden's 2010 *How to Understand Israel in Sixty Days or Less* and Miriam Libicki's *jobnik!* series, first collectively published in 2008 and ongoing, are travel narratives that trace the journeys of their North American narrators to Israel. By challenging the notion of Israel as "Jewish homeland," these graphic memoirs investigate what Caryn Aviv and David Shneer have described as "the assumptions people make about diaspora" (2). They play with expected notions of the travel memoir genre, revealing the complicated ways that Israel, as a concept and an actual place, affects both the real and imaginary geographics of American Jews.

Rejecting oversimplified notions of Israel as Jewish "homeland," Glidden's and Libicki's works propose dis-affiliation as a stance related to an ethics of accountability, a positioning that exposes the individual story as a narrative framed in large part by its relationship to many seen and unseen others. By shaping identifications through disavowals, as well as through a splintering of networked relationships and perspectives, their works decenter the narrative "I" from the stories they tell, even as those stories are clearly bound to the particularized experiences of the teller. This central paradox ties all of these women's works together: How can you tell a "Jewish" story when you are not even sure what it means to be Jewish? What does it mean to affiliate through an obstinate rejection of cultural norms? Can you claim a Jewish identity without letting go of the parts of yourself and your experiences that do not align with that identity? These cartoonists all claim comics—an "outsider art"—as the language that most fittingly and powerfully lets them express these complex puzzles through their uniquely rendered modes and styles.

Finally, in my conclusion I turn to Liana Finck's *A Bintel Brief*, a book that looks back at an early twentieth-century immigrant community without detaching that narrative from the twenty-first-century point of view that shapes it. Combining the fantastic with retraces of a material, fading, and increasingly abandoned archive, Finck revises the voices, styles, and scenes that make up a remembrance of a Lower East Side Jewish past. Her slender but replete volume of graphic and tragic personal histories, superimposed on a ghostly "present" narrator's search for a connection to her Jewish identity, reflects the ways that the present informs the past even while that past continually and forcefully imposes itself on the present. The book gestures to the possibilities built into the graphic narrative form of reimaging ourselves and our identities by reconnecting to the past without letting it overdetermine how we see ourselves.

When Vanessa Davis incorporates her mother's words into her comic—"What do you consider yourself FIRST: A woman, a Jew, or an American?"—it is her way of signaling the central tension that informs her entire self-narrating project, although she ironically rejects the very premise of the question itself. All the cartoonists discussed here take as axiomatic the notion that they do not have to choose one way of relating to the world, or of visualizing their places in it, over and above another. Instead, they offer their graphic narratives as spaces to reimagine those connections and collisions: between self and other, past and present, word and image, experience and the retelling of it. On the page they can begin to carve out a space, however fragile and tentative, that feels like home.

"My Independent Jewish
Monster Temperament"

The Serial Selves of Aline Kominsky Crumb

line Kominsky Crumb has never disguised her Jewish iden-
tity on the page. From her earliest published works, she
incorporates Yiddishisms into the language of her comics,
often draws her alter egos displaying symbols of their Jewishness, such as wearing Stars of David around their necks, and does not shy
away from continuous criticisms of and reflections on the Jewish middle-class
community she was born into.[1] A close inspection of her comics also reveals a
consistent awareness of the anxiety that accompanies representing the body as
Jewish. As Derek Parker Royal points out in his introduction to a 2007 special
issue of *MELUS* on ethnicity in graphic narratives, comics provides an especially
fertile space for the examination of "those very assumptions that problematize
ethnic representation" because the form has historically relied on visual stereotypes (9). By exaggerating Jewish bodily and behavioral "flaws," especially in her
female personae and characters, Kominsky Crumb confronts such stereotypical
notions of Jewish identification by visualizing them.

This chapter will focus on the ways that Kominsky Crumb's autobiographical
comics play with long-held stereotypes about Jewish women and their bodies,
about women and their bodies more generally, and about the representation of
such bodies and subjectivities in the interface of various autobiographical styles
and modes. Some have referred to her work as "sexist and anti-Semitic" (Crumb
and Kominsky Crumb, "Introduction" 5) because she does not simply reject such
bodily and behavioral codings in favor of more politically correct or antitypological
portrayals of Jewish women. Instead, her comics reflect how, as Sander Gilman
so aptly sums it up, "there is no hiding from the fact of a constructed difference"

(*The Jew's Body* 193). Kominsky Crumb confronts stereotypical representations by recognizing how ingrained they are in her subjectivity and portraying them as a constant and sometimes even productive influence in how she sees herself and others. In a 2007 interview published in *Heeb Magazine,* she discussed her Jewish identity in relation to her experiences growing up in an upwardly mobile, mostly Jewish, suburban community, and particularly in regard to her relationships with "Jewish boys [who] were real snotty" ("Drawn Together" 49). As she explained, "They were these short, skinny boys who wanted little blond girls. Those boys all grown up still make me feel like a Jewish monster. Whereas when I'm with a goy, I feel exotic and sexy and voluptuous." With this statement, Kominsky Crumb reinscribes classifications of Jewish men as petite, feminized, and *shiksa* loving, while she reinforces her own feelings of marginality stemming from another gender stereotype: that of the Jewish woman as "monster."[2] Additionally, what she enjoys about non-Jewish men is their fetishization of the Jewish woman as an exotic, or sexy, "other."

In this response, and, as we shall see, in her comics, Kominsky Crumb suggests that long-standing categorizations of Jewish women, and, consequently, of Jewish and non-Jewish men as well, can become empowering based not only on who is creating the image, but also on how it is being made. In this interview as well as in her characteristically stylized comics, she reveals the contradictions inherent in depictions of Jewish women as both desirable and grotesque in their otherness. By favoring a seemingly unself-conscious portrayal of how conventional notions of the self and of communal identities continue to define the way she depicts herself and others, Kominsky Crumb risks being misread as an amateur artist confirming these stereotypes even as she distorts and dislodges them. Her postwar autobiographical comics present the potential of stereotype as a means of representation that, through dynamic reconstruction, can lead to new ways of seeing and understanding the self, although these new ways of seeing are also always connected to a limiting and destructive past.

Kominsky Crumb experiments with stereotypes to reveal their productive possibilities, as well as their limitations and degradations, not only in relation to her Jewish identity but also in relation to her identity as a woman and artist. Her Jewish body is always inevitably a gendered body, drawn in an often allegedly "crude and sloppy" manner (Kominsky Crumb, "Public Conversation" 124).[3] In her 2007 graphic memoir, *Need More Love,* she illustrates the interdependence of these identity positions through serial depictions of various alter egos in the framework of one overarching narrative. As Nicole McDaniel points out in her 2010 essay "Self-Reflexive Graphic Narrative," the definition of the word *serial* is currently undergoing a transition: "Now also linked with repetition, seriality can be either recursive and episodic or sequential and chronological" (199). For the purpose of this book, I understand the serial to be aligned with the recursive and episodic, that is, with a lack of any sense of closure—a definition that aligns with Stuart Charmé's spiraling model of Jewish identity, as outlined in my introduction. While Kominsky Crumb previously published most of the comics included in her memoir, a reading of her representations of Jewish identity not separately but as part of this larger, serial, collage-like work reflects experimentation with notions of Jewishness as integrated into the scheme of a structured but nevertheless open-ended narrative. Teetering on the verge of the autobiographical and imaginary, her graphic memoir invokes and performs countless anxieties and fluctuations about genre classification and intent, much like the graphic narratives of all the cartoonists examined in this volume. The book comes to almost four hundred pages and collects an amalgam of everything from photographs and reproductions of paintings to reprints of previously published comics, both in full and as shorter excerpts, as well as typed journal entries. Her ambitious aesthetic project questions the constructions that form and inform self-identifications—of woman, Jew, or artist, for example. It also challenges and makes visible the artificial boundaries between how we define ourselves and how others define us. Finally, it reveals the ways that these various constructions can be informed, supplanted, or destabilized through a process of visually mapping them.

"It is Me But It's Not Completely Me"

Born in 1948 in Long Island, New York, Aline Kominsky Crumb is best known as an autobiographical underground cartoonist and the wife of legendary countercultural cartoonist Robert Crumb. As Hillary L. Chute points out in *Graphic Women*, which includes a seminal chapter on Kominsky Crumb's comics and especially her representations of sexuality, "the case of the Crumb family is possibly *the* defining example of th[e] double standard at work" (31). While Robert Crumb has achieved worldwide fame and is respected in the comics world for "writing the darker side of (his own) tortured male sexuality," Kominsky Crumb's work has been criticized for the very same reason. In fact, Chute's chapter-length discussion of Kominsky Crumb's comics is the first critical text to include an in-depth examination of this highly influential cartoonist. [4] Despite the lack of critical attention, Kominsky Crumb is clearly one of the initial and highly influential members in what can be seen as a genealogy of what I call postassimilated Jewish American women cartoonists. [5]

Kominsky Crumb's comics have often been looked down upon as scratchy, "crude scrawls" (Crumb and Kominsky Crumb, "Introduction" 4). Instead of recognizing her works as intentionally stylized, some critics have dismissed them as narcissistic, amateur, and confessional. As Sidonie Smith and Julia Watson point out in *Interfaces*, women's autobiographical projects are often viewed as transparent renderings of their life stories instead of carefully constructed interpretations and performances of their memories and experiences, which is what is more generally presumed about men's autobiographies. Kominsky Crumb capitalizes on this misreading by frequently putting herself down in her comics, both verbally and visually. As critics and readers have frequently pointed out, she looks much more attractive in photographs and in person than she does in drawings of her personae. In public forums, too, she often plays along with the idea that she lacks a deliberate consciousness about her artistic style, as though the reason she draws herself as "ugly" and in such a "crude" manner is because she does not, in effect, have the skills it takes to draw in what would be considered a more realistic, and therefore ostensibly more skilled, style. In one interview, in response to a question about her artistic vision, she told the interviewer, "You seem to think I have a more sophisticated approach to the whole matter than I do" (Crumb and Kominsky Crumb, "A Joint Interview" 122). In this way she contributes to the false notion of herself as an untrained and amateur cartoonist, a conceit that allows her more freedom on the page, although it often reinforces misreadings of her comics.

Despite these projections, her works themselves draw attention to the performativity and deliberateness of her autobiographical depictions. In individual comics she often changes the style in which she draws herself from panel to panel. Sometimes the variation is as subtle as the shape of her nose or the cut of her hair; sometimes she brings attention to more radical fluctuations through textual commentary. For example, in many of the collaborative comics that Kominsky Crumb draws with her husband, some of which were included in *Need More Love*, she draws little starred notes, similar to footnotes, at the bottom of certain panels and pages. [6] In one such note in the long comic "Krumb and Kominsky in Their Cute Little Life Together," originally published in 1992 in *The Complete Dirty*

Laundry Comics, she writes, "The Bunch changes her look a lot because she likes to draw herself in different cute outfits with new hairdos whenever she wants to!!" (186).[7] Sure enough, The Bunch, one of Kominsky Crumb's many personae, is drawn wearing different clothing and with several hairdos throughout the black-and-white, almost uniformly six-panels-per-page collaborative comic. Her hair is down and curly in all of the panels on one page, her feet bearing large and chunky platform shoes. On a previous page, she has her hair up in a ponytail, her unshaven legs sprout tiny black hairs, and her oversized feet are bare. Other physical details, from the width of her thighs and knees to the shape and size of her nose to the cut and cast of her mouth and eyes, are also continually modified over the course of the narrative. In these ways, flagrantly but also, at times, less obviously, Kominsky Crumb highlights the differing images she has of herself, each dependent on her mood and outlook at the time she is writing and drawing. Robert Crumb's relatively uniform depictions of his alter ego throughout the comic—he dons the same plaid shirt and slacks for the first seventeen pages and often maintains nearly identical awkward postures and gestures over the course of numerous panels, if not whole pages—further serve to highlight Kominsky Crumb's shifting compositions. In addition, although The Bunch's outfits, accessories, body and face shapes, and hairstyles so frequently alter, the most obvious characteristics tend to remain generally uniform over the course of full pages, at which point they often change. Presumably, The Bunch does not significantly modify her appearance until the artist begins a new day of creating the comic, which starts on a fresh page. In this way the reader is reminded, particularly through Kominsky Crumb's contributions to these joint ventures, of the process of drawing an autobiographical comic as something that happens over time, and that is therefore dependent on and bound to the very same shifts in subjectivity as the author herself. By continually refiguring the ways she draws herself, even or especially through subtle details, Kominsky Crumb's work reveals the multiplicity of images that individuals have of themselves, which are reliant on context and undergo endless transformations, both considerable and slight.

Kominsky Crumb uses another powerful technique within her comics to relay the gap between life and its representation and to draw the reader's attention to the constructedness of her self-depictions. Scott McCloud has outlined several different categories of word-image combinations often used in comics, although he admits the possibilities are endless (152).[8] In a "word specific" combination, for instance, the text gives away the story line and the image on the page merely helps illustrate what is already written (153). In a "picture specific" combination, on the other hand, the opposite occurs, with the words on the page merely acting as a "soundtrack" to the image. McCloud determines that the most common combination, an "interdependent" one, involves "words and pictures [that] go hand in hand to convey an idea that neither could convey alone" (155). Kominsky Crumb uses such interdependent combinations to reveal a disparity between what she is thinking and how she presents herself on the outside (often, at least in her earlier years, as amenable to others). For instance, in a comic reprinted only in part, and placed early on in the memoir, she depicts The Bunch talking to an art teacher who she later realizes was only interested in her because of her looks (*Need More Love* 110). In this vibrant and colorful piece, so typical of her individually created works, The Bunch, with curly black-and-red hair flowing and sporting a bright, flower-patterned dress, stands focused as she composes a cubist-inspired painting of the nude female model located at the front of the classroom. Each panel is cluttered with bright colors, lines, and shapes; imperfectly hand-drawn letters accented by exclamation points and inconsistent ellipses, and encased in word bubbles, thought bubbles, and narrative boxes, further crowd the scene. Hard at work, The Bunch is approached by an ogling instructor, whose directed gaze ironically neglects the naked woman standing in front of them as well as the one in The Bunch's painting. She turns her back to her artwork in the following panel in order to hopefully, but unsuccessfully, engage as an artist with this male authority figure, who now stands with his back to the artwork and his arms folded. The dramatic difference between how The Bunch represents herself to him—with a smile and the words "Hm . . . Wow Great!"—and what she is thinking, which is that she has lost some of the pleasure in painting because of the "complicated" dynamics of the art classroom, comes across through this interdependent word/image combination. The reader has to work to assemble these often conflicting layers of consciousness and experience, in the same way that the reader has to accept The Bunch's different body shapes and outfits as representative of the same person.

In these consecutive panels, the reader is additionally confronted with two differing versions of The Bunch's painting of the nude model's body, with the second image having acquired a tuft of curly orange pubic hair to match, in color and style, the art teacher's own unruly head and beard. These small, transformative details reward the attentive reader, adding humor to the recollection of an otherwise humiliating and disempowering encounter. Carefully, but also often buoyantly, Kominsky Crumb employs the unique form of comics, specifically juxtapositions of words and images as well as images and images, to convey the inherently ambiguous and selective nature of self-projection and reflection. The visual self on the page, divided by and of itself, is differentiated from the verbal self on the page, which is further separated into overlapping internalized and externalized subjectivities.

The global framework and structure of *Need More Love* additionally establishes Kominsky Crumb's self-imaginings and influences as multiple, fragmented, and often contradictory in sentiment, if not also in appearance, style, and voice. In the memoir, which interweaves many of her previously published works with a running diarylike commentary, she incorporates photographs and paintings of herself alongside her autobiographical comics as another way of highlighting the intentional contrast between the various ways she sees herself and the ways others see her. Her inclusion of serial but always slightly differing drawn and recorded autobiographical visions reinforces the idea that every single self-image is built out of a variety of notions of self. In another interview, she commented on the disparity between her drawn self and her so-called real life self by explaining, "The character that I draw is fictional to some extent. It is me but it's not completely me. There's another part of me that's a little bit more well-adjusted, vain and confident" ("Interview with Andrea Juno" 172). Here she reinforces what is already plainly visible in representations of her personae on the page: much like her real-life persona, her cartoon selves are pieced together out of multiple and often mismatched versions of reality and fantasy.

Juxtaposing photographs beside paintings and drawings also allows Kominsky Crumb to play with and challenge the hierarchy of signification so often taken for granted in discussions of self-representation. The predigital photographic image, for instance, has sometimes been assumed to be a neutral object of communication—a nearly unmediated copy of the thing that has been photographed, surpassing writing in its truth-telling capabilities. As Susan Sontag argues in *On Photography*, "Photographed images do not seem to be statements of the world so much as pieces of it, miniatures of reality that anyone can make or acquire" (4). Of course, as Sontag, Roland Barthes, and others have pointed out, photographs are never unbiased reflections of our "real" selves.[9] For example, the body that has been photographed can never find what Barthes, in *Camera Lucida*, calls "zero degree" (12). In addition, as with all mediums, readings of photographs are dependent on the context surrounding their production and reception, like the mind-set of what Barthes identifies as three key figures: the photographer, the subject of the photograph, and the person viewing the photograph. Therefore, for example, someone looking at a photograph found in a family album is going to see something very different from someone looking at a photograph in a museum. A photographic representation, and the response it evokes, is never at a constant.

Images in comics have, in contrast, generally been presumed to be distant and vague renderings of whatever they are meant to represent. For this reason, cartoonists who draw autobiographical comics all too often find their works being referred to as "graphic novels" instead of "graphic memoirs."[10] Thus, for example, Art Spiegelman's *Maus II* was originally placed in the fiction section of the *New York Times* best-seller list, much to the author's confusion and annoyance. In a follow-up letter to the editor published December 29, 1991, Spiegelman admonished: "I know that by delineating people with animal heads I've raised problems of taxonomy for you. Could you consider adding a special 'nonfiction/mice' category to your list?" (quoted in *MetaMaus* 150). Terminology aside, comics is often presupposed to be less realistic, and therefore less sophisticated, than other kinds of art and writing. As Douglas Wolk argues in his 2007 cultural history, *Reading Comics*, only in the last few decades, with the publications, especially, of Art Spiegelman's *Maus I* in 1986 and *Maus II* in 1991 and Frank Miller's *Batman: The Dark Night Returns* and Alan Moore's *Watchmen*, both in 1986, has comics begun to be perceived as a literary form capable of addressing "serious" and real world concerns (8). In general, in North America, before the *Maus* series, and, though to a slightly lesser degree, even after, comics has often been presumed to be childish and lacking in artistic and literary merit. Wolk calls the last few decades a "moment of crisis" for the comics world, as the field of what he terms "mainstream" comics battles the field of "art comics" (11). The hierarchy established by many critics, and especially those unfamiliar with the medium, is of "art comics" as highbrow, and "mainstream" comics (such as adventure, superhero, and newspaper strips) as lowbrow. Indeed, many use the term *graphic novels* rather than *comics* to describe what they deem to be more "serious" works. As Wolk and others, like McCloud, point out, this issue reflects a misperception of comics as a genre rather than a medium that can accommodate many genres. Indeed, the reason I use the terms *comics, graphic memoirs,* and *graphic narratives* interchangeably throughout this book is to stress the importance of breaking down—instead of reinforcing—such superficial hierarchical classifications, as certain terms, and especially *graphic novel,* have frequently been used to rhetorically affirm the legitimacy of the medium as a form of "high" literature.

Both comics and photography are therefore mediums that have been misunderstood, with one, comics, often presumed to be an overly constructed and the other, photography, to be a nearly unconstructed representation of the subjects they are meant to convey. Kominsky Crumb utilizes these common misperceptions to her advantage when she includes both photographs and comics in her memoir. For her, playing with the repetition of images, and especially of her own image, in these different forms allows her to recognize and draw attention to difference within a general sense of sameness; it offers her the opportunity to trace the expressions and postures that never allow her body to find "zero degree" and, therefore, that gesture to other possible points of rupture hidden within images of the self. For example, throughout the memoir she includes photographs taken of herself at various stages of life, and these images are presented alongside, and sometimes on pages adjacent to, comics that she draws of herself in these same

1.1 *Aline Kominsky Crumb, untitled photograph, Woodmere, New York, 1966. In* Need More Love, *p. 101. Used by permission of Aline Kominsky Crumb.*

stages. Kominsky Crumb has admitted that the way she draws her personae, a style she calls "very expressionistic" (*Need More Love* 135), does not at all align with how she appears to other people. As she explains of her earlier comics, "I was actually pretty cute at that time, but I portrayed myself as a hideous monster" (151). The reader of *Need More Love* experiences this contrast firsthand in sorting through the various images that make up the memoir. Consider, for instance, the photograph of Kominsky Crumb posing with a guitar at age eighteen (101, figure 1.1). In the photo, with her head titled downward and her eyes half-closed, she looks shy and demure. She sits at the edge of a soft, cushioned chair covered in a flowery, antique pattern, her bare feet poised on dark, drab carpeting. The tone of the image, with its muted colors, faded furniture, and reclusive subject, is morose. A pair of dark sneakers is somewhat haphazardly strewn in the corner, adding to the general atmosphere of posed intimacy. The photograph manages to simultaneously evoke a sense of closeness and distance from its subject: she looks caught in a moment, but there is something careful and expectant in her pose, in the way a few long chunks of hair solicitously fall into the frame of her face, in the careful curve of her knees as they chastely fall together, in the sculpted neatness of her fingers pressed lightly into the guitar strings.

Turning the page of the memoir, the reader encounters a markedly distinct, drawn and brightly colored image of Kominsky Crumb's persona at around the same time period (102, figure 1.2). In this oversized square cartoon, set against a beaming, bubble-gum pink background, The Bunch stands outdoors with bulging eyes and oversized teeth, her hands splayed out in an awkwardly cartoonish gesture. Her orange hair is wild and frizzy, her nose oversized and hooked, and her bright dress looks short enough to suggest a tantalizing exposure, advanced in the form of dark, shadowed lines. The contrast between the two pictures is not limited to her bodily features; it extends to her behavior, as her drawn self contrasts dramatically not only with her photographed self but also with the relatively unsuspecting, tame male passersby occupying the same Lower East Side city street in the cartoon. She shouts out, to the discomfort of another customer, "I'm free at last!" and her exclamation, drawn in large, capital letters, mirrors the noisy, protopunk lyrics, originally composed and sung by the rock group The Fugs ("Slum goddess of the Lower East Side . . . "), that crowd a large part of the page. Above the scene a series of cracked, glassy windows and a crumbling rooftop hint at the sharply divergent, subdued indoor setting left behind with this sudden turn of the page. As this image suggests, Kominsky Crumb's comics personae, which

1.2 *Aline Kominsky Crumb, untitled cartoon. In* Need More Love, *p. 102.*
Used by permission of Aline Kominsky Crumb.

are exaggerated or distorted versions of the "real" thing, are paradoxically the depictions that allow her to reveal her deepest secrets and expose herself, again and again, in ways she cannot with photographs or other, more "realistic" modes. With the comics versions of herself, Kominsky Crumb can feel "free at last," even if subject to a potentially judgmental audience. In the cartoon she is not, as with the photograph, "caught" in a private setting—she is, instead, clearly in charge, open and unmasked, and willing to let it all hang out. Because of this dramatic difference in self-representation, readers are motivated to look twice at the snapshots and family photographs that are supposedly traces of her actual self. In this way the juxtaposition of photographs and comics in the text brings to the surface the gap between self-perception and perception by others and the question of what any image can convey all on its own.

By incorporating different mediums into her memoir, Kominsky Crumb also takes advantage of the uncertain status of both comics and photography in the arts world. In 1965 Pierre Bourdieu published his influential sociological study, *Photography: A Middle-Brow Art*, which argued that photographs were somewhere in between what are considered "noble" and "vulgar" arts. If music, painting, and sculpture were thought of as legitimate arts, for instance, and potentially mass-produced items like clothing and furniture were considered nonlegitimate arts, then photography, along with film, was, for Bourdieu, located in the middle of this spectrum. As Jane Gallop points out in her hybrid academic autobiography, *Living with His Camera*, Bourdieu's survey was published just as family photography started to become integrated into the world of art photography (132). Nevertheless, his book calls attention to the false oppositions that continue to divide what are considered serious and unserious forms—like so-called literary versus genre fiction, for instance, or popular versus high culture—and the ways that an (arguably) enduringly "middlebrow" medium like photography, with its utilitarian as well as nonutilitarian functions, can prompt us to question such problematic classifications. Comics is similarly valued, even if its status is changing: although they have historically been tied to popular and consumerist culture, for instance, print comic books bear the traces of the hand or hands that draw and write them and are therefore also often coveted as collectible art objects. Both mediums, then, frequently activate questionings of these problematic constructions between lowbrow and highbrow art, and each has consequently been traversed by many as an exciting avenue for autobiographical exploration—a storytelling mode that similarly calls into question definitions of art and literature.

By including both photographs and comics in her memoir to create a hybrid text, Kominsky Crumb runs the risk of marginalizing herself even more than she would as a cartoonist exclusively. Unlike the acclaimed works of cartoonists Art Spiegelman and Alison Bechdel, for example, which include actual photographs or drawings of photographs as bookends or singularly central images within their texts, Kominsky Crumb's memoir is so replete with photographs of herself and others that her work cannot be said to fit into any easily defined category. This marginalization works in much the same way as her self-deprecation regarding her artistic skills. In both cases, although she potentially restricts her audience, she allows herself the freedom to experiment with form in a way that might not otherwise be possible.[11] While she subtitles her book a "graphic memoir," many readers might initially be turned off by the lack of a clear categorization of the text based on the differing mediums gathered, in a seemingly disorganized fashion, in its pages. In addition, the overwrought and glittery appearance of the book itself, as well as its title, *Need More Love*, presupposes a certain flattened and solipsistic leitmotif, thereby possibly alienating potential readers even further. A cartoon drawing of Kominsky Crumb's persona is centered on the purple cover in a gilded and studded pink, purple, and blue frame. Four small speech bubbles emanate from her brightly dressed character's thick, lipstick-covered mouth, which is busy chewing on a large red valentine heart. "More shoes," "More beauty," "More spiritual enlightenment," "More pleasure and fun," the word bubbles read. An oversized, technical drawing of a realistic human heart hovers inexplicably behind the wide-eyed caricature. This visual and textual language of heated, sentimental excess signals the diverse catalog of confessional materials bound within the book's pages even as it mocks the autobiographical practice in itself as garish and narcissistic. In this way Kominsky Crumb's cover image responds to and satirizes a tradition of autobiography in which authors frequently begin by apologizing for their self-interest and qualifying the content of the material to come.

Most famously in comics autobiography, for example, Justin Green's introduction to his 1972 classic, "Binky Brown Meets the Holy Virgin Mary," pictures the cartoonist with bound arms and legs, hanging upside down and writing with a pen in his mouth that has been dipped in "dad's blood" (10).[12] The hero apologizes for the "indulgent, morbid, and obscene" content of the following pages, beseeching the reader, "Please don't think I'm an asshole." The subsequent text makes good on the narrator's promise, for instance picturing rays shooting out of Binky Brown's penis as he divulges his personal history of going to Catholic school, coming to terms with his sexual needs and desires, and dealing with his obsessive compulsive disorder. For Kominsky Crumb, the excess of her memoir project is also built out of the explicit and personal journey she takes us on—one that includes, for example, a humorous and disturbing exploration of her parents' sex life and drawn images of them engaged in the act. But the excess of *Need More Love* is unapologetically presented, and it extends even beyond the graphic

1.3 *Aline Kominsky Crumb, drawing, 2005. In* Need More Love, *p. 290.*
Used by permission of Aline Kominsky Crumb.

material contained in its pages, in both senses of the term *graphic*. The book is also excessive in its sheer size—the roughly 7-by-10-inch book is almost 2 inches wide—and the expanse of personal materials it brings together. In a sense *Need More Love* is a fully fleshed out, if whimsical, archive of the self, one that takes into account the many verbal and visual materials that the autobiographical artist has collected over time and internalized, which have then helped her form a distinctive but ever changing projection of herself in her comics and other artworks.[13] In this way the memoir stands not just as an independent entity but also as a supplement to the many individual works Kominsky Crumb has produced in various contexts. The photographs in *Need More Love* reinforce the atmosphere of abundant cataloging that is ingrained not only in this particular memoir but also in Kominsky Crumb's lifelong project of self-inquiry and self-representation.

In drawing on the art of collage in her memoir, Kominsky Crumb reveals the possibilities available to the artist creating "in excess," the artist willing to purposefully and creatively straddle the line between fantasy and reality. Toward the end of *Need More Love*, she includes a sketch of herself standing beside her friend (290, figure 1.3). The black-and-white image is much closer to her likeness in photographs and real life. In it she stands with her arms crossed, her mouth closed, and a pair of sunglasses covering her eyes. There are a few details captured in the sketch—several photos sitting on a bookshelf in the background, flowers carefully drawn onto her friend's blouse, a train of chunky bracelets decorating one of her own wrists. The sleeves of her top are covered in painstakingly applied dotted marks, and there is light shadowing cast behind the women. This placid, careful image suggests that the persona presented here is holding something back from the spectator, and it is as much her stance as it is the more realistic depiction of this likeness that enables her to maintain this boundary. If drawing herself cartoonishly allows Kominsky Crumb to explore and expose the most secretive and hidden parts of herself and her experiences, then this sketch suggests that the closer she moves toward a realistic or photographic depiction, the more she hides herself from the viewer. Her inclusion of a photographic album within the memoir therefore allows her to submit an entire spectrum of self-revelation as accessible within its pages. But it is through the comics form alone that she comes closest to conveying her "real" self on the page, through her vibrantly curated personae. The force of Kominsky Crumb's work emerges from the creation of characters on the page who reveal themselves as somehow a part of, or attached to, the real-life author, but who are also distanced, exaggerated, and made-up versions of the "original"—characters who represent "me but . . . not completely me."

"In the Beginning I Felt Loved"

Goldie is one of Kominsky Crumb's earliest semiautobiographical recurring characters. In a 2009 interview Kominsky Crumb described Goldie as a kind of alter ego representing the worst or most hated parts of her. As she explained, "my maiden name is Goldsmith. They used to call my father 'Goldie,' so it went back to my father. And also since I didn't like my father very much, I sort of hated that name, and my character was a part of me that I felt was repulsive, and the name sort of fit that character" ("Interview," *Believer* 62). Here, in the choice of her alter ego's name, she demonstrates the importance of acknowledging the most hated and feared aspects of herself and her childhood. She is loyal to this past, even the elements of it she wants to forget. Her incorporation of negative concerns in her comics, and especially her frequent retellings of the traumatic events of her childhood, including teenage experiences of date rape, and physical and emotional abuses from her parents, indicate her awareness that to take oneself out of the past and into the present requires a constant revisiting of those past events. In addition, the incorporation of a "present"-day diarylike narrative, interspersed throughout *Need More Love*, in which she frequently retells the same series of events that are portrayed in her comics, performs a privileging of the past, in all its different incarnations, through a rendering of the self mired in the present.

Kominsky Crumb's comic, "Goldie: A Neurotic Woman," was first published on the opening pages of the 1972 premier issue of *Wimmin's Comix*, the first ongoing comic drawn exclusively by women.[14] This five-page black-and-white text, which is often considered the first published autobiographical comic by a woman, traces her initial twenty-two years through various images of herself, as her alter ego Goldie, that dramatically diverge. While Kominsky Crumb's signature scratchy style and crammed design is recognizable in this, her first, piece, republished in full almost halfway through *Need More Love*, it is decidedly more muted in sensibility than her later work. This is not only because of the lack of colorful backgrounds and jagged shapes making up the individual images but also because of the comic's more generally polished look, molded in large part by her careful use of black-and-white contrasts throughout. In the panel following the title panel, we see a smiling, curly-haired little girl with a doll protected in her arms and a tiny, almost indecipherable Jewish star around her neck (140, figure 1.4). The caption reads, "In the beginning I felt loved . . . " In this image Goldie, her face bordered in tight curls and a small, neat hair bow, is framed by a rectangular box and surrounded by lumpy-looking relatives ogling and admiring her from the sidelines. The two older women crowding around her are drawn as stretched-out figures dressed in distracting and unflattering patterns, with breasts sagging and eyes rolling as their more composed male counterparts hide in the background. The box-within-a-box arrangement suggests that such unadulterated love and attention, framed most powerfully through female presences, requires stringent boundaries; Goldie's sense of unconditional love is related to an understanding of herself as divided from, but still maintaining proximity to, others. It is a sense of self that, as we soon witness, is unsustainable, as it inevitably and

1.4 Aline Kominsky Crumb, first page from "Goldie: A Neurotic Woman," 1972. In Need More Love, p. 140. Used by permission of Aline Kominsky Crumb.

theatrically breaks down. In the final panel on the bottom of the same page, in contrast to the happier images portrayed of a much-loved and sought after Goldie, surrounded by others, puberty finally hits. A grotesque figure, with protruding legs and a sharp grimace marking her face, fills a bubble of white light. Her hair has lost its bounce, her body has ballooned, and large round blemishes cover her cheeks and chin. "With puberty came uglyness and guilt," the narrator writes, and this lonely panel, framed by an uncertain layer of crosshatched, shadowy darkness, accentuates her new, unwieldy frame. In this drawing, the young Goldie is pictured completely alone for the first time since her debut, and this isolation seems to accentuate and cement her warped self-image.

The dramatic metamorphosis occurs abruptly, emphasizing how Goldie's changing and aging body makes her feel increasingly out of control and isolated from others. On the following two pages, as she goes through puberty and attends high school, she is increasingly portrayed alone or, when connected to others, in humiliating and degrading situations. Her experiences at school and at home overrun one another, as she juxtaposes her first sexual encounters and hungers with her father's verbal abuses ("Ya can't shine shit," he says to her one day as she applies makeup in front of the bathroom mirror) and her desire to "attract a boy" (141). These episodes culminate in a panel pictured halfway down the third page that reads, "I was a giant slug living in a fantasy of future happiness" (142). Here, building on the grotesque self-image first developed with the onset of puberty, her body indeed comes to resemble a giant, molluscan mass, with formless pillars for legs, an odd, oval-shaped head, and an exaggeratedly rounded nose. In the background we see two happy, good-looking, skinny couples cavorting and looking off into the sidelines. The framework of this panel, however, contrasts with both the isolated, puberty-struck Goldie and the framed and admired golden child, suggesting once again that happiness and self-image are connected to the status of her boundaries in relation to others. As a slug, her body overtakes the frame and, although she is spatially a part of this school crowd (there is no dividing frame here), the borderlessness of her protruding body actually highlights her otherness, the sense that her experience is taking place in another dimension. She looks off to the side just like the other teenagers, but the dramatic distinction between what she is thinking—"When I'm 18 I'll be beautiful"—and how she looks suggests that she is not seeing whatever it is that the others are seeing. Ironically, this teenaged Goldie is in a sense no longer subject

1.5 *Aline Kominsky Crumb, last four panels from "Goldie: A Neurotic Woman," 1972.*
In Need More Love, *p. 144. Used by permission of Aline Kominsky Crumb.*

to the gaze of the other, even in her heightened, self-conscious state, because she cannot recognize where she ends and others begin. She cannot orient herself because she is so overwhelmed by the scale of her own self-delusions, the distended and grotesque image of herself that isolates her from the very frameworks that first helped shape her self-imaginings.

If the first half of "Goldie" traces the narrator's transformation from a smiling, protected little girl, literally boxed in on the page, to a wretched, borderless adolescent—one who cannot distinguish how she sees herself from how others might be seeing her—the second half expands on the traumas of this early narrative, opening up the potential for reorientation. As an adult, Goldie acts out different roles that nevertheless continue to tie her to her early life. On one page she is first pictured as a Jewish wife, her sagging bosom now mirroring those earlier pictured ones belonging to her mother and grandmother, and then, after rebellion, as a sex object, her body appealingly on display in a tight negligee, as she had earlier fantasized of her eighteen-year-old future self. In each case she does not last long in her new roles because of the contrast between how she feels and how she wants to be seen, a gap often demonstrated in the text through a pronounced disparity between what she is thinking (as depicted verbally in thought bubbles or narrative text) and how she presents herself (as depicted usually visually in facial and bodily expressions). The divergence between her inner and outer selves impels her to keep trying out new roles in the hopes of finding some sense of relief, of repossessing the sense of wholeness she felt as a child surrounded by clear and closed boundaries separating her from others. In one panel, which shows her lying naked on a bed with men lined up at her front door and one leaving the house with a satisfied grin on his face, she passively explains, "The more I was ostracized the more I degenerated" (144). Like Goldie-the-child, the adult Goldie depicts her actions, as well as her self-image, as out of her control. Only in the last three panels, when she actively returns to isolated images of herself, does she begin to "analyze the past events of [her] life" and gain some sense of command over these fragmented snapshots.

Most crucially, in the third-to-last panel of the entire comic, the narrative shifts suddenly, as Goldie maps out her internal life onto a close-up sketch of her head (144, figure 1.5). This close-up dramatically differs from the storytelling panels that make up the rest of the comic, and here she pictures just the profile of her face, with little lines dotting the skin beneath her eyes and tiny dots and circles suggesting scaly imperfections on her skin's surface. Half of her bulbous nose bleeds into the previous panel, though skipping over a small white gutter space, suggesting that this moment of retrospective analysis has merged fragments of the past and present into a more unsettling, inconclusive time frame. Above this profile of the lower half of her face, using arrows and words, she sketches links between the different influences in her life. "Parents" and "husband" occupy two-thirds of this hemispheric diagram, while the final section is left relatively bare, but for a question mark and the words "void of fear" and "uncertainty" traced across it. As she diagrams the forces and experiences that have shaped her until now, she distinguishes herself clearly from others and finds herself, finally, "indignant at everyone else" (144). For the first time, she comes to possess, of her own agency, those boundaries that were forced on her as a child. This mapping powerfully exposes the previous lack of active self-imagining on her part, as a question mark, a "void," fills the space where her subjectivity has, until now, been filled with visualizations largely stemming from or determined by others.

Tellingly, the Star of David appears twice in "Goldie." It first appears in the opening panel when Goldie is still the "golden child," her image framed by loved ones. The star disappears as Goldie's childhood story unravels, signifying that her conception of herself as Jewish and her subsequent omission of that identification is intimately tied to her relationship with her changing, increasingly sexual, and sexualized, female body. The second Star of David appears in a panel depicting the beginning of Goldie's first and unhappy marriage (143). The star looms large behind the bodies of the newlyweds, suggesting a point of union or connection between them. However, the couple's body language, the thought and speech bubbles next to each character, and the captions accompanying the image tell a different story. "It happened so fast," her new husband thinks, as Goldie declares, "You're all mine." Goldie's neediness, in comparison to her husband's sense of shock and inevitable suffocation, presages the unfolding of a marriage characterized by miscommunication and emotional isolation. The Star of David, so prominent in this mismatched union, comes to symbolize the life and home that this couple will build together, as the chuppah, the ceremonial Jewish wedding canopy, is meant to symbolize in Jewish weddings. Unfortunately, as the larger context of the panel shows, it is a home premised on misunderstandings and the pressure of familial expectations—expectations that are closely linked with that symbol of Jewish identity. "Thank God he's Jewish," Goldie's mother's thought bubble reads. In both cases, the Star of David represents an identity symbol forced onto Goldie by her family, and the narratives that unfold after the star is depicted and then omitted suggest this enforced and isolated version of an inherited identity as ominous and, inevitably for Goldie, unsustainable. Kominsky Crumb's inclusion of Jewish symbols and concerns in "Goldie," which will become even more central in the next few comics I explore in this chapter, reveal her desire to grapple, through what I have been calling dis-affiliation, with the complexities and contradictions of what it means to be a contemporary secular Jew in America. In place of these prescribed symbols of affiliation, the question mark in the third to last panel of the comic stands for a designation as yet undiscovered, a self-selected, undetermined, and therefore potentially freeing representation.

In the final panel of "Goldie," soon after she has laid out her past life in a simple, close-up sketch, she is pictured in a storytelling panel once again, sitting in the driver's seat of a car with her cat in tow. This time, in contrast to the opening, she looks directly at the reader, and the caption reads, "Finally after 22 years of trying to please other people. / I set out to live in my own style!" Given the dramatic identity changes so apparent in most of the comic, it is unclear that Goldie *has* any kind of personal style—except for the one drawn onto the page and tying together the young and old Goldie, the character undergoing traumatic past experiences and the character drawing and telling of those experiences. This final image then suggests that it is Goldie-the-artist who inevitably ties together the young, happy child, the miserable slug, and, finally, the adult pursuing independence. The style is both overarching and still being sought out, thereby confirming the impossibility of ever fully reconciling these many versions of herself. With the artist's hand, which dangles here out the front window of the car, the past that haunts and hurts her, including those versions of her identity that were forced on her, also serves as the basis of her relational self-explorations.

This boxed-in version of Goldie inside the car therefore represents her desire both for boundaries and for continuous movement in relation to those boundaries. She becomes an insider and outsider in relation to her own life, able to articulate the traumatic experiences of puberty through adulthood from the inside, through the perspectives of a child, an adolescent, and finally an adult, because of her distance from them as an autobiographer-artist, as one who has learned to seek and observe from the outside. Goldie looks at us, in this last panel, from within the frame of her car, which symbolizes movement and possibility, but she is still somewhat stagnant in this image, as she can never fully escape the boundaries of her own constructed narrative.

As the insider-outsider artist, Goldie's position at the end of this comic demonstrates a potentially empowering way for her to locate her Jewish identity, one that Kominsky Crumb's personae enact in many of her works. For her alter egos, as for many contemporary Jews, the questions surrounding Jewishness and the representation of that Jewishness begin with the paradox of Jewish identity as both inherited and chosen. In his foundational 1987 book *Beyond Ethnicity*, Werner

Sollors refers to "the conflict between contractual and hereditary, self-made and ancestral, definitions of American identity—between *consent* and *descent*—as the central drama in American culture" (5–6). With this "Goldie" comic, Kominsky Crumb shows how certain elements of one's Jewish identity—adopting various cultural and religious practices or identifying *as* a Jew in a certain community, for example—can be accepted or rejected, whereas other aspects of that identity—familial ties, how others see you—are without choice. Her representation, at the end of "Goldie," of being an artist as a primarily consent-based identity allows her a safe vantage point from which to explore the elements of her senses of self that have been thrust onto her. And it is, oddly enough, through an exploration of and experimentation with those inherited aspects of her identities, particularly as a woman and Jew, that she can establish choice both from within and alongside these identities.

"So I Managed to Make It Through High School With My Nose!"

The comic "Goldie" appears in chapter 2 of *Need More Love*, titled "Escape." This chapter focuses on the beginning of Kominsky Crumb's career as a comics artist, the vocation that allowed her to escape from (and then return to, in her work) the strict confines of her family and childhood community. By putting her first comic in the second chapter of the memoir, Kominsky Crumb suggests the importance of "Goldie" in terms of the story of her career rather than primarily in terms of the events of her early life. Conversely, her comic "Nose Job," originally published in issue 15 of *Wimmen's Comix* in 1989, forms part of the first chapter of the memoir, "Post-War Jerks," which centers on her childhood and adolescence. This chronological play—the comics are situated not in the order they were drawn or published, but rather in terms of the unfolding of her subjectivity and maturation as an artist—suggests that "Nose Job" reflects Kominsky Crumb's struggle with her Jewishness before she came to identify herself as an artist. In a sense, then, this comic can be read as prefiguring that artistic "style," the freedom that being an artist affords her in terms of the ways she imagines and depicts herself.

Early on in *Need More Love*'s "Post-War Jerks" chapter, in one of the brief diarylike pages interspersed throughout the memoir, she describes her family's "upwardly mobile" move to Woodmere, New York, a community in Long Island, when she was still a young child. Her description of the community presumes everyone in it to be Jewish; along with socioeconomic status, Jewish identity is what ties the community together and forms the backdrop of her childhood:

> The financial and social pressure to keep up was monstrous in the Five Towns. . . . An education was seen merely as a way to make more money. The ultimate for Jewish boys was to go to medical school and become doctors, or gods as far as everyone was concerned. For us girls, a good education was the way to land a rich husband and secure a "better life," meaning a large, showy new house, a big brand new car, the right schools, summer camps and beach and country clubs, the absolute latest fashion ("It's what they're wearing deah dahling!"), and every beauty treatment available—including a nose job, fairly routine in this socioeconomic group.
>
> (30–31)

Kominsky Crumb here delineates the status of "Jewish boys" as separate from that of "us girls," pointing to the gendered differences built into the Jewish identity of her childhood as well as the specificity of her point of view as a woman. Yet the description of both groups as subject to the expectations of a silent but persistent majority "pressure" also highlights the interconnection between the Jewish boys and girls—both are subject to certain expectations. Her comic "Nose Job" picks up on this question of gendered difference in light of a common otherness in the Jewish community of the Five Towns.

"Nose Job," a comic whose full title reads "Just Think . . . I could've ended up looking like Marlo Thomas instead of Danny! If only I'd had a Nose Job," stars The Bunch.[15] In an interview in the *Comics Journal*, Kominsky Crumb described the origin of her character's name in a narrative that echoes the story of how she came up with her alter ego Goldie: "I saw Honeybunch [Kaminski, a Robert Crumb character] as a cute, cuddly little victim, dumb and passive and compliant. I wanted to make the thing the exact opposite, a strong, obnoxious, repulsive, offensive character, but with a name that related to Honeybunch, so I shortened it to The Bunch which sounded disgusting" (66). Honeybunch Kaminski was the character drawn by Robert Crumb before he had ever met or seen her; for years Crumb had been drawing this character, which coincidentally resembled

1.6 *Aline Kominsky Crumb, top of title panel from "Nose Job," 1989. In* Need More Love, *p. 86. Used by permission of Aline Kominsky Crumb.*

Kominsky Crumb both visually and by name. In the context of the naming of both Goldie and The Bunch, Kominsky Crumb took names that had been "passed on" to her (retroactively, in the case of Honeybunch) by the men in her life and revised them, thereby claiming some agency over the naming process. In both cases the characters she created came to be associated with this newfound self-empowerment—the ability to rename and reimagine herself—but also with the inevitable ties she shared with the negative, or "disgusting" and "repulsive," aspects of these past selves. In addition, by including a definite article, *the,* as part of The Bunch's name, she continues, in a sense, to objectify herself, but it is a depersonalization that takes place on her terms.[16] The names of these characters therefore encapsulate the impossibility of ever fully detaching from the senses of self that others, mostly men, projected onto her in the past—the inherited aspects of her identities—despite having reoriented herself in relation to these prescribed roles in large part through her art.

Even within her chosen personae, as we have already seen, Kominsky Crumb frequently hints at the split she inevitably experiences in having to draw just one version of herself on the page. The title panel of "Nose Job," for example, reveals the rupture she feels in drawing a single account of her history at the expense of dispensing with other fantastical accounts of the roads not taken (86, figure 1.6). The oversized opening panel, which takes up two-thirds of the page, is framed at its top by two images of The Bunch in the present day: on the left side she is depicted as she is usually represented, with a somewhat oversized, hooked nose, unruly red hair, large eyes and lips, and a shapely set of breasts; on the right side The Bunch is drawn as she would ostensibly look had she chosen cosmetic surgeries, with a ski-slope nose, dark and straightened hair, and wearing a red blouse with a bow tie that hides the shape of her body. The peace sign necklace she is wearing on the left is gone on the right, signifying, like the change to more conservative dress, that the bodily alterations would inevitably lead to differences in her personality or at the very least in the other ways she might choose to represent that personality had her life taken a different turn. The inclusion of these two self-representational possibilities at the opening of the comic serve to level The Bunch's imaginary and "real" selves. As Jared Gardner writes of autobiographical comics, "The split between autographer and subject is etched on every page, and the handcrafted nature of the images and the 'autobifictional' nature of the narrative are undeniable" ("Autobiography's Biography" 12). These two images—the "real" and "imaginary" The Bunch placed side by side—acquire equal status in this comics world; they reinforce the fictionality intrinsic in any hand-drawn image. Further, they reveal Kominsky Crumb's continual reassessment of the events of her past in relation to the present, her speculations about what might have been had she made different decisions in her life.

The comic continues in the following panel with the "real" The Bunch musing about plastic surgery. Standing in front of a mirror with her face tipped sideways, her back to the reader but her nose, face, and behind still visible, the narrative box reads: "Growing up with cosmetic surgery all around me . . . At 40 I can't help dreaming about surgical possibilities." The opening images of this comic, published over fifteen years after "Goldie," reflect a persona used to grappling more consciously with her self-image, a character not moving toward, but already mired in self-analysis and speculation. Nevertheless, this character, too, makes sense of her present sense of self by connecting to her past and reorienting her present deliberations—of standing in front of a mirror and inspecting body parts—in

1.7 Aline Kominsky Crumb, six panels from second page of "Nose Job," 1989. In Need More Love, p. 87. Used by permission of Aline Kominsky Crumb.

relation to her history. On the following page she connects her present reluctance to have plastic surgery with her experience of growing up on Long Island, where, as she explains, "a disturbing epidemic" took place in 1962, as her Jewish classmates all began to show up in school with "pug noses + lots of eye make-up + cover up under the eyes" (87).[17] The move from the present to the past occurs abruptly in the comic; while the page is split into four rows of three hand-drawn square panels each, this shift from current contemplation to memories from the past occurs in the sixth panel, with the general framework, architecture, and coloring of all the panels nevertheless remaining relatively even over the course of the entire page.

As Kominsky Crumb remembers her past self, she moves from images of an isolated character to five panels that all include other characters from the past (87, figure 1.7). First she pictures a group of three young women, including herself, and the framing of their faces in the center of the image as well as the narrative box describing the young women ("me 'n my pals in Jr. hi") reflects a sense of collective identity, a starting off point from which the character will eventually dis-affiliate. In the following panel these three women maintain this collective self-image, but their visages are gathered more tightly together on the page as this increasingly claustrophobic collective is contrasted with a slender young woman pictured in profile with long blond hair, a somber smile, and a tiny nose. As Kominsky Crumb references elsewhere, this image is of Peggy Lipton, the Jewish actress and model who attended her high school and went on to star in the popular television program *The Mod Squad*. Eventually, the original group comes to be replaced by women whose faces resemble those three, but who have clearly undergone physical changes in terms of their makeup, hairstyles, and the shapes of their noses. The following, fourth panel from the past cements the splintering of the original group as The Bunch is depicted alongside her childhood friend, Stephanie Karasick, facing two young women with noses that have clearly been altered, though each new nose is slightly distinct from the other (one is long and straight, the other a tiny "button"). Although there is meant to be a strong contrast between the two sets of women in this panel—those, like The Bunch and Stephanie, with "big nose pride" and those without it—the drawing nevertheless portrays four women with similar hairstyles, including bangs, shoulder-length hair tied up in bows, and slightly parted, thick lips. What distinguishes them at all, besides the detail of their noses, is, instead, the way they are positioned on the page. Stephanie and The Bunch face the front of the page, standing together as a pair, while we see only close-up profiles of the other two women, who almost block our view of the others. The symmetrical positioning of these two pairs of women reflects their interchangeability; the two could just as easily have become the "other" two. The entire series of images of these young Jewish women from the past suggests that, whatever details of appearance they choose to transform, their senses of self are nevertheless integrally rooted in the collective identity that bound them to each other early on.

In the following panel, whatever comfort The Bunch managed to derive from being part of a pair—from being defined not individually but as two, and in relation to another two—is taken away when Stephanie shows up to school looking like a different person. Unlike the previously pictured makeovers, Stephanie's metamorphosis, which results in The Bunch's final break from the group, is the most startling. The Bunch wonders, "Who is that button-nosed beast? Sounds like my friend Stephanie Karasick, but it doesn't look like 'er!!" In this image the contrast between the women is not only in how changed Stephanie looks from her previous self, with a new face that does not correspond at all with her old face, but also in how the two are situated in relation to each other. Large white speech and thought balloons fill up most of the panel, and the faces of the women are nestled at opposite edges, casting sidelong glances at one another. Although they are having a conversation, only The Bunch's lips are parted, while Stephanie's remain closed. As with the previous panel, the opposition between the women is a matter of positioning—of where they stand in relation to each other, of who gets to speak (or, really, who gets to draw the comic). But here the women also look markedly distinct from one another, a difference that extends beyond details. The Bunch is no longer wholeheartedly part of any group; her refusal to change her looks, to disguise herself, paradoxically marks her isolation from those around her. This sense of solitude peaks in a last panel from the past, the only one in which she is pictured alone. Word and thought bubbles frame her face, the background behind her a deep black, signifying how her final, full isolation from others is tied to the stubbornly independent mind-set that prevented her assimilation.

As this comic continues, it moves quickly forward in time, and The Bunch is increasingly drawn alone in panels or beside oppressive characters—a male street artist, her parents, a nose surgeon—who seek to shape her looks and identity. In the second to last panel, as the story concludes, she is pictured no longer wearing makeup and also now allowing her hair to take on its "natural" dimensions, as accepted styles around her have changed. She narrates, "So I managed to make it thru high school with my nose! / I was the only one o' my friends with their 'original' face" (88). Maintaining a link to her original face, particularly doing so despite pressure from others, is obviously a point of pride, even though, as an adult, her styles regularly change, and she continually wrestles with questions of whether or not to get an eyelid job or facelift. She can feel a certain pride in her Jewish body, including her nose, even as she recounts her struggles with body image as a teenager and although she continues to struggle with these issues as an adult. But it is always primarily in relation to her discomfort and distancing from others, from a group, for instance, that once included her, that she forms a connection to her Jewish self.

Interestingly, a collaborative *New Yorker* comic by Crumb and Kominsky Crumb from November, 28, 2005, "Saving Face," returns to the question of plastic surgery. In this comic, published sixteen years after "Nose Job" was initially published, Kominsky Crumb decides to have plastic surgery (a facelift) and returns home to justify and explain her decision to a somewhat horrified Crumb and, presumably, to herself as well. Kominsky Crumb's decision to record and publish this experience in her comics reflects her dedication to a notion of self as always changing and even outgrowing or contradicting its previously narrated private and public iterations. Her dis-affiliations unfold not only in relation to past conceptions of Jewish identity as prompted and enforced by others but also in relation to her former decisions to rebel against those conceptions. In other words, identity as invention is a recursive, open-ended process that precludes the possibility of closure and elicits continual reinvestigation.

In "Nose Job," then, Kominsky Crumb portrays herself as both an insider and outsider Jew. She is the product of her upbringing, tempted by many of the same desires and values that she criticizes. But she is also one who has moved away from and often actively works against this way of life, and particularly the memories that remain tantalizingly manifest, even as she gazes at herself, in the present day, in the mirror. This insider/outsider status crystallizes later in life in her identity as an artist (as we have seen at the end of "Goldie"), an identity that allows her a sense of choice and freedom from within the framework of the inherited aspects of all her identities. At one point in "Nose Job" The Bunch muses, "How come boys get to keep their noses?" (87). For Kominsky Crumb, the question of Jewish identity and how to represent that identity is always inevitably related to her identity as a woman. Karen Brodkin has argued that Jews in America have experienced "a kind of double vision that comes from racial middleness: of an experience of marginality vis-à vis whiteness, and an experience of whiteness vis-à-vis blackness" (1–2); in other words, it is a double vision that stems from existing simultaneously inside and outside the realm of normative ethnoracial boundaries (distinct, Brodkin crucially notes, from the "classic portrait" of African American double vision as depicted by W. E. B. Du Bois). In "Nose Job" The Bunch experiences her identities as a woman and Jew as similarly granting her such a double vision, the ability to define herself through an ambivalent and dis-affiliatory relationship to an assigned identity. If, as a woman, The Bunch has to deal with the problem of the assimilation of her body, of whether or not to keep her nose, she can frame and draw that story as one of both personal agency and group dis/ identity. She is forced to confront her nose because she is a woman, and her body is therefore most valued for its conformity to a certain aesthetic norm. But it is also as a woman that she is able to claim her own independent Jewish identity, to stand *as* a Jew *outside* the Jewish community. The inherited aspects of her identity positions, which include the stereotypes associated with being a Jew and woman, ironically allow her a starting point from which to explore choice or individual agency in the face of what is forced or passed on by others.

"But I Don't Want to Seem Jewish Anymore"

The third and fourth chapters of *Need More Love*, "Love, Marriage and Mother-hood" and "The Sunny South of France," are organized around Kominsky Crumb's experiences of "settling down" and starting a family of her own in settings very different from her childhood community in Long Island. Despite her move from the United States to France between these chapters, they collectively mark a new and important stage in her life narrative as well as a new stage in the trajectory of her aesthetic subjectivity and career. Chronologically speaking, at this point in the memoir she has already established herself as a cartoonist, and her artistic explo-rations now focus on two other roles, besides artist, she has chosen for herself as an adult: namely, those of wife and mother. What she reveals over the course of these chapters is the relational nature of these chosen roles and how she similarly claims them primarily in terms of her dis-affiliations from them.

Throughout these chapters Kominsky Crumb includes various republished comics created collaboratively by herself and her husband, one of which was already discussed at the beginning of this chapter. As she recounts, after break-ing her leg in six places, she was forced to wear a cast for six weeks. "To keep me from getting too bored, we started to work on a two-man comic story, something Robert had done with his brother Charles when they were kids. We just ram-bled on without any particular aim, plunging into crazy fantasies about invading aliens and Tim Leary, mixed with real details about the floods we were living through, and for the first time drawing our mutual 'sexploitation.' We just let ourselves go and had fun with it" (176). As we shall see, these playful collabora-tions expand on the engagements with identity that Kominsky Crumb struggles with in her noncollaborative work. They stress the relational nature of the various identities at play in the comics, of Jew/non-Jew and male/female, as well as the very style of the artist, born of the struggle to negotiate between inherited and chosen identities.

In "Euro Dirty Laundry," which is featured in its complete republished ver-sion at the beginning of chapter 4 and was originally created in 1992, Crumb's and Kominsky Crumb's self-identifications in terms of individual artistic styles literally bump up against one another on the page, revealing how much these identifications are dependent on the delineations and articulations of boundaries between self and other.[18] Although they have very different drawing styles, their collaborations partially mask these differences by offering no obvious boundaries between the works of each individual artist on the page. While it may be clear that Crumb, with a more classical and realistic-looking drawing style heavy on details and cross-hatching, has drawn his own figure and thought or speech bubbles, and it is also clear that Kominsky Crumb has drawn hers, it is often less apparent who has filled in the backgrounds, drawn the headings, or started the comic to begin with. In this way their comics question the boundaries between self and other, artist and muse, creator and collaborator. By inserting such collaborative comics into her graphic memoir, Kominsky Crumb's work also questions the rigid definitions of life writing as by and about a single, representable subject.[19]

The content of these comics further expands on the question of boundaries. At the beginning of "Euro Dirty Laundry," Kominsky Crumb's alter ego declares, "But I don't want to seem Jewish anymore. . . . It's too yucky and unpopular. . . . Everyone hates the Jews!" (249, figure 1.8). Here, she draws herself to look like Frida Kahlo, with thick eyebrows and a cross around her neck, though her characteristic hair, nose, eyes, and lips remain. In this panel her visual self-depiction emphasizes the possibility, in autobiography, of representing the self by using whatever image suits one's particular needs and desires at any moment in time (as well as the desires of the public, of what sells). But her alter ego's words, in addition to her enduring "Jewish" features, quickly complicate that possibility by declaring her Jewishness on the page. This opportunity for self-fashioning is additionally undercut by the reader's potential knowledge of Kahlo's own rumored Jewish patrilineal background.[20] This word-image collaboration thus asserts the agency of the artist to reclaim or reject certain facets of her identity, all while demonstrating the impossibility of ever truly hiding or passing. In other words, the artist is never free, in creating depictions of herself (and others), of inherited notions of what this self looks and sounds like. Kominsky Crumb's choice of Frida Kahlo also emphasizes how much an author or artist's power is related to her status in the real world, and especially to the other identifications that are both chosen by her and imposed on her by others. Like Kominsky Crumb, Kahlo was married to a famous artist, the Mexican painter Diego Rivera. During her lifetime, Kahlo's artistic merit likewise took a backseat to her husband's, and she only

1.8 Aline Kominsky Crumb and Robert Crumb, two panels from first page of "Euro Dirty Laundry," 1992. In Need More Love, p. 249. Used by permission of Aline Kominsky Crumb.

became famous for her own talent after her death. By choosing Kahlo's visage as her "self-portrait" on the page, Kominsky Crumb inserts herself into an interethnic narrative and creates a lineage of female autobiographical artists whose works are always inevitably influenced by the ways they are perceived by others off the page, particularly on the basis of gender.[21]

The panel is complicated even more by Crumb's "side" of the page. Crumb, who is not Jewish, draws his persona waving his hand in a Nazi salute, as he says, "I'm not anti-Semitic! Some of my best wives have been Jewish. . . . Ha ha Seig heil!" In the context of Jewish American women's literature, the representation of interfaith marriages has often been a place to air out the anxieties and fantasies of assimilation. As a third-generation American, Kominsky Crumb, with her husband, inserts herself into that conversation, but reconfigures the boundaries of this fantasy/anxiety as a space that can and should be talked about from the point of view of both the Jew and non-Jew. The anxiety of the Jew to assimilate and, consequently, to presumably and potentially lose her heritage is in this way understood as connected to the anxiety of the non-Jew *not* to be seen as anti-Semitic or as part of a history of anti-Semitism.

In the next panel Crumb draws his alter ego in traditional Hasidic garb, asserting, "Why I'm practically a Jew myself, I've been hanging around with Jews so long." As the two are facing each other in this panel, this visual stereotype can be seen as an image dependent on the mirrored face of the other. Crumb's caricature brings to the forefront the question of how much one can reinvent or play with one's identity in autobiography without in some way reducing the self or other to stereotype, without preying on the other or on notions of the other. Ironically, though, it is Kominsky Crumb's alter ego who is here drawn to resemble what is described in a narrative box to be a "blood sucking parasite," as her eyes and nose come to bear a resemblance to elongated tentacles and her character admits to loving "only very financially successful ahtists that we can mooch off of!" The gendered stereotype about Jewish women (the "we" in this declaration) as parasites seems to trump Crumb's Hasidic caricature, as the textual labels of "parasite" and "host," stamped onto the image, indicate. As with the choice of Frida Kahlo as self-image, Kominsky Crumb continually brings up questions about the relationship between gender and perception in her investigations of inherited identities and stereotypes. Her sense of self, particularly in relation to her non-Jewish husband, is always influenced by the often problematic ways others have represented such relationships.

Two panels later, at the top of the following page, Crumb's alter ego takes stock of his culpability in this series of depictions, after he has pushed the joke even further by depicting himself pondering his "Jew paranoia" in a panel in which his wife is absent. Apparently, her absence from the panel and not the content of it, which is no more offensive than earlier ones, prompts him to finally ask, "Are you offended by that last panel, Aline?" Kominsky Crumb's persona responds, "No . . . I started it didn't I??" (250). The question of who "started it" emphasizes the difficulty, in such a collaboration, of deciphering between self and other or, more generally, deciding who should take the blame for such characterizations. In the context of Jewish American art and literature, this set of panels stands as a thoughtful commentary on questions of who is responsible for characterizations and caricatures of Jews in mainstream culture. As seen in these collaborative comics, the self-identification of the Jew is as much a product of the fantasies and paranoia of the self as of the other.

In terms of the self-identifications of the artist more generally, this comic illustrates the impossibility of ever claiming an artistic style as completely free of outside influences, even and especially those the artist wants to reject or escape.

In these collaborative works Kominsky Crumb can question the boundaries between self-creation and collaboration and play with visual and verbal stereotypes as one way of examining the pervasive outside influences that inevitably shape any autobiographical project. Such explorations also take place in her comics about motherhood, though in a different, generally noncollaborative format. As an identity that has been chosen by her, like becoming a wife and artist, motherhood has the potential to signify a role that allows Kominsky Crumb to feel free and further indulge in her "own style." Yet, as her comics reveal, motherhood is also always inevitably associated with inheritance—that is, the inherited relationship she shares with her own mother, as well as the stereotypes about Jewish mothers, not to mention mothers more generally, that characterize much of popular North American art and literature. In her comics about motherhood, Kominsky Crumb links these personal and collective inheritances through the Jewish mother stereotype, thereby demonstrating the inevitable struggles and interactions between her own perceptions of her mother, her perceptions of herself *as* a mother, and the perceptions passed on to her by others about Jewish mothers and mothers more generally.

When Kominsky Crumb depicts Jewish women, and especially the women of her family, she pictures them lacking in self-control. These portrayals in many ways connect these women with Kominsky Crumb's own personae. For example, as mentioned, she frequently represents herself, in real life and in her comics, as a limited and undisciplined female artist who lacks control in the very way her hand shapes figures on the page. Similarly, she often depicts her personae as giving in to their carnal, basic desires, whether they are sexual, sensual, gustatory, affective, or verbal. In the case of both her own personae and her drawings of other Jewish women, she presents this lack of self-control as a component of her Jewish identity, especially her gendered Jewish identity. In the comic "Moo Goo Gaipan," republished about halfway through *Need More Love*, for instance, she pictures her character in the opening panel sloppily eating noodles with chopsticks, her curly hair having taken on the same shape as the food, as her speech bubble reads, "Us Jews love Chinese food" (191). The next row of the comic depicts two panels that directly refer to the stereotype of the Jewish woman as one who consumes but does not produce (figure 1.9). In the first panel, she narrates, "The women in my family really know how to eat." Here she takes the subject of her comic, a generalization about all of "us Jews," and narrows it down to make it a gendered classification, one that can be traced down the matrilineal line of her own particular family. The women depicted in the panel have exaggeratedly thick lips, emphasizing not only the excessiveness of their hungers for the many plates of food crowding the table but also their propensity to focus on looking "done up," even if their overly applied makeup only adds to the grotesqueness of the scene. Jewish women, as portrayed in Kominsky Crumb's comics, are narcissistic and obsessed only with their own desires and needs, which are boundless. In the next panel the narrator adds another sweeping statement about the women in her family: "But they hate to cook . . . " The woman pictured in the panel, presumably Kominsky Crumb's mother or some other female relative, is revealed to be help-less, excessive, and wasteful, shouting into a crammed refrigerator, the door cast wide open, as her husband sits comfortably reading the paper in the next room. Without looking up, he suggests that she "call Vinnie's" and affirms her overdone suggestions for what they should order with a brief, "Yeah shure tahrifac." The black line drawn between the two characters further distinguishes and isolates them from each other; if the Jewish woman has her head stuck in the refrigerator, ruminating over her many cravings in the face of mountains of food, the Jewish man is left untouched by the scene. Jewish women's excesses and feeble-mind-edness are well-documented and serve to make Jewish men appear, in contrast, more analytical and balanced. The stereotypes are relational; they are dependent on each group's perception of the other.

1.9 *Aline Kominsky Crumb, two panels from first page of "Moo Goo Gaipan." In* Need More Love, *p. 191. Used by permission of Aline Kominsky Crumb.*

Riv-Ellen Prell has written about portrayals of Jewish women and men in America over the last half century or so and how these portrayals often "mirror" the relationship between Jews and dominant American culture. To Prell, for instance, stereotypes of Jewish women's bodies reflect the anxiety many American Jews felt as they came to assimilate into mainstream American culture. In one essay about postwar representations of Jewish women, entitled "Why Jewish Princesses Don't Sweat," she writes about popular depictions of the Jewish woman's body as passive. As she explains, although this body "is one of consuming desire . . . [it has] no object of desire other than the self" (80). According to Prell, stereotypes about Jewish women's bodies can be said to mirror "power struggles over the control of economic and emotional resources" (*Fighting* 12) experienced by a generation of people who were new to the middle class. Stereotypes of Jewish women more generally then reflect the fear that, for people who are not raised with it, access to money and other cultural capital can lead to greed, self-absorption, and bad taste. Kominsky Crumb's Jewish women embody more particularly the postwar anxieties of a group of people that has moved up in the world, often at the expense of, or at the very least in the shadow of, earlier generations of Jews, including especially their parents and grandparents, as well as other minority groups. That this excess is reflected more plainly on women's bodies in many of the comics merely affirms the notion that stereotypes are dependent on and built out of power structures that must, by definition, paint one group of people as monstrous in relation to another, more powerful group, which is then legitimized. The title of the comic, "Moo Goo Gaipan," written on an exaggeratedly large Chinese take-out box, also points to this phenomenon. Moo goo gai pan is a dish that is an Americanized version of what is already an American invention, what many Americans believe to be authentic Chinese food. The title of the comic therefore alludes to an interethnic stereotype that gets written into an essentialized, intraethnic narrative. In this way, Kominsky Crumb establishes a kind of network between various ethnic and gendered representations; self-depiction, her comic shows, is always a collaborative and often contradictory mixture of what Brodkin terms ethnoracial assignment and ethnoracial identity: how one is viewed by dominant society and how one views one's self.

If to be seen *as* a Jew and/or a woman is, in some ways, to be misread, then part of Kominsky Crumb's project is figuring out how, as an artist, she can seek out ways of somehow controlling or manipulating these misreadings, particularly by, in turn, assuming and rejecting them for herself and others. As the one in control, creating and arranging these various images on the page, she defies the classification of Jewish women as unproductive and lacking in self-control, although her specific depictions also ironically reinforce these old stereotypes. Additionally, her categorically based illustrations of women and Jews highlight a continued uneasiness about inheritance and descent. For Kominsky Crumb, there is always a tension between perceptions that have been passed on and internalized and perceptions that are still being questioned, rejected, and then refigured on the page. In her autobiographical comics she often confronts that friction using explorations of the women in her own family. By this means she grapples with what happens to old ways of seeing as they get written into the scripts of subsequent generations as well as how certain iconographies function intergenerationally.

The two-page brightly colored comic, "The Bunch Her Baby & Grammaw Blabette," republished in full in her memoir, presents a particularly revealing and offensive portrayal of her mother's persona. The title of the comic is telling, as Kominsky Crumb has always given careful attention to the names of the people she draws in her comics, including herself (in this case, her alter ego is The Bunch). In her autobiographical comics she often refers to her mother's character as Blabette. As the name suggests, Blabette, who likes to blab and whose face resembles a blob, is a hyperexaggerated representation of various stereotypes about Jewish women, and especially Jewish mothers. She is materialistic, demanding, and oblivious. In the comic, The Bunch, her baby daughter, and Blabette go on a vacation together to visit the outdoors. Blabette attempts to calm the baby, who cries when she tries to hold her and then ends up throwing up all over "Grammaw's handpainted jogging suit" (215). The narrator remarks that Blabette is "totally useless" in this situation because she "just had her nails wrapped."

Blabette's comments and facial expressions drive the narrative, and they contrast starkly with depictions of The Bunch as reserved. She does not say very much, and her outfit, hairstyle, expressions, and speech bubbles are similarly tame, particularly when compared with more typical depictions of this persona. Indeed, what is especially interesting about this comic is the lack of thought bubbles throughout, as though the force of Blabette's character on the page prevents The Bunch from expressing her usual layers of self-consciousness and subjectivity. Further, all three characters, including the baby, are for the most part consistently drawn throughout the short comic, an uncommon characteristic of Kominsky Crumb's comics more generally, reinforcing, again, how the force of

Blabette's character stifles the usual means of expression in her artist-daughter's self-depictions.

The title and architecture of the comic, which is composed mostly of panels depicting these three characters interacting together, suggests that Kominsky Crumb is interested here in relationality and interdependence as it is mirrored between mothers and daughters, and particularly how depictions of Blabette influence and refigure the way The Bunch is constituted on the page in relation to her own daughter. In one panel, for instance, mother and daughter are drawn with their profiles facing each other, the baby in the middle, as Blabette's words spread and take up most of the space between them, eventually devolving into repetitive yammering and long strings of words, letters, and ellipses (215, figure 1.10). The Bunch's head, and especially her trademark hair, are cut off in the corner, and we see only one eye, frozen in what looks to be angst and frustration. Both she and the baby make the same incomprehensible noise as they stare into Blabette's oversized mouth, lined with sharp, fanglike teeth and attended by a short, thick, quivering pink tongue. Beside her caricatured mother, The Bunch finds herself reverting to an infantlike state, reminiscent of a childhood in which, as Kominsky Crumb shows elsewhere, she did not have a voice. The inclusion of the baby as one of the central figures of this comic also reflects a fear of the inevitable repetition of personal histories: if The Bunch draws her mother in this way, is this what will someday happen between baby and The Bunch? Is the only way for a daughter to gain subjectivity in relation to her mother to draw her as a monster, so that she can be the human one in relation to her?

In the end this depiction of Blabette as monster can be read more generally as a commentary on Kominsky Crumb's process of self-creation on the page. The final panel of the comic emphasizes the potential for caricature, both of the self and other, as a catalyst for reorientation. Concluding the two-page narrative is a large close-up of Blabette's grotesque face. A bright yellow emanating light surrounds her head, encasing it and freezing her in time. Here Kominsky Crumb is clearly depicting what she sees as her mother's excessive and suffocating personality—"So relax . . . Don't get upset . . . Don't get nervous!" Blabette implores in thick and large black lettering, as her body language explodes on the page. This image can be seen as a concentrated and ultimate reflection of all the negativity displaced onto The Bunch by this mother figure as well as by stereotypes representing Jewish mothers more generally. But it is a force that,

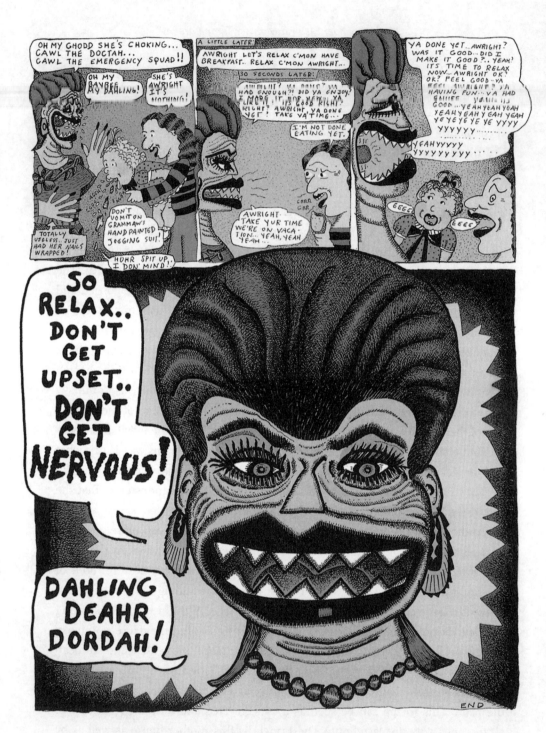

1.10 *Aline Kominsky Crumb, final page from "The Bunch Her Baby & Grammaw Blabette."* In Need More Love, pp. 215. Used by permission of Aline Kominsky Crumb.

once captured on the page, can also potentially and consequently be cast off, as its very figuration affirms a rejection of its power over the artist. A recent interview with Kominsky Crumb corroborates a reading of this and other caricatured depictions of her mother as a vehicle for refiguring, through visualization, her relationship to a damaging past. As she explained, "The only thing I can say is that getting those images out there, those mean images about my mother . . . our relationship has improved. Maybe I wouldn't be able to have a decent relationship with her now if I hadn't gotten it out" ("Public Conversation" 123). While elsewhere in the memoir her mother is pictured in photographs and illustrations that portray her as ranging from a passive to an active, damaging presence, this mother-monster image serves as a decisive, irrefutable portrait; transformed into an ultimate other, she can never be reintegrated into the narrative without this likeness somehow affecting all other readings of her character. Even so, such an extreme caricature, oddly enough, makes it easier to then isolate that mother-monster, to sequester this version of her to the realm of fantasy in order to free up new readings of the past.

This disproportionate portrait thus simultaneously disorients and reorients Kominsky Crumb's persona in relation to images from her past, specifically those depicting her relationship with her mother. But, by virtue of its arrangement in a story line about two sets of mothers and daughters, it also serves as a self-portrait that reframes The Bunch's relationship to her own daughter as well as to the vision she has of herself as a Jewish mother. In this way the monster represents yet another, though perhaps a quintessential, dis-affiliatory persona in her vast repertoire of personae. By maintaining a close proximity between this mother-monster and her own self-image, Kominsky Crumb confirms the inevitability of always somehow mirroring, in her self-depictions, the very images she continually works to reject. In *The Female Grotesque* Mary Russo writes about the grotesque female body as a depiction that exceeds the very norm defining it and therefore "leaves room for chance" (11). For Russo, in much the same way as Kominsky Crumb's ever changing personae, the grotesque body "is open, protruding, irregular, secreting, multiple, and changing" (8). In a sense, by assuming the role of the ultimate grotesque monster, for herself and for those who are closest to her, Kominsky Crumb refuses normative, constrained categories of "womanhood" or "Jewishness," even as she actively claims the very possibility of difference written into these identity labels. Her reenactment of prescribed symbols and stereotypes of Jewish women's inherited identities ironically offers her a space for reimagining an indeterminate, continually transforming, and potentially liberated relationship to those identities.

At a panel discussion at the Museum of Comic and Cartoon Art (MoCCA) in New York City in June 2012, Kominsky Crumb again brought up the topic of the negative depictions of her mother, and of other relatives, that are incorporated throughout her comics and can be found throughout *Need More Love*. As she admitted, "I wouldn't make the same comics now. . . . I don't have anger about [my adolescence] anymore." The panel accompanied the opening of Kominsky Crumb's most recent exhibit, "Miami Makeover: (Almost) Anything for Beauty," a series of paintings by Kominsky Crumb and her collaborator, French artist Dominique Sapel. In the eponymous 2012 documentary, which was shown as part of the exhibit, the two women travel from France to Miami Beach to receive hair and style makeovers from Kominsky Crumb's mother's beautician, Cookie. As Kominsky Crumb explained during the panel with regard to the purpose of trying out the very styles she ridiculed in earlier drawings of her mother, "Now I'm curious about the path I didn't choose . . . I could have gone there." The paintings that accompany the documentary, which include images of Cookie and other women encountered in Miami Beach, along with self-portraits of the two artists in their made-over outfits, reflect a continued desire to embark upon questions of self-fashioning and dis-affiliation. These paintings are sobering versions of her comics: the images are placid but still wildly colorful mosaics representing women playfully but earnestly acting out the performance of beauty. A project premised on what might have potentially resulted in reinforced caricaturing ultimately and unusually resulted instead in a renetworking, an alliance not only between different women but also between different sides of the same woman. As with Kominsky Crumb's earlier work, this latest exploration reflects her continued devotion to self-explorations that acknowledge potentially limiting categorizations of self and other, but refigure them to establish new and powerful ways of seeing.

"My Independent Jewish Monster Temperament"

Toward the beginning of *Need More Love*, Kominsky Crumb describes the end of her relationship with a "real cowboy named Ray Edington" in the late 1960s. She writes, "His violent ways quickly lost their charm, and his macho nature inevitably clashed with my independent Jewish monster temperament" (122). With this wording, she makes clear the link between her independence and her status as a woman and Jew. Through her comics, she has recast these identities as hybrids of consent and descent, acceptance and rejection, which, when mapped in relation to one another, represent the possibility of agency in the face of essentialized identity labels. She claims her Jewish identity alongside her status as a "monster," set apart from other women and Jews. In this way she "transform[s] what was considered pathetic and abject into something sexy and glamorous" (Bloom, *Jewish Identities* 3).[22] Her use of the term *temperament* is especially interesting given Goldie's interest in finding her own "style." The *Oxford English Dictionary* defines temperament as a "state or condition with respect to the proportion of ingredients or manner of mixing."[23] For Kominsky Crumb, finding a "style" or "temperament" is a matter of combinations—of doling out parts in search of a certain whole. Her Jewish identity can be understood in the same way, as a matter of rejecting and inevitably accepting certain aspects of her identity, of finding choice within inheritance.

In an interview published before her memoir, she linked herself to a "tradition of complaining Jewish comedy," which, she explained, "is deeply imprinted in me" (Crumb and Kominsky Crumb, "A Joint Interview" 128). Then, in a move typical of her insider/outsider self-fashioning, she added, "what I think is funny is quite often sick to most folks." To claim any status as an insider, to put herself in line with a group of inherited traditions or characteristics, Kominsky Crumb always also needs to set herself at a distance. As she makes clear, her temperament is what sets her apart, a state of being and a style that is both within and beyond her control. This emotional climate sets the tone throughout her work; her comics, like her identities, stem from a world of experiences mostly outside of her control that, as an artist and writer, she then shapes.

In her book on nonfiction writing, *The Situation and the Story*, Vivian Gornick, another contemporary Jewish writer with an interest in the preservation and expression of independent temperaments, writes about the importance of finding and creating a narrator, or what she terms a persona, "who can bring under control the rushing onslaught of my own internal flux" (25). As she explains, "we pull from ourselves the narrator who will shape better than we alone can the inchoate flow of events into which we are continually being plunged" (24). For Kominsky Crumb, that narrator, or set of narrators, from Goldie to The Bunch, must be rewritten and redrawn, all the while maintaining the common thread of an independent and rebellious style and temperament. This artist's temperament links those many versions of the self together—past and present, Jewish and non-Jewish, independent and codependent, artist and novice, visual and verbal—to provide an optimistic space for play, even within the confines of her personal and communal histories of self-imagining. Her independent Jewish monster temperament is a manifestation of her role as an artist, and especially a cartoonist, as one who deliberately makes room for chance and doubt—and therefore creates a world of possibility—in every last hand-drawn "crude scrawl."

"What Would Make Me the Most 'Myself'"

Self-Creation and Self-Exile in Vanessa Davis's Diary and Autobiographical Comics

anessa Davis is another cartoonist invested in what it means to serially represent the self on the page through vignettes or snippets. Characterized by multiple artistic modes and styles and a general lack of clear-cut panel divisions, her comics portray the self as a textured, patchwork entity that changes from moment to moment, depending on framing and context. Her sketches, as well as her narrative and diary comics, collectively and often humorously visualize this animated and inexhaustible autobiographical project.[1] Born in 1978, Davis's comics represent another version of the postassimilated Jewish American female artist. Like the works of Aline Kominsky Crumb, many of her comics visualize the struggle of responding to and rebelling against preconceived notions of selfhood based in gendered, ethnic, religious, and regional identifications. But unlike Kominsky Crumb, Davis's work does not evoke her religious or ethnic identities primarily as a response to stereotype. Rather, she frames her identities more centrally as revisable and individual processes that, though developed out of granular diachronic and synchronic realities, inevitably converge in the present tense of the artist's composition.

In *Need More Love* Kominsky Crumb often looks back at the values of her parents' generation and her childhood experiences in Long Island in order to understand how she has moved away from or past them. In contrast, in Davis's graphic works the persona on the page is *always* in process, both in the past and present versions of herself, rather than an entity that has definitively changed, or moved beyond a previous iteration, over time.[2] In this way her graphic memoir, while also framed through dis-affiliations, can be considered a narrative of continual self-creation and revision, or a testimonial to the present, rather than a narrative hinging on a relatively static and unyielding past.

Davis has published two full-length books: *Spaniel Rage*, her 2005 graphic diary, and her most recent work, *Make Me a Woman*, a 2010 collection of comics and drawings, including diary entries and pages taken out of her sketchbook. The title of Davis's more recent collection reinforces Simone de Beauvoir's famous words about the construction of female identity, namely, that "one is not born, but rather becomes, woman" (283). But the title, presented ambiguously somewhere between a directive and a plea, also highlights the notion that there is always an active subject forging the creation of that woman. Whether the final authority over that subject lies with the author herself or with someone else is a puzzle that repeatedly surfaces in the many layers of her work, and it is a puzzle generally left unsolved. As Davis has pointed out, "The comics form might not come up with a lot of answers, but it can really illuminate the questions" ("Vanessa Davis Keeps It Complicated"). Thus Davis's texts, like all the comics explored in this project, represent postmodernism as a form of inquiry that "calls all categorical thinking into question along with the modes by which categories are consolidated and maintained" (Gilmore 4). Both *Spaniel Rage* and *Make Me a Woman* are books that illustrate the process of becoming, while they also accentuate its mysteries, the blurry boundaries where private or inward explorations and public, published performances, exposures, and influences overlap.

This chapter will trace the movement from *Spaniel Rage*, a book of daily journal entries with almost no overt recognition of various categorizations of identity, to *Make Me a Woman*, a text very much rooted in typologies of the self, including especially gender and religious/ethnic identities. In *Living Autobiographically*, Paul John Eakin distinguishes between "self" and "identity" as follows: he marks "self" as a "larger, more comprehensive term for the totality of our subjective experience," whereas "identity" points to "the version of ourselves that we display not only to others but also to ourselves whenever we have occasion to reflect on or otherwise engage in self-characterization" (xiv). This distinction similarly marks the change in emphasis between Davis's two books. Many of the narrative comics included in *Make Me a Woman* were originally written for and published by the online daily magazine *Tablet: A New Read on Jewish Life*, between 2007 and 2010. These comics, intended for such a publication, contain explicitly Jewish content, unlike the diary comics in *Spaniel Rage*.

As the shift in form from a book primarily consisting of diary comics to a hybrid text including both diary comics and narrative ones reveals, the move from an exploration of self as an undefined and uncategorizable entity to self as consisting, in part, of a struggle against a series of fixed categories reflects the more ostensibly public form of the second book. Although the diary can never exist as an entirely private work, its pretense of privacy is conducive to explorations of a more unspecified and "comprehensive" representation of selfhood. In other words, the self depicted in the diary is comparatively free from concerns of how it does or has appeared to an outside "other." In contrast, a reflection of self as created in and for the public eye, as in *Make Me a Woman*, is more clearly based in predetermined visions of identity that are shared by disparate, sometimes overlapping communities. Throughout *Make Me a Woman*, Vanessa engages in a process of self-discovery by questioning and juxtaposing multifarious versions of self-knowledge. Even so, she is always aware of the various, predetermined categorizations of self—her Jewishness and femaleness, mainly—as public identities. In this way, although both texts convey self-revelation as a process located in an ever transforming and transformative present, they also reflect the manner in which genre conventions and imagined audience influence how such explorations get played out. Ultimately, despite their differing slants, self-creation in both works is simultaneously cast as self-exile: even while the artist literally composes and recomposes herself, she is never any closer to forming a complete image or understanding of her personhood as a single, unified, or chronologically representable entity. Both texts consequently reflect an antiessentialist point of view or an awareness that, as Zygmut Bauman has described it, "'belonging' and 'identity' are not cut in rock . . . they are not secured by a lifelong guarantee . . . they are eminently negotiable and revocable" (*Identity* 11). While part of a newer generation of Jewish female cartoonists, Vanessa Davis's works, like Aline Kominsky Crumb's, reflect how preestablished significations of identity can paradoxically lead postassimilated writers and artists away from essentialized or simplistic notions of the signified.

"But that is Only A Small Part of Why I Feel Like Total Shit"

Published in 2005 by the now defunct Buenaventura Press, *Spaniel Rage* is a collection of what Davis describes, on one of its title pages, as "diary comics and drawings that I made in sketchbooks from 2003 to 2004."[3] Assembled in a thin, soft-cover book about 10 inches tall and 7 1/2 inches wide, the text can most accurately be categorized as a graphic diary or journal. In this chapter, like autobiography theorist Philippe Lejeune and others, I do not distinguish between the diary and the journal. Some critics make a debatable distinction by correlating journal writing with an intended public audience and content that is less so-called personal. This distinction sets up a hierarchical dynamic—with the diary often cited as a "feminine" and the journal as a "masculine" form—between two modes of writing that have, despite their differing histories and genealogies, become otherwise indistinguishable. Davis's collection does not include pagination, and one or more often but not always dated entries fill each page. As Lejeune explains in his essay on diaries, "On Today's Date," page dating is one of the characteristics that helps define the modern day diary and distinguishes it from other literary and nonliterary forms, including autobiography. The date scrawled or typed at the top of the page reflects "people's relationship with lived time" (80); specifically, it demonstrates a particular awareness of the continual passing of and subsequent accounting for time. It also stands as a "pact of truth" (79) in that it *certifies* the time of enunciation." By tracking time on the page (or, for some, on the computer screen), the diarist testifies to what is beyond her control, while she also acknowledges her powerlessness over the situation, the inevitability of death and, consequently, of the diary project. That Davis dates some but not all her diary entries is significant, most importantly because it hints at her work's ability to complicate stylistic conventions in order to create new composite forms of self-representation that defy normative expectations. As she explained in an interview, "I think that it's important for people to try to be realistic and not strive to fit some template of what works or what sells or what's popular or what's considered legitimate. I think people should just do what works for them and see where that takes them" ("Interview: Vanessa Davis"). The structure of Davis's journal as a whole also reflects this independent style. For instance, three-quarters of the way through *Spaniel Rage*, a book that otherwise includes no chapter or section divisions, she includes various short comics labeled "Other Stories" and marked as each having been published previously in other locations. The title of these comics, in stressing "otherness," points to the difficulty of categorizing the various types of texts included in the book and therefore establishes what will become, in both of Davis's works, a more general preoccupation with categorization and typology. The inclusion of these longer-form comics—each divided from the other by a single blank page—at the end of what is primarily a graphic diary also complicates the possibility that her works, in publication, will fit a particular, clearly defined genre or market standard. By incorporating images created for publication alongside images presumably drawn for her eyes only in what started as a sketchbook, *Spaniel Rage* thwarts the simple distinction often constructed between the two forms of creation. In this way her text questions the notion that authorial intention or imagined audience is ever clear-cut or formulaic. A resistance to such conformity is also pronounced in her later work, *Make Me a Woman*, which, also like Kominsky Crumb's memoir, represents a dramatic departure from a categorizable literary product with an intended audience.

The structure of *Spaniel Rage* additionally draws attention to the published diary as a work that has inevitably been exposed to edits, and that has been transformed in the process of its publication. Lejeune and others have written extensively on the near impossibility of reading diaries, especially contemporary ones, in the form that they were originally composed, prepublication. Consider, for example, the fact that printed versions of diaries often do not reveal the various nuances of the original text, from handwriting (and changes in handwriting) to the spaces left between words (Culley, "Introduction" 16).[4] The title page of *Spaniel Rage* is drawn in the handwriting of the artist, with watercolors filling in carefully bubbled, black-and-white cursive letters. Thus the title as well as the name of the press and city of publication are adapted in the pages of the graphic diary and reestablished as part of the diary composition itself. Davis's work therefore blurs the distinction between "paratext" and main text, and preempts the possibility of ever fully differentiating between the two. As Gérard Genette explains in his seminal book on the topic, the paratext, a term encompassing elements like the author's name, the title, or the introduction to a work, "surround . . . and extend" the text "to ensure the text's presence in the world, its 'reception' and consumption in the form (nowadays, at least) of a book" (1).[5] In the case of Davis's work, the intimacy of the hand-drawn paratext prompts readers to approach the book as a unified project that does not distinguish between its creation by a single author and its publication history. The overall structure of the book therefore resembles the way that the self gets established in its pages, as an entity that cannot fully be understood by looking at isolated experiences, memories, or reflections but rather needs to be considered in the context of the work as a whole, including factors that take place outside of, or alongside, the author's immediate creative control. The hazy boundary between text and paratext additionally destabilizes a notion of self as insider or as one who belongs, even in an iteration of one's own life story. Just as the paratext is marked by the hand of the author, the journal entries themselves, creations emerging from and reflecting the inner life of the artist, are equally and easily subject to the taint of outside influences, including those of the publisher and of anticipated and actual readers.

The question of audience and influence is especially important in a genre often mistakenly presumed to be written for the self alone. Margo Culley writes in her introduction to *A Day at a Time*, "The importance of the audience, real or implied, conscious or unconscious, of what is usually thought of as a private genre cannot be overstated. The presence of a sense of audience, in this form of writing as in all others, has a crucial influence over what is said and how it is said" (11–12).[6] The framing of Davis's text draws attention to the question of audience from the outset of the book. The image adjacent to the title page, for example, proposes Davis's graphic diary as a work that does not simply fall into any preconceived notion of a public or private document (in intention or execution), but rather wavers somewhere between both spheres. Beside the handwritten, and in this way individualized, title page, there is a full-page black-and-white drawing, which is the first image we see of Vanessa (figure 2.1). She is pictured standing in front of her car in a supermarket parking lot. There is no verbal etching attached to the image but for the word *Publix* scrawled across a terra cotta roof and a Fresh Sushi sign leaning against the supermarket wall. Publix is an employee-owned supermarket chain, with most of its stores located in Florida, which is where Davis grew up and her mother now lives. The lack of context or narrative connected to this drawing prefigures the style and tone of the rest of the graphic diary, which does not focus on a directed accretion of experiences and reflections in order to form a narrativistic whole, but rather documents a paratactic and fragmented panorama of self, recorded in narrative and nonnarrative spurts over a single year.[7] Vanessa stands looking down at the door of her car, ostensibly fitting her key into it, although this action is obscured by the vehicle (we see her arms but not her hands). The image presents her moment of passing or moving from a public space into a semiprivate one, an act that, in itself, is partially hidden and partially visible, cropped and directed from a corner angle overlooking the scene. Like this self-representation, the composer of the journal is similarly situated in a transitional framework. Whether or not she ever intends to show her diary to others, she is always at risk of having her work exposed merely by putting down words or images on a page. In this sense, she is always affected by, and maintains an awareness of, the possibility of an audience larger than herself. Her seemingly private universe, in being transcribed onto the page, is always part of a larger public landscape. As Lynn Z. Bloom argues, "it is a mistake to think of diaries as a genre composed primarily of 'private writings,' even if they are—as in many women's diaries—a personal record of private thoughts and activities, rather than public events" (24). Diaries written with no intention of publication always involve some kind of awareness of a possible public audience since "the writing act itself implies an audience" (Culley, "Introduction" 8). Conversely, even if the author intended the work to be published from the outset, there are always private meanings hidden in the diary to which certain audiences will never have access.

Vanessa, as pictured at the opening of the diary, is documented at the cusp of both of these worlds, the private and public, reflecting the status not just of the writer of the diary but also the reader-viewer, who is about to enter someone else's semiprivate world through the space of a semiprivate document. But this visualization of the diary writer's stance, the image of Vanessa standing at the threshold, is further complicated by its transmission as an image, and a large, full-page image at that. From its outset, this diary is presented primarily as a *visual* document, framed not in and through the word but, instead, in and through structures of looking.[8] As W. J. T. Mitchell, among others, has shown, images are presumed to invite viewers as spectators, as passive surveyors. The mere presence of an oversized visual depiction of the author at the opening of this diary thus also implicitly undermines the notion of the diary as a private text, as one not meant to be seen by others. Yet, even as the overwhelming presence of an almost wordless image at the beginning of the diary invites that problematic connection between the visible and public, between images and exposure, the angled, partially concealed content of the drawing nevertheless reinforces the disestablishment of such simple binaries. The scene is highly specific, a fragment of a fragment of a particular perspective. Further, the facing page is the aforementioned title page, which consists *only* of words, even if they are intimately, hand-drawn ones. It reveals nothing "personal," relaying only the title of the book, its author, its publisher, and its publisher's location. More broadly, then, when put in context, the opening of Davis's book subverts the expectations audiences often assign to their readings of different kinds of texts, particularly the diary. In many ways this destabilization of genre conventions—the breaking down of reader expectations—is mobilized through the spatial and visual structures available uniquely through the graphic narrative form. By placing a full-paged image facing a hand-drawn, word-based title page, the reader is compelled to establish connections and comparisons. In this case these include the differences and similarities between texts that communicate primarily through images and those that communicate primarily through words

2.1 *Vanessa Davis, page adjacent to title page.*
In Spaniel Rage, *n.p. Used by permission of Vanessa Davis.*

or texts that presumably profess exposure and "truth" and those that potentially undermine such claims. By depicting various registers relationally, across several or numerous pages, *Spaniel Rage* reflects the means by which comics more generally can activate productive confrontations with categories like genres or mediums that are so often taken for granted.

The content of the diary beyond the title page and opening image also plays with the assumptions that frame expectations about audience and intention, particularly as they relate to narrative and nonnarrative representations of self as well as the constructed distinctions that are often made between public and private spaces and acts. A number of the journal sketches figure Vanessa in her apartment and, often, even more privately, in her bed—a repeated setting in both of Davis's books. Other recurring scenes illustrated throughout include Vanessa at work, on the telephone, at a restaurant with a single companion or various friends and family, in bars with friends or on dates, at concerts, and commuting on a subway train. Many of these scenes are left either unnarrated or involve narration that consists only of dialogue without any overarching narrative voice to interpret or connect the various settings and spaces. These repeated representations emphasize the diary as a space in which the seemingly inconsequential gets recorded, where daily public and private experiences that might otherwise be forgotten—either because they are so often repeated and familiar or because, in memory, they fade easily into more significant events—are documented. But a closer look at such scenes also reveals the potential for connection and relevance, for construction and engagement within the presentation of such seemingly trivial or disconnected recordings.

In one early sketch, dated May 12, 2003, for example, Vanessa sits in front of her computer at her work desk (figure 2.2). The same event is depicted in three adjoining panels, drawn in heavy and light pencil lines with next to no gutter space separating them. The changes between the three carefully drawn images can be seen in the details: Vanessa's arm moves from the mouse to the keyboard and back to the mouse again. Her chair swivels slightly. Her head tilts to the right, as she moves closer to a subtly changed screen, and then back again. A shelf in the background almost disappears by the final panel, as the perspective is slightly modified. In itself, the black-and-white entry featuring Vanessa at work presents a seemingly trivial slice of life. The cinematic quality of the diary entry, which looks like part of a filmstrip, imbues the images with the sense of time passing, but their static nature slows that time down and signifies the sense of monotony that comes from

May 11, 2003

May 12, 2003

2.2 *Vanessa Davis, opening page. In* Spaniel Rage, *n.p. Used by permission of Vanessa Davis.*

working long hours at a desk job. Nevertheless, the slight variations between the three images also ingrains these moments with a certain significance, recalling the keen eye, and careful hand, of the observing artist. The diary becomes a space not just for recording but also for studying and even sharpening acts and moments that might otherwise remain cloudy and inconsequential. The act of chronicling transforms the events and scenes being portrayed.

In addition to the sense of attentiveness and constructedness that permeates individual entries, when an entry is amassed as part of a larger collective, when it is read in relation to another entry or in relation to many entries, it acquires other new meanings. This particular office scene is depicted on the same page as a much more intimate, smaller, and single-paneled entry, dated May 11, 2003. A woman's breast, lightly shadowed and in profile, is the focal point of this loosely drawn rectangular panel, and a sketched face with pursed lips and clearly delineated long eyelashes looms over the pointed nipple. In the background a series of diagonal lines calls attention to the corner of a window frame, with several small branches recalling another world outside this very intimate space. Taken together, in such close proximity, this page of the diary evokes the complex and often paradoxical web of intimacy, familiarity, and distance that an individual experiences over short time frames. A secret, sexual act can be observed, in the diary as in the mind of a participant, from a cool remove, or it can be juxtaposed with scenes that feel otherwise incompatible but nevertheless potentially connect to those previous private moments. The images of Vanessa at her office desk, clicking away at e-mail messages that cannot be deciphered by the reader, similarly demonstrate how trivial experiences that occur in public places can potentially relate to more intimate moments.

These engagements additionally complicate the notion of the diary as a space reserved solely for the reflection or refraction of one's intimate or "personal" thoughts and experiences. As many critics have pointed out, while the diary can focus on an exploration of a person's "inward journey," meaning her interior thoughts and emotions, "the reader must remember that the idea of the diary as the arena of the secret, inner life is a relatively modern idea and describes only one kind of diary" (Culley, "Preface" xiii). In other words, to presume diary making to be an act of confession and self-contemplation, one that focuses exclusively on an individual's secret or private experiences and reflections, is an assumption that ignores not only many of the historical precursors to the modern day diary but also overlooks the many different functions of the diary that exist even today.

Another characteristic of Davis's diary, for instance, is its frequent attentiveness to the process of its very construction. The entries are often spaces where the author can work out aesthetic issues and create or develop a method of cartooning. Indeed, various aspects of many of the illustrations throughout point to the diary's use as, among other things, a workbook, in the sense of a book where work-related problems can be recorded and explored, or simply a place where writing and drawing habits are noted. In her introduction to *Drawn In*, a collection of sketchbook excerpts from various artists (with a preface by Vanessa Davis), illustrator and sketchbook creator Julia Rothman describes sketchbooks as serving this function, among others. As she explains: "Within sketchbook pages, one can trace the development of an artist's process, style, and personality. Sketches emit a freshness and vitality because they are the first thoughts and are often not reworked. Raw ideas and small sketches are the seeds for bigger projects. Sketchbooks ultimately become the records of artists' lives. They are documented visual diaries" (12). Within its pages, Davis's journal, which, as mentioned, was culled from her sketchbooks, includes images and diary entries that reflect such a progression of her "process" and "style." For instance, on a sketch dated May 24, 2003, the author draws a starred footnote in the corner of an image that says, "Not even close resemblances to Rebecca and John." Several of the images include self-criticisms related to her work habits, like the introduction to an entry dated July 2, 2003: "I haven't drawn in more than a week. But that is only a small part of why I feel like total shit." This particular notation reveals how self-reflections in terms of work-related habits often overlap to combine with other, less specific considerations, such as a general ontological anxiety. Both the structure and content of Davis's graphic diary thereby redefine the scope and practice of journaling as a space of relative freedom from conventional genre standards, expectations, and norms where diverse practices collide and interact to reflect a self in the making.

By juxtaposing various kinds of explorations and observations within the same text, often even on the same page or within the same image—those taking place in public spaces and those taking place in private ones, those formulated in a social setting and those framed in relative isolation, those focused on aesthetic issues and those testifying to daily experiences and modalities—Davis's journal presents self-chronicling as a process that, despite its fragmentary nature, inevitably unifies to form a kind of assembly on the page. As Culley explains, "Keeping a life record can be an attempt to preserve continuity seemingly broken or lost"

("Introduction" 8). Indeed, by bringing together the various aspects of our lives that are normally thought of as disconnected, like significant life events alongside mundane everyday realities, or publicly located experiences and private ones, the diary, graphic or otherwise, can help create a sense of cohesion between various senses of self over time. In their introduction to *Inscribing the Daily*, Suzanne L. Bunkers and Cynthia A. Huff argue that the unique forms of diaries, unlike autobiographies or other forms of personal writing, "challenge us to question the boundaries between the public and the private; and they encourage us to assess the social, political, and personal repercussions of segmenting our lives, our texts, our culture, and our academic disciplines" (2). Davis's diary entries reflect the ways that mapping together various forms of experience, through the many places and perspectives that inflect and inform those experiences, can actually lead to a stronger sense of a unitary self. In her graphic diary the multifarious geographies that make up the individual's worldview are all leveled and consequently equalized on the surface of the page to be considered in relation to one another.

One way of better understanding how this unification through fragmentation occurs is by recognizing the integral difference between the practice of autobiographical and diary writing. As Lejeune writes in his essay, "The Diary as 'Antifiction,'" "the problem of autobiography is the beginning, the gaping hole of the origin, whereas for the diary it is the ending, the gaping hole of death" (201–2). Since the diarist never knows what will happen next, life is presented as a series of unfolding events without any "retrospective point of view" (Cates 213). For this reason, as various critics of diary writing have pointed out, fictional diaries often sound overly contrived and constructed. It is this sense of an unknown future that is so difficult to replicate in the fictional realm.[9] Generally, there is no way of knowing what past events will gain in significance over time or become irrelevant, so in a nonfictional journal all events, experiences, and reflections stand within a certain range of equality on the page. In this way diaries, unlike autobiographies, represent a relatively unsentimentalized or unfiltered view of everyday life, as much as that is possible. This unfolding more closely resembles life as it is actually experienced, with the act of representing one's self and the places one inhabits as something always entrenched in the present, with no clear or definite sense of what the future holds or how the past will link to that future. This structural difference between diaries and other forms of personal writing and composing ensures that even the most public nonfictional diary—a diary, for example, created with the intention of publication—always maintains some pretense of itself as a private document. The underlying narrative structure of the diary can never be fully decoded since the future arc of the story always remains a mystery to the writer herself. Even, or perhaps especially, for its writer, though also for its audience, the diary is a somewhat contained and mysterious text.

As a mode of life writing that always involves some mysterious elements and hinges on an unknown future, the graphic diary therefore differs dramatically from the recently popularized "graphic novel memoir," like Alison Bechdel's *Fun Home* or Marjane Satrapi's *Persepolis*, in which the story line frequently pivots around an often traumatic event or series of events from the past. As Isaac Cates explains, "A memoir, in comics or in prose, requires a degree of structure, a degree of deliberate storytelling, that is not available to diary comics, because the diarist can never entirely see the larger plots and arguments that his life will eventually fulfill" (214). By presenting life as a set of vignettes without any obvious links between individual images, the graphic journal more clearly reflects the absolute integration of past experiences and settings of all kinds into an animated present, especially because there is rarely a definite sense of how one location or experience will relate to another over time. It is in part for this reason that Davis's diary showcases a self reflective of Eakin's "totality of [a] subjective experience," rather than, as in *Make Me a Woman*, a self composed of predetermined public identities. The added autobiographical narrative element incorporated into Davis's second book allows for a more focused self-analysis. It could be said, then, that in *Spaniel Rage* Davis introduces many of the themes she later and more directly explores in *Make Me a Woman*. The graphic diary allows her the freedom to pose questions without necessarily answering them. It serves as a kind of dress rehearsal for a more fully developed and manifestly public exploration of what eventually reveals itself, for the author, to be a most urgent and vital set of questions about self-representation and self-knowledge, and which is evoked most explicitly in relation to representations of Jewish identity.

"So the Big Day Finally Came"

From its opening pages, *Make Me a Woman* is a text that both resembles and differentiates itself in important ways from Davis's earlier work. Like *Spaniel Rage*, *Make Me a Woman* is a book that illustrates the very private and individual nature of the process of becoming. But it also highlights the boundaries that are blurred between personal or inward explorations and public performances, exposures, and influences. The book includes previously published and often brightly full-colored comics alongside black-and-white journal and sketchbook entries. Will Eisner has discussed the connections between color and tone in comics. In an interview about his sepia-colored *A Contract with God*, he explained, "it was the only way of introducing color in a way that gave the book a tone. I felt it developed an intimacy between me and the reader, as if we were talking in hushed tones" ("The Walk Through" 86). Eisner and McCloud agree that black-and-white comics demand closer, more careful readings, whereas comics drawn in colors call attention to the text as surface.[10] The divergent uses of color in Davis's work propose various narrative tones, with more muted black-and-white sketches and ink washes suggesting intimacy and brighter, colored pictures reinforcing the distance between reader and text. In addition, the entire text of *Make Me a Woman* does not include page numbers, a formal omission that adds to the sense of timelessness in the way identity gets figured, again and again, in the present, as though each time it is being (re)made anew.

As at the beginning of *Spaniel Rage*, the introduction by Davis describes what is included in the book, which could otherwise be seen as a slapdash or arbitrary collection of comic art. The introduction to this second memoir is longer, more informative, and conscious of the larger audience that will be reading the book due to the artist's increased exposure in, among other places, the "alternative" comics world. The publisher of this second work, Drawn and Quarterly, attests to this fact. A publisher of independent comics, Drawn and Quarterly represents many of the most internationally popular cartoonists. In her introduction Davis writes: "This book collects comics and drawings that I made between 2004 and 2010. Some are as yet unpublished strips and sketchbook pages. I moved: Diary entries take place in New York, where I used to live; California, where I moved in 2005; and Florida, where I grew up and where my mom still lives. A lot of the stories were printed in zines and anthologies. And a bunch of them appeared on-line as part of a monthly column I did for *Tablet* magazine." The introduction implies that the text loosely tracks some kind of structured narrative based in the author's geographical relocations over time—the move from Florida to New York to California—although it also reinforces the possibility that the works contained in the collection, as well as their arrangement, are somewhat arbitrary. This introduction complicates audience expectations, given the size of Davis's text, which is a hardcover, 9-by-11-inch book, and the often inaccurate association of that format, the "long-form" comic, better known as the "graphic novel," with the "structure, breadth, [and] coherence" of the novel" (Hatfield, *Alternative Comics* 5). What the reader encounters over the course of the memoir, instead, is a chronicle of the process of recording the self as it is made, unmade, and remade within a particular time frame that nevertheless encompasses a past and future outside of its pages.

Just as the opening of *Spaniel Rage* can be read as a prelude to what is contained over the course of the book, the opening images of *Make Me a Woman* can also be considered precursors to the graphic narrative that follows. There is, as in *Spaniel Rage*, a self-portrait of the artist on the page opposite the title page (figure 2.3). This opening image reinforces the instability of all life writing and drawing as precariously situated on the border of public performance and private act. In this colored self-portrait, Vanessa sits naked, on a stool, with a guitar covering her "privates" and a harmonica lodged in her mouth. She is positioned outside of any particular time or space and she looks nonchalantly at the reader. The image portrays her as preoccupied: her hands and mouth, the tools of creation of her verbal and visual narratives, are engaged. Like visual artist Alice Neel's famous 1980 *Self-Portrait*, a commanding oil painting that depicts the nude eighty-year-old artist sitting on a striped couch with a brush in hand, confidently exposed, Davis's image, which could also be read as a "portrait of the self as 'other,'" evokes the female nude as "conscious and aware" (Lewison; Bauer 21).[11] If the opening sketch of *Spaniel Rage* presents an artist teetering between two worlds, a bit unsure of her place even as she is located in a very particular setting, this solidly drawn artist exhibits confidence in her self-exposure, while she also conveys herself as almost too busy to notice the audience that inevitably watches her. Since *Make Me a Woman* is a text that includes both previously published comics and diary entries, from its outset it reveals itself as a work intended for and aware of a public audience, although it also continues, like *Spaniel Rage*, to flaunt the unstable boundary between the public and private. Much like the cover of Kominsky Crumb's *Need More Love*, this somewhat satirical image advertises a kind of easy access into the author's most intimate self. But in Davis's text the added element of the conspicuously covered privates, the muted color scheme, and the artist's location outside any frame, floating in a clean, white space, also offers up the pretense of private engagement and inevitable secrecy. Certain parts will remain covered.

Additionally, the book includes a whole series of full-colored portraits of women interspersed between various narrative comics and diary entries, challenging the

2.3 *Vanessa Davis, page adjacent to title page. In* Make Me a Woman, *n.p. Images from* Make Me a Woman *copyright © Vanessa Davis, provided courtesy Drawn and Quarterly.*

notion that an autobiographical narrative must consistently feature the self as principal actor.[1] With one exception, these images do not reflect a clear relationship to the comics that come before and after them, and they are accompanied neither by narrative explanations nor clear indications of who is being portrayed or where they are located.[13] Although some of the drawings feature a woman who resembles Vanessa—generally, a brunette with brown hair, freckles, and a curvy figure—many are images of women who are clearly *not* the same as Vanessa, as indicated by their hair color, body types, and certain ethnic/racial features, like skin color. A good number of these "anonymous" portraits display bodies in motion, with colorful outfits contrasted against the white background of an otherwise empty page (figure 2.4). As the subtle but significant movements of the bodies captured in these images reveal, these are not women who are merely being looked at and drawn as they have been adorned, or as adornments in themselves, but, rather, these are women engaged in the process of being looked at, who are somehow consciously and actively involved in the making of themselves as visual subjects. Their accessories—hair styles, jewelry, purses, shoes—as well as their basic outfits point to individual histories that have been woven together on these pages through the eyes and hand of a single artist. Their fashion choices, along with the disorienting white backgrounds, have the capacity both to unite and distinguish them from one another.[14] The dancing, moving portraits, set between other types of image-text combinations, contextualize a self in the making amongst a larger community of women or, more generally, a self-portrait created alongside other self-portraits.

By including this collective of anonymous women in an autobiography, the text reflects its interest in exploring what Hillary Chute describes as "the self in conversation with collectivities" (*Graphic Women* 104). Chute uses this description to talk about Lynda Barry's *Naked Ladies! Naked Ladies! Coloring Book*, a work that Barry created after discovering a pack of pornographic playing cards in Las Vegas displaying and advertising fifty-two women. As Chute explains, *Naked Ladies!* "is a book that involves but decentralizes the self," revealing a "desire to move beyond the individual" (104, 105) by displaying a sequence of images of women alongside a seemingly unrelated prose narrative about a single self. Like Barry's work, Davis's *Make Me a Woman* is a text that foregrounds an individual narrative, but immerses it in a sea of the dynamic postures and poses of anonymous women. In this way both texts attempt to show how conceptions of self and identity are inextricably, and often ambiguously, located in portrayals of the self in

2.4 *Vanessa Davis, full-page color drawing. In* Make Me a Woman, *n.p. Images from* Make Me a Woman *copyright © Vanessa Davis, provided courtesy Drawn and Quarterly.*

relation to various communities, however dislocated these are. As Sidonie Smith and Julia Watson argue in *Interfaces*, "Identities materialize within collectivities and out of the culturally marked differences that constitute symbolic interactions within and between collectivities. But social organizations and symbolic interactions are always in flux" (10). The portraits of women included throughout *Make Me a Woman* visually represent Vanessa's affiliations at the boundaries of many different communities, both real and imagined. In addition, the range of colors depicted in these images connects these women not only with the self-portrait that opens the book (though, because of its coloring, that portrait comes across as a more subdued version of the others or like a precursor) but also with the many full-colored narrative comics contained within it. These communities are bridged together through surface-level resemblances, like colors, shapes, styles, and clothing, which act as a unifying backdrop to the diverse themes explored in greater depth and given particular settings through the lens of Vanessa's individual life, particularly as portrayed in her narrative and diary comics.

The inclusion of anonymous women in *Make Me a Woman* also points to one of the key differences between Davis's graphic journal and her memoir. Whereas *Spaniel Rage* is focused on tracing the moments that make up a self in the present, through narrative and nonnarrative reflections on the significant and mundane experiences of that self's daily life, *Make Me a Woman* is additionally invested in exploring the documentation of a self through questions of identity and categorization—questions inevitably linking that self with larger publics. The book takes up the Jewish question, not as a way of isolating one version or aspect of the self, but instead as a connective approach to reading identity as always relational and locational.

One of the earlier comics in the memoir, the black-and-white "Make Me a Woman," reflects this spatially based understanding of identity in just a single page, setting up the larger framework of the book as a whole. Drawn in careful, often heavy pencil lines, the comic first pictures Vanessa standing at a podium in front of a crowd reading her bat mitzvah Torah portion (figure 2.5). The narration begins, "So the big day finally came . . . " while her speech bubble reads, "Tamar showed lots of INITIATIVE when she tricked her fiancee's father into impregnating her by posing as a prostitute." The irony of the seriousness of Vanessa's pose juxtaposed with what the twelve-year-old narrator is saying highlights one of the recurring themes of the text, which is the contradictory nature of Jewish identity for women, and especially young, unmarried women, who often figure as

2.5 *Vanessa Davis, panel from "Make Me a Woman," 2005. In* Make Me a Woman, *n.p. Images from* Make Me a Woman *copyright © Vanessa Davis, provided courtesy Drawn and Quarterly.*

second-rate citizens in Jewish culture and history. At twelve Vanessa, who attends an all-Jewish day-school, has no means of evaluating her place in the community or of assessing the narratives passed on to her as "empowering." She has no community to contrast with her own, no sense of what else empowerment or "initiative" could potentially mean for her. In this setting, even though she momentarily maintains a position of relative power beside the rest of the community—she is, after all, on a stage, standing at a podium—her pose remains somewhat subservient and isolated, as her hands grasp the piece of paper in front of her in a submissive and dependent gesture. Though differentiated from the other Jews around her, who are depicted as distanced, sketchy fragments, she remains an inevitable part of this closed community, gridlocked in a limiting posture.

Taken as a whole, this full-page comic nonetheless reflects the ways that Vanessa's stance in that first image represents only a fragment of the process of "becoming a woman," or only one of many points of perspective that ultimately contributes to her ever shifting sense of identity both in time and over time, her ultimate dis-affiliations. In the following image a young woman sits in a chair being drawn by a cartoonist, while the narrator explains of her bat mitzvah that "my party didn't have a theme, but we did have kind of a mean-spirited caricaturist."

Since there are no clearly defined boundaries between Davis's panels, a reading of the "following" panel as the one just under the first is my own interpretation. While the page generally suggests this particular sequence, as it is chronologically sound, one might also read the comic from left to right in three segments going down the page. This "alternative" reading is especially likely upon the reader's first encounter with the page, since most English-speaking comics are meant to be read from left to right. In any case, the young woman, who could be, but is not necessarily, the same person as Vanessa, is drawn by the cartoonist with wild, unkempt hair, an upturned nose, and long, exaggerated arms. Her representation is trapped in a rectangular frame, while her actual self sits meekly in a chair with arms folded, her body leaning into the background that surrounds her. In both the narrator's recitation of the story about Tamar as well as the drawing made by the bat mitzvah cartoonist, the young Vanessa, or someone like her, is frozen in place, the object of projections that are being passed on to her by others. It is not a coincidence that the "mean-spirited" caricaturist is engaged in a vocation that Vanessa will take up later in life, perhaps, in part, in order to revise this earlier, passive, and static portrayal of herself and others like her.

By the end of the comic, Vanessa is finally able to acknowledge this earlier limited perspective when she includes a reflection about her bat mitzvah from the point of view of the present-day artist drawing on this memory. "Years later," the narration begins, stressing the temporal distance between this narrative voice and the one that dominates the rest of the page. Vanessa goes on to describe how she thought differently about her own bat mitzvah upon watching a television show called *The Wonder Years* and recognizing the distance between the main character's experience and her own. *The Wonder Years* was a popular and acclaimed show that aired from the late 1980s to the early 1990s. It followed a man recalling his coming-of-age in a middle-class American suburb in the 1960s. As Vanessa explains, after verbally indicating that temporal shift, "I watched the wonder years where Paul has a sweet bar mitzvah party at a rec center and I was embarrassed because mine was so fancy." In being presented with another version of this religious rite of passage, even so long after her own, Vanessa recognizes her own perspective as rooted in the context of a particular time and place, and specifically, in this case, in her economic background. This consciousness about growing up in a privileged class, and the realization that it was not a universal background for all American Jews, reorients her in relation to her own history and sets her on a path to understanding her Jewish identity as highly individualized or a matter of location.

Despite this verbally indicated shift in time and perspective, in this final image Vanessa is still pictured at her bat mitzvah; indeed, despite the accompanying text, she is drawn here engaged in the tradition of being lifted in a chair, alongside her mother, by a medley of guests. The bat mitzvah setting unites all of the images on the page and reveals how "Make Me a Woman" is not simply a narrative of present-day Vanessa revisiting and then revising her past. Instead, past and present perspectives reciprocally influence one another and accrue, as the spiraling construction of the page—free of typical grids and borders, reflective of joyful as well as complicated emotions, and banded together by stylistically complementary images all tied to a single past event—reflects. The comic's black-and-white nature also levels the various time frames and spaces depicted, as though all experiences are taking place simultaneously and on the same plane. Formed collectively in the same penciled shades of gray and united on a single, clustered page, word and image, past and present, here and there converge until their oppositional postures settle. Vanessa cannot erase her past outlooks, though she can represent them as points that come together in a much larger and always expanding constellation of self. It is as a self in relation to other versions of the self, as well as in relation to other, often overlapping collectivities, that she can productively reflect on her earlier life and integrate past perspectives into a dynamic and textured present.

Davis's explorations of her Jewishness throughout *Make Me a Woman* thus reflect the two dimensions—the diachronic and the synchronic—integral to Charmé's model of Jewish identity and the means by which the comics medium supports the visual integration of these two dimensions. The narrative comics, both on their own and also when considered in relation to the diary comics and sketches included throughout the book, represent a self whose perception of her Jewish identity has changed over time as well as a self who is always conscious of the many other identities that intersect with and help define her understanding of Jewishness as something that is never independent or isolated in its existence. The structure of Davis's individual comics, as well as the arrangement of the text as a whole, reinforces this notion of a spiral development of identity—what Charmé, in borrowing from Jean-Paul Sartre, describes as "a series of revolutions that preserve the past but also move on to higher levels of integration" (122). These "higher levels of integration" are reflected on the page, for example, as Davis's comics generally lack clear borders between panels; instead, as in the single-page "Make Me a Woman," various panels bleed into one another, both across and down. Most of the comics included in the book generally do not include gutters, the spaces between panels that have so often been theorized in conversations about the way comics function and are read. Building on the theoretical ground-work laid by cartoonists like Art Spiegelman and Will Eisner, many comics the-orists have written about the gutter as "host to much of the magic and mystery that are at the very heart of comics" (McCloud 66). These spaces between panels require the participation of the reader, who must use her imagination to fill in gaps or account for time lost between panels, and this kind of reader participation is generally unique to the experience of reading comics.

In contrast, Davis avoids drawing panels completely on most of her journal entries, and even her longer-form narrative comics often meld into one another or are separated by white spaces filled with the swirling and loopy handwriting of the author. Davis has described this style as reflective of a desire "to be sponta-neous . . . to feel out the process. . . . Also, I found panels intimidating, as I had to pre-plan things too much to structure the comic that way. And I liked how the open space left room for details, and improvisational visual connections. I wanted to have as much page space as possible" ("A Womanly Chat"). This visual tactic makes the author more accountable for the work in one sense—the reader, after all, cannot fix spaces that do not exist—while allowing the reader greater freedom in how she chooses to read the page as a whole. The lack of spaces between panels additionally visually compounds the past and present, as the moments of transi-tion between time frames, generally marked by the gutter, are excised. In this way the design reinforces the notion that impressions of past experiences are always connected to, and somehow based in, previous understandings and reflections—a "spiral" integration of the past into the present.

A diary entry pictured around the middle of the memoir, dated September 1, 2005, demonstrates this spiraling anatomy of the book as a whole through its anti-climactic visual execution, which structurally mirrors the "Make Me a Woman" comic previously discussed (figure 2.6). The September 1 entry marks the moment of the text when Vanessa first mentions, and reflects on, her move from the East to the West Coast, a shift that shapes the overall structure of the narrative. This entry is unique—it is a full-colored drawing instead of a black-and-white sketch—yet it is also the first in a miniseries within the text, preceding a number of similar, full-colored diary entries. These diary entries involved preplanning rather than

2.6 Vanessa Davis, "September 1, 2005." In Make Me a Woman, n.p. Images from Make Me a Woman copyright © Vanessa Davis, provided courtesy Drawn and Quarterly.

spontaneous drawing. They figure somewhere between sketchbook drawings and long form finished narrative comics (coloring takes time and is unusual in a diary entry or sketchbook), and were made to appear as finished works.[15] The juxtaposition of the September 1 diary entry among a series of full-colored entries downplays this particular page's significance and instead presents it as one of many equally weighted experiences. Like the "Make Me a Woman" comic, the September 1 entry also lacks panel divisions. The opening narration bubble introduces the thematic illusion of time passing while it simultaneously encapsulates the emotional paralysis that overcomes Vanessa in reflecting on this life change. "I've been gradually freaking more and more out about moving away," she states, and the sentence is presented in short line breaks, like poetry. In format as well as in syntax—the phrase *freaking out* is divided by a slow but steady increase in anxiety marked by the words *more and more*—the wording emphasizes the fragmented sense of time that dominates this individual comic as well as the book as a whole. Similarly, the serialization of Vanessa's image reflects an anxiety that is both fluid and weighted; her head is drawn a total of five times from different angles and displaying a subtle variety of expressions of general angst and worry. Speech bubbles emanate from Vanessa and her friends, crowding the middle of the page. These almost overlap and offer only snippets of longer conversations. All these formal elements combined thwart a simplistic or chronological delineation of Vanessa's emotional states. Instead, the page visually represents the impact of Vanessa's move as a series of small shocks whose significance can only be fully distilled through their compounded effect. Additionally, the images are shaded in dark and rich reds and browns, a color scheme that embeds the manifold, disparate figures and elements of the entry into a single amorphous mass, almost, but not quite, frozen in time.

The impression of time simultaneously passing and slowing down, with past and future experiences and emotions blending into one another, evokes the notion of "integration" that Charmé attributes to his spiral model. Vanessa, about to leave her job, experiences varied, sometimes conflicting thoughts and reactions regarding her impending move between coasts. "Don't people leave New York all the time? Everyone's lives go on! Things change!" she asserts at one moment, although at another she is pictured sobbing in response to an email asking her if she feels scared. "I—I doooo!" she types onto the computer screen. These confused and sometimes contradictory reflections mark a moment in the text when Vanessa's perspective is dramatically unsettled. She is moving from the East Coast, where she lives among a community of others ostensibly like her, including but not limited to Jews, to the West Coast, where she exists in what she later describes as "self-exile." Yet the chaotic nature of time, frozen but still passing, that this diary entry relates highlights the ways that Vanessa's past experiences, perspectives, and identifications continue to affect and influence her, no matter what changes she endures over the course of the entire text. In a way, this spiral representation of time captures Vanessa's sense of self over the course of the entire memoir; it reveals how an impending and pivotal shift in her point of view is tied not, as it may seem at first, to a single event, but rather to a journey of self-exploration that begins much earlier, and ends much later, than this particular geographical relocation. It is a sense of self, and identity, that is always extending off the page and outside the binding.

"Isn't Homesickness Just Part of Self-Exile?"

Various critics have written about contemporary Jewish American women's literature as preoccupied with a desire to reflect on, remember, and sometimes even return to the past. In her 2006 essay "Recalling 'Home' from Beneath the Shadow of the Holocaust: American Jewish Women Writers of the New Wave," Janet Handler Burstein argues that unlike works from the earlier part of the twentieth century, which featured narrators leaving home in order to find themselves, contemporary Jewish American women's writing from the last thirty years or so often depicts women who set out on journeys to understand and connect with their pasts. Burstein explains, "women's writings of the new wave . . . seek continuities, often imagined as reconciliation with people long estranged from the writer" (39). What many of these women writers want, in an effort to better understand themselves, is to reunite with a notion of home that "has been lost or denied," or "to retrieve what they believe has been withheld" (43). Similarly, in her 2003 essay "'The Girl I Was': The Construction of Memory in Fiction by American Jewish Women," Sylvia Barack Fishman argues that "fiction by American Jewish female writers in the second half of the twentieth century often depicts women remembering their past" (145). For these authors, many of whom are the children or grandchildren of immigrants, if not immigrants themselves, "home" is often an estranged relationship to a person, history, or place. The desire to find or return "home" resides in a need to better understand their relationships to the present, and how their identities as women and Jews connect with the experiences of the generations that came before them, especially the worlds of their mothers.[16]

In some ways, *Make Me a Woman* is a text that enacts this move away from and subsequent search for "home" within its pages, beginning with the diary comic from September 1, 2005. In Davis's book, as in many other contemporary works of Jewish American women's literature, this notion of home is principally metaphorical and consistently aligned with the pursuit of a secure and familiar sense of self. But Davis's memoir is not primarily interested in a return to or reflection on the past so much as it is focused on an integration of past experiences and reflections in the present moment or a revised understanding of "home" as something that both is and is not bound to a particular place or concept. This rejection of a conventional notion of home is at the root of Davis's Jewish dis-affiliations. Her work establishes home as an idea that is not simply tied to a particular time and place but is instead an expansive concept that changes over time, encompassing many differing versions of familiarity and estrangement, intimacy and isolation. *Make Me a Woman* is a book that emphasizes not a return to, or move away from, some lost or locatable place or past, but rather identifies the question of home as one that persists over the course of a lifetime and one that, for the artist, must be contended with afresh through every piece of self-representation. The search for home thus serves as a repeating trope in her work, bridging together the ontological and narrative pursuits of coming to terms with one's various identities along with the aesthetic enterprise of representing those identities. No single artistic form or style—from fragmentary, loosely drawn black-and-white sketches to carefully posed full-colored portraits—therefore represents the artist's "home," as each instead forms part of a larger mosaic of self.

The second half of *Make Me a Woman* tracks Vanessa's journey as she leaves New York City for California, her move away from home. But this coastal move is not presented as a clear or seamless shift. Instead, various diary comics noting experiences that happen in New York City venues, on the subway, in SoHo, or at an East Village café, for example, are suddenly interrupted by the September 1 entry. The diary entry is then followed by other comics that also take place in New York locales and then several comics that do not give any clear indication of where they take place. In fact, these entries, including one dated September 3, 2006 (a full year ahead of the September 1 comic, though positioned only seven pages later) and a narrative comic titled "Nightmoves," convey a sense of confusion and chaos regarding time and space, as Vanessa finds herself thrown together among groups of people, many of whom are strangers. Several pages later, the three-page comic "Crispy Christmas" begins with Vanessa explaining that she normally goes home to Florida, where her mother lives, "for Christmas," while her boyfriend, who is first officially mentioned in this comic, though in passing, stays in California. What the book's sprawling structure demonstrates above all, as in the nonchronological and somewhat sudden depiction of this move from the East to the West Coast, is the somewhat arbitrary nature of the concept of home.

As the book begins to focus on Vanessa's experiences in California, the three-page, full-color narrative comic "Stranger in a Strange Land" conveys the feeling of "homesickness" that she experiences in her new surroundings. As she explains on a page in which the narrator's tightly rendered cursive prose fills up the spaces between wide panels, "Every place I've lived, from my upbringing in South Florida, college in the Midwest and South, to even a short stint in Central America, I'd always been around New York Jews. I couldn't imagine any place being THAT different." She describes Santa Rosa, her new locale, as a "funny place" with a "limited number of professional opportunities, bars, and guys to date." One broad, watercolor drawing of bright green and brown fields on the opening page—the only image in the comic that does not picture people or speech or thought bubbles within it—accentuates the difference between her new and old cities, as this new locale is at least initially distinguished by its vast unpeopled landscape. In fact, the main element that sets apart Santa Rosa seems to be Vanessa's converted sense of her relationship to the spaces around her, a sensibility that, as the remainder of the comic shows, is actually rooted in her relationships with people. As she confesses, what baffles her sense of orientation in this new place is not the number of Jews she encounters but the new and unfamiliar ways they relate to their Jewish identities. She states that there are "some Jews here . . . and they're my friends. [But] I think that they might connect with their Judaism in a different way than me—I've never been in a situation where I had to feel like it made me different." Below this textual explanation, in a set of three interconnected images, Vanessa is seen having a conversation with a friend about growing up Jewish on the East versus West Coast (figure 2.7). Her friend explains, "Yeah, when we were little, we just didn't tell people we were Jewish!" Vanessa replies, "That is so weird! And you guys are only half Jewish anyway so what's the big deal?" In the third and final image tracking this dialogue, her friend looks annoyed, and Vanessa sheepishly admits, "Oh my gosh I didn't mean it like that! I'm sorry—I'm an idiot!"

2.7 *Vanessa Davis, middle of second page from "Stranger in a Strange Land," 2009. In* Make Me a Woman, *n.p. Images from* Make Me a Woman *copyright © Vanessa Davis, provided courtesy Drawn and Quarterly.*

As with the black-and-white diary sketch picturing Vanessa at her desk at the beginning of *Spaniel Rage*, this experience is broken into three pictured moments that are nevertheless tied together in one larger, horizontally positioned rectangular panel. The subtle shifts in each of the three matching images reflect a careful unfolding, as each player's facial expression slowly transforms in reaction and relation to the visual and verbal behaviors of the other. The conversation demonstrates the alienation—the feelings of disorientation—that Vanessa experiences in her new element. No matter the location, a common Jewish identity, much like any other shared affiliation, does not necessarily or easily unite her with others. Instead, as in this particular case, it can become a fracturing identity, dividing two people presumably belonging to the same community. Visually, the comic reflects this separation between the two women as Vanessa's friend is slowly silenced over the course of the three panels, her smile transformed by the third panel into a scowl as Vanessa's expression subtly shifts to one of budding remorse. Despite their spatial closeness on the page—drawn adjacent to one another, their bodies are almost superimposed—they are nevertheless portrayed as detached, their postures and language moving in separate directions.

Vanessa's friend's body faces forward while hers remains in profile, and her friend's speech bubbles disappear while hers take on more urgency and space. These relational stances suggest a powerful distancing between the two women even within these narrow frames.

Here, even though Vanessa finds herself in close conversation with a Jew from the West Coast, an affiliation reinforced by the narrow proximity of this intimate space, she still feels homesick for what she calls "the ubiquity of Jewishness in East Coast culture—how lots of people seem kinda Jewish, the diversity of Jews there." It is not necessarily "being" or identifying as Jewish that unites Vanessa with others or makes her feel comfortable around them, but rather a more intangible characteristic of being "kinda" Jewish, an identity that cannot easily be summed up, pictured, or defined. It is a matter of perspective, as the differing standpoints of the two women reflect. By revealing identity to be at least partly dependent on an individual's point of view, the comic reflects the slippery nature of the term *Jewish* as something without an essential core or home, a term as dependent on the person who uses or adopts it as on the setting in which it is claimed and the person who receives, reacts to, or witnesses that identity label.

Additionally, in the context of the spiraling chronology of the memoir as a whole, Vanessa's homesickness can be read as a feeling that is not altogether new to her, but rather a state of being that has followed her from the East to the West Coast. Although this particular narrative comic seems to align a comforting sense of being "kinda Jewish" with those living on the East Coast, as opposed to those living on the West Coast, the earlier narrative comics and journal entries in *Make Me a Woman* make it clear that this set of binaries—Jewish, East Coast, and home versus not Jewish, West Coast, and exile—is not straightforward as it seems. For example, even early on in *Make Me a Woman*, in various configurations and settings Vanessa often undergoes the sense of being an outsider or different from others. She encounters this feeling of marginality both as a member of a tight-knit Jewish community and, later, as one who has moved outside that community. "Modern Ritual" and "Preparation Information" are two comics stylistically linked with "Make Me a Woman," and they were all originally published in *Arthur* magazine in 2005 and 2006. The three one-page black-and-white comics are presented on consecutive pages at the very beginning of the book, and each is similarly drawn in pencil on a single page, dated 2005. In the first two comics of the set, which trace Vanessa's thoughts about Judaism just prior to her bat mitzvah, even when steeped in settings that suggest formative and immersive experiences of

Jewishness, she already recognizes the apprehensions she feels about her relationship to certain religious and cultural aspects of being Jewish. "Modern Ritual," another spiral-shaped comic, begins with Vanessa explaining how she grew up "almost exclusively around Jews"—and the characters drawn on the page are all presumably tied through this Jewish affiliation. Despite her continued exposure to Jewish life, rituals, and personalities, however, before her own bat mitzvah she finds herself experiencing "some doubts," a sentiment visually reinforced by her continually confused and uncomfortable facial expressions over the course of the page. Her rabbi somewhat alleviates these concerns with his observation that "the Torah is full of metaphor!" and his suggestion that she take her religion less literally. But, as her continually rounded and often contorted mouth and eyes reflect, she continues to experience strong misgivings.

In "Preparation Information," the following one-page comic (which is succeeded by the third and final comic in the series, the previously discussed "Make Me a Woman"), these misgivings culminate in a fainting spell, which occurs on the day she practices her Torah portion—the section of the Torah she has been assigned to read in honor of her coming-of-age—in front of a cantor. The accompanying image hides her face, as though only in this moment of presumably uncontrollable bodily disengagement can she stop marking her resistance in the passive but nevertheless consistent manner of disgruntled facial expressions. The comic ends by focusing not on the religious aspects of this rite of passage, but on the social and commercial traditions surrounding the bat mitzvah, like the excesses related to those having the parties. The shift from the spiritual to the material reveals the complexity of Vanessa's relationship to her Jewish identity. Her questioning stance, which in this context defines her understanding of what it means to be Jewish and is often reflected in her face, is more than a strictly religious issue—a difficulty with believing in a monotheistic god, for example. Instead, Jewishness is, in this case, a highly stressful classification linked to the expectations of others, whether those in her peer group or religious representatives and authority figures. In the final image, though her face finally looks somewhat content, her eyes cast a sidelong glance at her peers, as though she needs to read and mirror their facial expressions in order to secure a sense of belonging. This early ambivalent and often dis-affiliatory response to Jewishness is one she maintains over the course of the book, which reveals itself almost entirely through her interactions with others. It is an outlook that simultaneously encompasses her affinity with, and her separation from, a consistent or communal notion of what it means to be Jewish or to identify as Jewish.

Several years after her bat mitzvah experience, Vanessa finds herself having switched from a private Jewish day school to a public school. Like her move from the East Coast to California, the change in environment leaves her with conflicted feelings. As she recounts in "Dyspeptic Academic," a three-page full-colored narrative comic included early in the memoir, she finds a resemblance between these two communities in the fact that "at both schools I was ensconced in a small, tightly-knit community, where we were told we were special." Below this narration Vanessa is pictured sprawled in a domestic space, hugging a pillow as her friend lounges on the couch and knits. The phrase *tighly-knit* is visually echoed, suggesting an evolving kinship between the two women that is both connected to and contrasted with the sense of belonging precipitated by the vastly different educational environments. Like a close friendship—a chosen affiliation—being part of a closed community appeases Vanessa's desire to belong. But this very exposure to public school, particularly conversations that Vanessa has with those who are not part of her early, religious community, compels her to recognize how much she is concurrently connected to and distanced from that earlier affiliation. In another panel from the same comic, separated from this one by several lines of the narrator's cursive prose, Vanessa argues with her public school social studies teacher about a map of Israel that marks the West Bank and Gaza Strip as disputed territories. "No it isn't! Israel won it in the Six-Day war!!" she argues. Several panels later, on the following page, in a conversation with a public school peer who likens the "situation in Gaza" to "ethnic cleansing," Vanessa, pictured with a scowl on her face, thinks to herself, "What do I even know about ANYTHING anymore!" These two incidents highlight her confusion when hearing, possibly for the first time in her life, opinions about Israel that question what she once seemingly took for granted. At the same time, she experiences an equal discomfort in a dialogue she depicts between herself and a peer from her Jewish day school after she has left that school—a conversation pictured just above the Gaza panel, with no clear space separating the two scenes. As her childhood friend talks about the religious persecution of the Jews and how, as a result, they too deserve affirmative action, Vanessa counters, "Jews weren't brought here as slaves and then terrorized for 100 years after!" The distance that Vanessa experiences from her childhood peer, visibly reinforced by the dense speech bubbles dividing the two women in dialogue, reflects her aversion to the view of Jews as victims or as a persecuted minority in modern day America.

These disparate conversations are visually connected to one another, as they appear close together on a series of pages with limited indicators separating the different scenes from one another. As these swirling, tied reminiscences disclose, during interactions with others in both public and private school Vanessa consistently finds herself sounding out the voice of a questioning minority or at least expressing her disagreement through noticeably irritated facial expressions and sidelong glances. Her status in both these communities is strongly defined by her ability to question, and oftentimes reject, the majority opinion. Even in the context of being at "home," then, Vanessa is not necessarily always an insider, just as she is not always an outsider in situations that imbue her with a feeling of homesickness, as in the conversation she has with the woman she identifies as not authentically Jewish. By depicting fragments of conversations and experiences side by side on adjacent pages, with her questioning stance linking these otherwise disparate fragments, she continually disorients and reorients her relationship to past and present conceptions of self and identity by documenting them as most decipherable in relation to her own recurrently questioning posture.

As revealed in these early comics, Vanessa's Jewish identity surfaces often at the moments she confronts and interrogates the opinions and expectations of those around her. Regardless of their affiliations, she feels most "Jewish" when she engages with others in dialogues that allow her to express her differing opinions or lead her to moments of internal crisis about the status of her own points of view. These moments of crisis or challenge are marked by layers of verbal and visual expression that acquire new, more complex meanings when read and looked at in relation to one another. In each encounter she experiences a kind of satisfaction from voicing, thinking, or facially expressing her oppositional viewpoints, even though the conversations generally lead her into further lines of inquiry regarding her own identity instead of presenting her with definitive answers. These earlier encounters thus connect to the conversation she has with the woman she describes as "only half Jewish" in the later comic "Stranger in a Strange Land." As this particular conversation concludes, Vanessa apologizes for her comment, while her friend stands silently as the minority or outsider, as the one challenging a majority (in this case, a Jewish one). The idea that someone is Jewish only if she was born to a Jewish mother is a belief expressed by some in more conservative or orthodox religious Jewish communities, presumably like the one of Vanessa's day school upbringing, as the result of a religious statute. For Vanessa, whose own experiences have revealed to her the myriad ways that a person can be Jewish, this utterance reveals her own internalization of an ignorance and insensitivity to the importance of allowing others to take charge of their own identities and self-expressions and to question a dominant opinion.

The comic "Stranger in a Strange Land" ends with Vanessa sheepishly, and somewhat reluctantly, accepting the reality of her new home, open-ended and confusing as that reality feels. In the same dense cursive writing, sprawled over the final rectangular, horizontal panel, she narrates, "Oh, well. I moved here partly to get away from East Coast sensibilities and values. Isn't homesickness just part of self-exile? Isn't it a Jewish legacy to not fit in really anywhere? Isn't it always that you can take the girl out of Brooklyn, but not Brooklyn out of the girl?" The open-ended questions here link this comic to earlier childhood experiences, depicting incidents in which questions were posed but never fully answered. Under this set of questions, three consecutive images of Vanessa in bed, holding Philip Roth's famous 1969 novel *Portnoy's Complaint* (figure 2.8), are pictured, with, once again, no clear divisions separating these panels. In the first image Vanessa enjoys the novel, as illustrated by her entertained facial expression and speech bubble, "Ha!" In the second image she looks annoyed, her eyes rolled upward instead of focused on the novel. In the final image she is asleep, one of her hands still touching the book and the other clasped at her side.

This series of expressive drawings prompts a connection between Vanessa's reactions to a touchstone of contemporary Jewish American literature with her feelings of rootlessness in relation to her personally located sense of Jewish identity, thereby linking the experience of stigmatizing someone else on an individual level with the experience of having been part of a stigmatized collective. Vanessa's recurrent sense of exile, and her consequent, responsive adoption of an active sense of self-exile, connects to her experience of being a Jewish woman whose own image has been narrowly written and established in mainstream Jewish American literature.[17]

Much has been written about images of women that emerged from a Jewish American literature or, at least, from a publicly visible "canon" that is too often based on misogynist stereotypes. As mentioned in relation to Kominsky Crumb's works, Riv-Ellen Prell argues that the fracturing that occurs within minority groups, as between Jewish men and women, often reveals the dynamic of the group as a whole in relation to mainstream society. She writes, "One is not simply

2.8 *Vanessa Davis, bottom of final page from "Stranger in a Strange Land," 2009. In* Make Me a Woman, *n.p. Images from* Make Me a Woman *copyright © Vanessa Davis, provided courtesy Drawn and Quarterly.*

in or out of a group, assimilated or merely acculturated. Rather, relations between members of the minority group continue to mirror relations between the minority and majority groups" (*Fighting* 20). According to this model, the ways that some visible Jewish men have depicted Jewish women over time is partially a reflection of the ways Jews have been treated by and reflected in American culture and society more generally. In her introduction to *Talking Back*, Joyce Antler chronicles the resulting stereotypes that some Jewish men have created of Jewish women, which so often mirror Jewish men's own anxieties and humiliations. These include, for example, "The Yiddishe Mama, the Jewish Mother, and the Jewish American Princess" (1). Antler argues, "Such contradictory images of Jewish women—domineering and vulnerable, manipulative and quiescent, alluring and unattractive—highlight the impressive yet threatening aspects of Jewish women's roles and their power." Both Antler's and Prell's books additionally trace the ways Jewish American women, especially since the second wave of the feminist movement, have responded to such representations in their own art and writings. Prell, for example, discusses 1970s feminist novels as counter-representations to earlier depictions of Jewish women's bodies, as they "envision . . . a Jewishness that does not depend upon the consuming woman as an icon because Jewishness is not defined primarily in terms of acculturation or membership in the middle class. Jewishness, instead, constitutes an identity from which an artist can question and critique the dominant culture" (242). Kominsky Crumb's comics, which utilize and exaggerate stereotypes of Jewish women in order to render them absurd, can therefore similarly be understood as a kind of "talk back art"—an art that is very much focused on, and inspired by, earlier (mis)representations of Jewish women.

Davis's representation of Vanessa in bed reading *Portnoy's Complaint* is also, at least in part, a response to such earlier representations of Jewish women. However, unlike other "talk back art," Davis's work is not primarily focused on looking *back* at stereotypical representations of Jewish women. Instead, as the comic "Stranger in a Strange Land" demonstrates, her exploration of stereotypes begins with the very personal and present question of what it means to be an artist engaging in acts of representation that involve the danger of oversimplifying the subject at hand, whether that subject is the self or someone else. The comic begins with Vanessa talking to a friend about a column she has been hired to write for a Jewish organization, Nextbook, publisher of the online *Tablet* magazine, and it is a conversational tidbit that emphasizes Vanessa's controlling status as artist and creator. At other points in this same comic, as in the scene with her friend, she recounts conversations that reflect her propensity to categorize others as well as her struggle to understand this inclination. As another example, in a set of panels pictured halfway down the final page of the comic, she somewhat apologetically e-mails a former Israeli lover to tell him that the film *You Don't Mess with the Zohan* reminded her of him. This 2008 American comedy starred Adam Sandler playing an Israeli soldier who has left his life combating terrorism to become a hairdresser in New York City. The film is loaded with satirical stereotypes of Israelis, not to mention Jews, Palestinians, and Arab Americans. In the Israeli lover's response, he tells her, "An obnoxious reason indeed! It's like if I told you I saw some dumb American girl at McDonald's doing her stupid American thing and thought of you!" By depicting Vanessa's personal experiences stereotyping others alongside her experiences of being stereotyped as part of a larger collective, Davis's comics reveal the porous divides between those on the inside of a particular community and those on the outside, between those who have been stereotyped and those who stereotype. Her work thus both responds to and creates anew representations of identity across various communities, as her comics engage with and account for her artistic imagination, which is always tied to the personal and cultural influences that affect her artistic choices and enterprises.

The images pictured at the end of the comic, of Vanessa reading Roth's novel, can thus be read as an epilogue to the narrative reflecting a complicated response to stereotypical depictions of Jewish women in American media and culture. Significantly, in the first image in this series of three, Vanessa finds enjoyment in the book—an important acknowledgment that although Jewish women as depicted in Roth's novels in many ways hurt Jewish women's perceptions of themselves, not to mention Jewish men's perception of *themselves*, they also contribute to a persistently influential cultural celebration of Jewishness in America, however flawed and contradictory that celebration. As Davis pointed out in an interview, *"Portnoy's Complaint* was important—those depictions had never been put out there, that Jewish voice was important to hear, for so many reasons" ("In Search" 180).

The following central image picturing Vanessa grimacing at the novel reflects more typical and public feminist responses to his works, not to mention reactions to other important Jewish American male literary figures, as well as comedians, from the 1950s and 1960s.[18] Yet this image is followed by a third that is perhaps unique to a generation of Jewish women coming of age in the late twentieth and early twenty-first centuries, whose relationship to feminism differs from the generations before them. In this final image Vanessa has fallen asleep, and drool emerges from the corner of her mouth. One of her hands still clutches the book, but the other is aimed away from it. The connection to the past is still there, in traces, but the postassimilated Jewish woman artist, as depicted here, has also moved forward; she is fully engaged in an imaginary dreamworld that still barely grasps at what engrossed her before she fell asleep.

Presented as a series with no panels dividing them, these carefully composed watercolor drawings are visibly and structurally linked to the set of images pictured on the previous page of the comic and representing Vanessa in conversation with her friend. By including these two mirroring sets of panels in the same narrative about homelessness and self-exile, Davis's work connects the violence of publicly feeling exiled from one's own identity with the private everyday interactions that often lead one member of a group to marginalize another within that group. That Vanessa presents her response to Roth's novel in the intimate space of her bed—heart-covered pillows propping her up—suggests an inevitable muddling of public and private spaces when it comes to self-perception. Homesickness is therefore a state of feeling like an outsider at "home" as much as it is a state of feeling like an outsider far away from "home." It is a recognition that the notion of home, of itself, like identity, is a concept that changes over time, but that also holds many sometimes contradictory meanings within the same present.

"That'll be A Funny Panel in Some Future Comic Where I Flashback on My Non-Jewish Boyfriend!"

In addition to recording Vanessa's journey between coasts, but not necessarily away from "home," or into "exile," *Make Me a Woman* is a book that tracks her experiences dating both Jewish and non-Jewish men over time as yet another fraught indicator of her ever changing understanding of and connection to her Jewish identity. For many contemporary Jewish American women artists and writers, the theme of relationships between Jewish women and non-Jewish men is a recurring one that allows them to explore the false presumption that non-Jewish men lead Jewish women into a state of separation from their Jewish ties and heritages or that relationships with such men represent a condition of not being "at home" with their Jewish identities.[19] Like Kominsky Crumb, Davis often paints her alter ego as uncomfortable around Jewish men, a discomfort that similarly stems from her overfamiliarity with them. In the previously discussed comic, "Dyspeptic Academic," for instance, Vanessa reflects on her negative experiences with Jewish men in grade school: "Sometimes I think that this overexposure to developing Jewish boys has contributed to a lifelong romantic aversion to them." Below this narrative, she is pictured in a classroom, seated at a desk with a scowl on her face as a young boy next to her, leaning over, inquires of her and another pictured female classmate: "Hey can you guys shut your legs? I really hate the smell of TUNA!" In the adjoining panel, Vanessa is depicted as an adult in bed with a man, and as she leans her body toward him—much like the adolescent boy once leaned toward her—he turns away, asking, "Can you get off me? I feel like I'm being smothered!" By presenting these two scenes in close proximity to one another, Davis draws a connection, however tenuous, between incidents that might otherwise remain isolated from one another. In a sense, by linking these experiences textually as well as visually—the boy and man wear matching hair colors and expressions—she engages in and compounds the very narrowed categorizations of "other" that, elsewhere and in relation to her own identity, she works hard to reject. But as a reading of the comic in its entirety reflects, such

stereotyping can also be a means of honestly and critically reflecting on how outside communal expectations often interact with and influence an individual's
most intimate desires.

In the final two panels of the same comic, for example, Vanessa sits at a "big
Jewish wedding," her face tilted longingly toward a man, labeled "Jewish TV
writer," who sits across the table. The adjoining panel portrays a daydream in
which, wearing an almost identical expression and posture, she is dancing with
yet another man, who is presumably not Jewish, and asking him, "If we ever have
kids, I can raise them Jewish, right?" In the first of these two images, Vanessa's
gaze is directed toward the TV writer, but also in the direction of the panel in
which she embraces her non-Jewish partner. In this way the images associate the
fantasy of affiliating with a non-Jewish man with the fantasy of fulfilling obliga-
tions that have been passed on to her—through her family (predominantly her
mother) and community—of maintaining a link to her Jewish heritage, especially
of transferring that heritage onto her hypothetical children.

In Davis's work, then, we see both a repetition and a revision of the anxieties and desires of earlier Jewish American women's writing about exogamy.[20]
Vanessa is able to question the expectations of Jewish womanhood that are
passed on to her without fully rejecting them. She modifies these expectations
to suit her own particular needs and desires, all the while maintaining an awareness and acceptance of the impressions these outside pressures have made on
her. Additionally, by framing her fantasy question about having children with a
non-Jewish man as an event that is a hypothetical and not a definite plan, an "if"
instead of a "when," she rebels against the cultural assumption and expectation
that, as a woman, she will ultimately procreate, or at least want and attempt to
procreate—even as she leaves it open as a possibility. Vanessa's fantasy, draped
on the page in the folds of a heap of gray and chalky storm clouds, possibly
ominous, possibly animate, simultaneously reconciles her need to accommodate
herself to the expectations of others, a need she has adopted into her own "sense
of identity," as she admits of the daydream, with her desire to question and rebel
against those very expectations.

Several other comics throughout the first half of *Make Me a Woman*, before
Vanessa finds herself in a monogamous relationship with a non-Jewish man in
California, additionally trace her interactions with various men, and these comics
similarly address the question of how to dis-affiliate. For Vanessa, this means how
to acknowledge the desire to maintain a Jewish identity without bowing to the

expectations of others or disavowing one's own needs, motivations, and appetites, however jumbled these may be. In the three-page narrative comic "Wild Ride," for example, she describes the time she spends with an Israeli in New York City. "Jewish American girls and Israeli guys—isn't that our REAL birthright?" she quips in the opening panel, as the Israeli man lets out a chuckle. Vanessa goes on to describe him as "insufferably charming" and "strangely familiar"—characterizations mirrored and echoed in his variously awkward postures, attire, and proclamations. These depictions correspond with the e-mail exchange with her Israeli ex-boyfriend in "Stranger in a Strange Land" in which she reveals her own predisposition toward lumping Israelis together, a tendency that evokes often misdirected feelings of nostalgia and familiarity. As Deborah Dash Moore and S. Ilan Troen argue in their introduction to *Divergent Jewish Cultures*, many presume a connection between Israelis and American Jews, in part because of the shared "impact of European Jews on both societies" (2). Nevertheless, as they go on to show, "Israelis and American Jews lack intimate knowledge of one another. They tend to hold stereotypes rather than real people in mind when they think of each other, despite their similar origins" (3).[21] For Vanessa, the candid descriptions of her stereotyped perceptions of Israeli men reveal yet another dimension of the way she conceptualizes her Jewish American identity. For her, as for other American Jews raised to perceive Israeli culture and history as an extension of their own heritage, Israel presumably marks a kind of "home away from home." According to this model, Israeli men represent the "strangely familiar," in the sense that they are Jewish but not American. A relationship with an Israeli man therefore could potentially serve to bring together Vanessa's conflicting needs to rebel against and simultaneously maintain her Jewish identity in the ways that others expect her to; it might conceivably satisfy her desire to affirm and cultivate the "insider-outsider" status she experienced as a child and teenager, the very sense of enforced "rootlessness" that she brands her own "Jewish legacy," although her comics reveal the simultaneous sense of connection she often feels both in and out of this very Jewish legacy.

The opening images in the comical "Wild Ride" visually reflect Vanessa's overly idealistic fantasies of what this relationship with an Israeli man could mean for her, even in the face of their obvious incompatibilities (figure 2.9). One early panel depicts an extreme close-up of their faces, with him telling her, "Just so you know, this is just for tonight." Her eyes look skeptically away from him, as her thought bubble reads, "No kidding!" Yet, despite what seems like an acknowledgment of the casual status of this relationship, the panel is followed by another, in which she sits at her computer with one arm on her chest and another on her forehead as her speech bubble emits her swoon. She is reading an e-mail in which her Israeli lover once again attempts to maintain an emotional distance, as he has written to her, "It probably won't go anywhere, but let's meet up." Vanessa's swoon is surrounded by red hearts that connect the previous panel, in which she reveals what can now more clearly be read as only a superficial skepticism, with a panel depicting her inability to break out of the fantasy she has created from an ideal of the Israeli man as her "birthright." The two images are additionally linked, once again, by her gaze, which is focused on the idealistic fantasy that evokes the swoon, even as she is engaged in a close embrace with the object of her purported affections.

The rest of the comic slowly breaks down Vanessa's illusion, as this man's individual quirks and behaviors disclose how much her Israeli fantasy lover is less than an ideal mate. The move toward reality comes slowly for Vanessa, who says almost nothing over the course of the comic once she has announced that

2.9 *Vanessa Davis, middle of first page from "Wild Ride," 2009. In* Make Me a Woman, *n.p. Images from* Make Me a Woman *copyright © Vanessa Davis, provided courtesy Drawn and Quarterly.*

initial "birthright" proclamation. What this story line humorously records, most significantly, is a superficial relationship between two characters who seem to be communicating on different planes. Vanessa's idealistic fantasy, which turns her Israeli lover into a characterization of who and what she wants to identify herself with, is matched by his comment, on one of their dates, that "I always wanted to be an artist. Instead, I just date artists." The glimpses that the comic imparts of the Israeli's personality hint at his own superficial reasons for spending time with Vanessa, a motivation mirroring her own desire to be defined by the person she chooses to date. Though the two are consistently visually linked throughout the comic, coupled together in all panels but one, their interactions ultimately reflect two people who never actually see or hear one another; they are proximate to each other, like Vanessa and her friend in "Stranger in a Strange Land," but neverthe-less maintain an unbridgeable distance.

Vanessa's fraught attitude toward being pressured into a relationship with a Jewish man is tracked throughout *Make Me a Woman*, as she negotiates the com-plicated desire to get around this expectation—to remain "open-minded," as it were—all the while somehow keeping up a link to her Jewish identity. The plot-lines that hinge around her dating reflect her struggle toeing the line between out-side expectations and personal needs, between the urge to rebel and the yearning to fit in or feel like part of a community. Her contradictory impulses and inclina-tions are traced on the page both explicitly—generally, through clear and careful verbal examinations and explanations—as well as implicitly—through omissions, silences, and often nuanced or ambiguous postures and expressions that poten-tially link to verbal narratives in unsettled ways.

The later comics in the book continue to explore this complicated question, as Vanessa's non-Jewish boyfriend, Trevor, becomes a more consistent presence. Like Vanessa's move from the East to the West Coast, however, her perception of what it means to be in a serious relationship with a non-Jewish man is not chronologically traceable. Indeed, while Trevor appears several times in the first half of the memoir, his presence is generally not explicitly referred to early on; instead, he is an often silent actor in Vanessa's narrative. In the previously discussed comic, "Dyspeptic Academic," for instance, the man pictured in the final panel looks like Trevor, and his humorous response to Vanessa's question about whether they would raise their kids Jewish—"I was thinking we'd raise them Zoroastrian!" he responds—aligns with the way Trevor's personality is portrayed in other comics. This surreptitious introduction into the narrative can

be explained by the nonchronological arrangement of the book: "Dyspeptic Academic" is dated 2009, although it was likely placed at the beginning of the book
due to its focus on Vanessa's early Jewish life. But Trevor's understated presence,
which continues, to an extent, in the latter half of the book, also crucially signifies
Vanessa's movement away from her fantasies and desires and into an actual, and
not imagined or underdeveloped, relationship with a man, who is also notably
an artist.[22] In another three-page narrative comic placed early on in the text, and
titled "Framed!?" Vanessa recounts her experience trying to push herself "to be
open-minded" by dating a non-Jewish man who proudly shows her his full-sized
tattoo of Jesus being crucified; the image is splayed across his chest in thick ink,
with the words "Praise the Lord" sprawled beneath it. Although the comic is centrally focused on Vanessa's attempts to wrestle with her dating history prior to her
long-term, monogamous relationship, Trevor's once again downplayed presence
in one of the opening panels is telling. He sits beside Vanessa, a scowl on his face,
as her mother, who coordinates a Jewish film festival, suggests that the three of
them watch "an animated documentary on circumcision" after dinner. In this case
Trevor's scowl mimics the pained expressions that Vanessa often wears when she
is made uncomfortable or feels out of place. But his posture, so closely aligned
with hers as they jointly face her mother, also suggests a close affiliation, or con-
sensus, between them. Vanessa's exclamation ("Mom!") serves to reinforce that
bond and even suggests that it is in the space of Vanessa's connection with Trevor
that she finds herself most able to fully express herself, to feel at home with her
questioning posture.

In the second half of the memoir, Trevor is often pictured in diary comics conveying an intimate and loving relationship between equals. The two are frequently
pictured together in bed, as in a panel from "Holy Rollin,'" a three-page narrative
comic in which Vanessa struggles with her connection to Jewish traditions and rituals. In this panel Trevor faces Vanessa, his expression attentive, as she somewhat
mindlessly prattles on about the future, her hands clutching at the bedspread
and an ambiguous drip—of sweat or a tear—pictured on her face. The narrative
text above their heads reads, "Judaism is a lot about personal responsibility, and
I like that. Also, I don't even trust my own beliefs much of the time—it'd be hard
to stay in sync with a whole community." Trevor's calm posture here contrasts
with the animate and always slightly off-key (in Vanessa's eyes) Israeli in "Wild
Ride." Too, their intimacy in bed, and particularly Vanessa's comfort with expressing herself verbally and affectively while he remains silent but interested, recalls

the image from "Dyspeptic Academic" in which Vanessa pictures herself with a neutral expression, leaning over her Jewish lover as he claims she is smothering him. In contrast, Trevor's often unpronounced presence throughout the book, in diary and narrative comics where Vanessa freely expresses herself, suggests a sense of comfort that is unattainable with other pictured male counterparts. While Vanessa often attempts to orient herself in relation to those others, through verbal and visual gestures and postures that suggest a contrived intimacy, with Trevor that sense of connection appears often seamless. Like his unannounced integration into the text, their daily interactions and intimacies are generally presented without metacommentary.

While he is in many cases a silent counterpart to Vanessa, when Trevor participates more actively in the narrative his expressions and contributions serve to enhance and complicate Vanessa's self-reflections, as in a diary comic dated March 18, 2008. Drawn rhythmically in six evenly spaced panels, and partially light watercolor, the comic opens with Vanessa sitting at her computer as Trevor is pictured in the background, his face hidden. "Purim is a fun holiday!" Vanessa exclaims, and he turns to hear her description of the food eaten on the Jewish holiday, asking questions and asserting, "That sounds fun," when she describes the tradition of drinking "till you don't know the difference between good and evil." When Vanessa describes hamantaschen, the triangle-shaped cookies traditionally eaten to celebrate the day, he responds, "Yeeuch! Sounds like more gross Jewish food," even as Vanessa dreamily pictures the cookies in a thought bubble floating over her head. The next panel is untitled, as Vanessa stares at her boyfriend, who sits with a self-satisfied look on his face. His eyes are closed, and two lines beside his lips reveal a slight grin while she looks on expressionlessly. This silent moment between the otherwise engaged couple reflects a pause in the narrative, as Vanessa presumably absorbs the conversation and contemplates a response. Captured in this constructed series of unfolding narrative bits, the recorded conversation affords the otherwise silent-on-the-topic couple space to finally address aloud what it means for Vanessa to be dating a non-Jew.

In the end, the final two panels of the comic depict a playful acknowledgment of a conversation between two intimates revealed to be equals (figure 2.10). Facing her computer again, and this time with *her* eyes closed—wearing an expression almost identical to Trevor's expression in the previous panel—Vanessa tells him, "Well, that'll be a funny panel in some future comic where I flashback on my non-Jewish boyfriend!" As in the collaborative comics drawn by Aline Kominsky

2.10 *Vanessa Davis, final two panels from "3/18/08." In* Make Me a Woman, *n.p. Images from* Make Me a Woman *copyright © Vanessa Davis, provided courtesy Drawn and Quarterly.*

Crumb and Robert Crumb, this image humorously addresses the question of who is allowed to speak for or about a minority group and how the context of the conversation affects what is or is not presumably permissible for its participants to say. Although noncollaborative, this diary comic reflects a dialogue originally held in a private space that has been made public by its visualization.[23] The statement that Vanessa will "flashback" on her non-Jewish ex-boyfriend in a future, imaginary panel reinforces the actuality that this is a conversation being translated onto the page by a cartoonist who is consciously turning her everyday life experiences into art that will be visible to others. The comic has been created in part for laughs, but it also captures and records an otherwise private moment between intimates whose relationship, as a Jew dating a non-Jew, has been repeatedly misunderstood and caricatured in the public eye. It revises that characterization in a public way. By exaggerating her reaction to Trevor with a comedic comeback, Vanessa presents the two as on par with one another even as she is the person drawing the comic. The depiction productively exposes and exploits the stereotypes associated with their coupling—namely, that the non-Jew will never be able to look at the Jew without categorizing her, through idealizations and/or degradations, or even by engaging in overt acts of anti-Semitism. By putting these portrayals in Vanessa's hands, so to speak, the story line turns the victim-persecutor formula on its head.

0.1 *Lauren Weinstein, "The Best We Can Hope For." Two-page map in the Ganzfeld 7, 2008, pp. 8–9. Used by permission of Lauren Weinstein.*

1.2 *Aline Kominsky Crumb, untitled cartoon. In* Need More Love, *p. 102. Used by permission of Aline Kominsky Crumb.*

1.7 *Aline Kominsky Crumb, six panels from second page of "Nose Job," 1989. In* Need More Love, *p. 87. Used by permission of Aline Kominsky Crumb.*

1.10 *Aline Kominsky Crumb, final page from "The Bunch Her Baby & Grammaw Blabette."*
In Need More Love, pp. 215. Used by permission of Aline Kominsky Crumb.

2.4 *Vanessa Davis, full-page color drawing. In* Make Me a Woman, *n.p. Images from* Make Me a Woman *copyright © Vanessa Davis, provided courtesy* Drawn and Quarterly.

2.6 *Vanessa Davis, "September 1, 2005." In* Make Me a Woman, *n.p. Images from* Make Me a Woman *copyright © Vanessa Davis, provided courtesy Drawn and Quarterly.*

2.8 *Vanessa Davis, bottom of final page from "Stranger in a Strange Land," 2009. In* Make Me a Woman, *n.p. Images from* Make Me a Woman *copyright © Vanessa Davis, provided courtesy Drawn and Quarterly.*

2.10 *Vanessa Davis, final two panels from "3/18/08." In* Make Me a Woman, *n.p. Images from* Make Me a Woman *copyright © Vanessa Davis, provided courtesy Drawn and Quarterly.*

THE ONLY PERSON WHO I HAVE EVER MET THAT WAS GOOD AT PLAYING BARBIES WITH ME WAS DIANA, WHO WAS MY BEST FRIEND UNTIL ABOUT TWO YEARS AGO, WHEN SHE DECIDED TO BE COOL.

The End

13

3.13 *Lauren Weinstein, final page from "Skate Date." In* Girl Stories, *p. 118. From GIRL STORIES copyright © 2006 Lauren Weinstein. Reprinted by permission of Henry Holt and Company. LLC All Rights Reserved.*

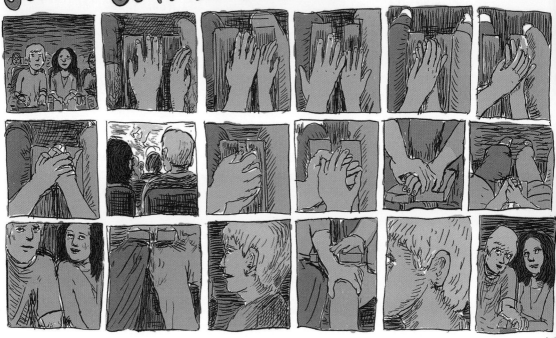

4.1 *Sarah Glidden, title page from chapter 4. In* How to Understand Israel in 60 Days or Less, *p. 78. Copyright © Sarah Glidden 2010.*

4.2 *Sarah Glidden, panel from chapter 1.*
In How to Understand Israel in 60 Days or Less, *p. 8.*
Copyright © Sarah Glidden 2010.

4.3 *Sarah Glidden, panel from chapter 1.*
In How to Understand Israel in 60 Days or Less, *p. 8.*
Copyright © Sarah Glidden 2010.

4.6 *Sarah Glidden, four panels from chapter 3. In* How to Understand Israel in 60 Days or Less, *p. 67. Copyright © Sarah Glidden 2010.*

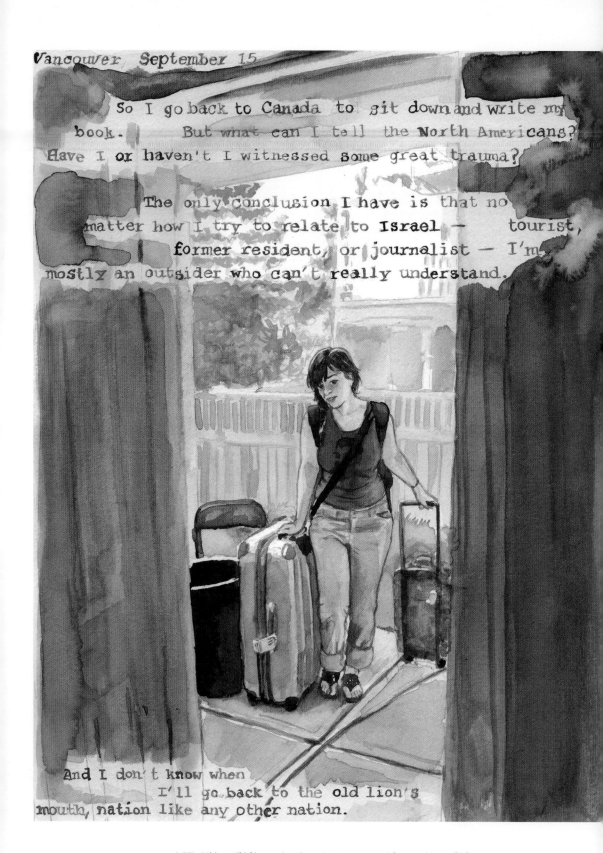

Vancouver September 15

So I go back to Canada to sit down and write my book. But what can I tell the North Americans? Have I or haven't I witnessed some great trauma?

The only conclusion I have is that no matter how I try to relate to Israel — tourist, former resident, or journalist — I'm mostly an outsider who can't really understand.

And I don't know when I'll go back to the old lion's mouth, nation like any other nation.

4.17 *Miriam Libicki, page in "Fierce Ease," n.p. Copyright © Miriam Libicki.*

Indeed, in the last panel on the page, titled "Epilogue," Vanessa's boyfriend giggles in bed as he reads a book about Hitler entitled *The Early Years*, while Vanessa looks over at him angrily, the covers drawn tightly up to her neck. The comedic depiction of this intimate space—Vanessa is leaning, in the panel, on the same heart-covered pillow pictured in the *Portnoy's Complaint* panels—exaggerates preconceived, stereotyped roles of the Jew in conversation, or in bed, with the non-Jew. This interaction, depicted playfully alongside the many other comics in the book that document a loving relationship, ultimately discloses a partnership between two people—both, notably, cartoonists—who are clearly at home with one another. In the end, it is, ironically, in the private space of her bed that Vanessa can "talk back" to the many unseen but influential presences that have informed, however surreptitiously, her current sense of what it means to belong.

"What Would Make Me The Most 'Myself'?"

Throughout *Make Me a Woman*, Vanessa often calls up her mother's words in narratives through which she explores her Jewish identity. Toward the end of "Holy Rollin,'" for example, in a square panel picturing a close-up of her mother's face poised in front of a cozy, flowery couch, she recalls her mother as "always" saying: "wherever I am in the world, if I'm around Jews I feel at home!" In the following, adjacent panel, Vanessa faces her mother's persona in her own close-up, wearing a scowl and with her eyes rolled. Though a blue background unites the two women, Vanessa's likeness is not tied to any particular space here, in contrast to her mother's familiarly depicted couch. Vanessa's cynical thought bubble, drawn in a cloud of smoke beside her, reads, "When are we EVER not around a bunch of JEWS?" Here Vanessa mocks her mother's words, but, as the rest of the page reflects, she does not completely reject them. Instead, depicted as a prelude to the remainder of the page, but also as an epilogue to the first two pages of the comic, these words prompt relational explorations. Over the course of the comic, she visually and textually experiments with notions of home and not home, the familiar and the unfamiliar, cast alongside one another, much like the neighboring images of mother and daughter. These disorientations and reorientations are important gestures, signifying not an omission of or disidentification with the world of her mother, but rather an integration of that point of view into her own ever evolving perspective.

In the final three-page narrative comic included in the memoir, "Fast Forward!" Vanessa attempts to move from her focus on the past and present, and especially the past as part of the present, to concentrate on the future. She begins by recalling her move to California and how her life since has felt "like a bit of a time warp." She lists the many changes that her friends, near and far, have gone through over those years, changes that have made her feel left behind. As she narrates, "I don't know what to do next. I don't totally know what I want," she once again inserts her mother's presence into the story line. When Vanessa poses the question "What would make me the most 'myself'?" the image underneath pictures her as an adolescent sitting beside her mother in the intimate space of a car. This time the two are in close proximity to one another, their bodies overlapping in the space of the same panel, and they look at each other with matching sidelong glances over the frames of two sets of eyeglasses. Her mother asks her, "What do you consider yourself FIRST: A woman, a Jew, or an American?" Framed also as a question, these words obliquely mirror Vanessa's own rebellious journey to understanding her identity as open-ended and never definitive, a continued investigation focused on unraveling possibilities instead of insisting on clear-cut truths. Beneath the image of the two of them in the car, the narrator adds an open-ended statement from her mother: "She's also told me, 'Be here now.'"

This panel brings together the main thematic explorations of *Make Me a Woman*—what does it mean to choose one identity over another? is there a way to best understand or represent the self as a distinct entity? how do relationships and experiences from the past affect present outlooks?—while it reiterates the memoir's continued emphasis on past-as-present as the most formative moment in any exploration of self and identity. Looking forward requires a kind of open-endedness that comes from integration, from recognizing the many connections between synchronic and diachronic versions of the self that are always in dynamic conversation with one another. For Vanessa, chronicling the self is a process based not on choosing one representation over another, but on recognizing the diverse truths inherent in all self-representations created over time and connected on the page. It is through the process of composition, of piecing the self line by line, that the artist can finally find and claim a space of belonging.

"I Always Want to Know Everything True"

*Memory, Adolescence, and Belonging in the Graphic Memoirs
of Miss Lasko-Gross and Lauren Weinstein*

espite the roots of modern cartooning as a means of political
and cultural satire, as well as the abundance of graphic narra-
tives clearly written for "mature" audiences, comics are often
mistakenly reputed to be reading material primarily meant
for the young. Many cartoonists have had the perplexing experience of seeing their
works advertised as children's or young adult literature. During a 2011 interview,
for example, Art Spiegelman claimed that when he first heard about parents and
teachers sharing the *Maus* series with twelve year olds, he thought, "wait, that's
child abuse" ("Art Spiegelman's *MetaMaus*"). Indeed, a 1993 *New Yorker* cartoon,
"In the Dumps," composed by Spiegelman in collaboration with children's book
writer and illustrator Maurice Sendak, reflects the struggle Spiegelman had in
coming to terms with this complex issue. Pictured walking together in the woods
outside of Sendak's Connecticut home, Sendak's alter ego tells Spiegelman's,
"Kids books . . . Grownup books . . . That's just marketing. Books are books!"
(80).[1] As Spiegelman admitted in the 2011 interview, he eventually came around to
an understanding of comics as "democratic—each person will take what he will."

Parsing out the relationship between storytelling and age appropriateness is
a complicated task. Many maintain the view that narratives composed as comics
are automatically unsophisticated, or one-dimensional, and that such texts must
therefore be intended for children. This outlook assumes, among other things,
that children are incapable of reading complex or demanding works. The problematic association between youth culture and the comics medium as a whole
endures, especially in North America, because of the popularity of mainstream
superhero and action genres, which often cater to children and adolescents (at least

as the starting point of an often lifelong attachment), the prevalence of animated films intended for young audiences, and the false presumption upheld by many of images as simple tools of communication and children as easy receptors of such simple transmissions.[2] In his introduction to a 2007 special issue of *ImageTexT* on "Comics and Childhood," Charles Hatfield addresses this connection, which he describes as "both misleading and contentious." As he writes, "the idea persists that comics are rooted in childhood, that is, that comics are grounded historically in children's culture and psychologically in some longed-for, Edenic state of childlike carelessness, innocence, and simplicity." As a case in point, among other pieces written for popular audiences Hatfield references "Not Funnies," a July 11, 2004 article by Charles McGrath published in the *New York Times Magazine*. In his piece, despite recognizing the complexity of "graphic novels," McGrath ultimately argues that, with comics journalist Joe Sacco as an exception, "this is a medium probably not well suited to lyricism or strong emotion. . . . [Comics instead] appeal to that childish part of ourselves that delights in caricature."[3]

This mistaken approach to comics as a narrow genre, rather than a tractable medium, creates, in addition to other problems, practical difficulties in terms of the marketing and distribution of texts—as Sendak's alter ego cuttingly intimates. For example, Lauren Weinstein's graphic memoir, *Girl Stories*, published in 2006, was originally placed in the children's picture-book section of Barnes and Noble, much to the dismay of the parent of a ten-year-old, who wrote an angry letter to the store. As Weinstein explained in an interview, "A book that blurs the lines for adults and kids is a really hard thing for people to figure out how to market" ("Interview with Emily Brobow" 51). Miss Lasko-Gross discussed a similar problem in a recent interview, describing the "touchy" situation of being asked by parents "what they think is right for their children" ("'A Portrait of the World'" 182). "I think it's more about context than about words or images," she added, lamenting that parents often "take things out of context and then get outraged." Given such widespread and stubbornly persistent beliefs about the kinds of stories that comics are, or are not, capable of telling, and the attendant issues that emerge from such beliefs, the creation of a comic that, intentionally or not, toys with what is suitable for certain audiences can be a means of challenging normative notions of authorial intent and audience expectation. By experimenting with genre conventions, and particularly intended readerships, a text that "blurs the lines" can expose the very assumptions that shape the way people read and respond to art and literature, potentially undermining those very assumptions.

The autobiographical comics of Miss Lasko-Gross and Lauren Weinstein both complicate the possibility of categorizing their works as intended for a particular age demographic. Lauren Weinstein's *Girl Stories* takes place during a young woman's adolescence, specifically from age thirteen to fourteen or fifteen. Miss Lasko-Gross's *Escape from "Special,"* also published in 2006, begins in childhood, with a recounting of the narrator's "earliest memory," while her second memoir, *A Mess of Everything*, published in 2009, concludes when the narrator finishes high school. Unlike the works of Aline Kominsky Crumb and Vanessa Davis, the voice of a present-day adult narrator does not drive these memoirs. Instead, the child's or adolescent's voice and physical presence dominates these books, as though they were composed by their author's young personae as the events unfolded or shortly after. The covers of the memoirs establish this conceit early on. Whereas the figures drawn on the covers of *Need More Love* and *Make Me a Woman* portray narrators close in age to the authors publishing the works, the fluorescent cover of *Girl Stories* pictures the face and torso of a cartoonish adolescent giving the thumbs up, a wide, toothy smile splayed across her face, and the more somber, gently colored cover of *Escape from "Special"* depicts a young woman morosely drawing in her notebook, several strands of bangs loosely covering one eye as she sits at her desk in a classroom (figures 3.1 and 3.2).

Given our general contemporary understanding of adolescence as a moment of transition, the focus on childhood and especially adolescence as the "present" in these memoirs establishes the liminal as a useful and unique vantage point from which to understand and represent the self. As Mary Pipher writes in her seminal book on girls and adolescence, *Reviving Ophelia*, first published in 1994, "Something dramatic occurs to girls in their early adolescence. Just as ships and planes disappear mysteriously into the Bermuda Triangle, so do the selves of girls go down in droves. They crash and burn in a social and developmental Bermuda Triangle" (4). The middle and high school years present a time when reflections about self and identity—questions of "who am I?" and "what am I?"—predominate and when categorizations of self, such as gendered, religious, ethnic, sexual, material, bodily, and even cultural affiliations, potentially assume an overwhelmingly devastating or comforting force, depending on how and in what context they are introduced. In this way the transitional frame of adolescence, which I am defining here generally as the time span between childhood and adulthood, is emphasized in these books as a privileged state of knowing, experiencing, and even recalling certain defining moments in the story of one's life.[4]

3.1 Lauren Weinstein, *cover of* Girl Stories. *From GIRL STORIES copyright © 2006 Lauren Weinstein.*
Reprinted by permission of Henry Holt and Company, LLC. All Rights Reserved.

By foregrounding questions of identity and classification in graphic renditions of childhood and adolescence as the present, the two works examined in this chapter underscore the aesthetic and narrative possibilities inherent in periods of transition. Yet, despite their emphases on social constructions and categorizations as the dominant lenses that adolescents in particular use to read each other and to be read by one another, unlike the graphic memoirs of Kominsky Crumb and Davis, *Escape from "Special"* and *Girl Stories* are texts that do not often refer explicitly to the Jewishness of their main characters. Although questions of Jewish identity are integral to these memoirs of adolescence, the theme of Jewishness emerges more often through absences or asides about ethnic and religious identity and experience rather than through direct, comprehensive engagements. While Jewish themes, symbols, and references can be found in these graphic memoirs,

3.2 *Miss Lasko-Gross, cover of* Escape from "Special." *Images copyright © Miss Lasko-Gross. Courtesy Fantagraphics Books.*

Jewishness is slantingly established and explored, often in relation to more general metaphors of feeling like an outsider or being singled out. As a label that is sometimes attributed to the personae of these memoirs by others and sometimes self-proclaimed, being "special," a "freak," or "other" comes to stand, in some instances, as a source of strength and power. At other instances it gets inscribed as an identity label that leads to self-doubt, agony, and the shattering feeling of a sense of rootlessness. Jewishness, as it is often indirectly signified in relation to these nonspecific representations of standing out, is thus open to imaginative revision. But it also runs the risk of effacement or displacement in light of more universally applicable—and therefore, in some ways, "safer"—metaphors for identity and belonging/not belonging.

Lasko-Gross's and Weinstein's graphic memoirs convey dis-affiliatory stances that are at times grounded in Jewish identity as an extrapolation, and sometimes even an abstraction, rather than a system of plainly distinguishable and traceable affiliations, gestures, symbols, traditions, and expectations. Nonetheless, in depicting Jewishness as a self-representation that can apply beyond easily recognizable Jewish worlds or contexts, these texts pose the possibility of postassimilated Jewish identity as connective; in the end these memoirs resist the possibility of any identity, as any aesthetic grouping, being a straightforward or seamless classification or construct. In both works Jewishness is by no means isolate in its construction, interpretation, or application.

"I Always Want to Know Everything True"

Escape from "Special," Miss Lasko-Gross's debut graphic memoir, is followed by a second memoir, *A Mess of Everything*, which continues the story chronologically.[5] The initial book, which is the focus of the first half of this chapter, traces the life of the author's alter ego, Melissa, from her "earliest memory" to the summer before high school, while the second book tells the story of her high school years.[6] Despite their immediate frameworks, both texts focus on the problem of what it means to represent the self accurately on the page when that self is located in the lost past of childhood and adolescence, in subjective, unverifiable memories. Each work, originally published in a soft-cover volume of about 6 inches across and 9 inches high, is composed not of a single, cohesive narrative, but instead of separate story fragments, some as short as one page and one as long as fifteen pages. I am limiting my focus here to the first memoir, as it is more invested in the issues of categorization and identity examined throughout this book. In any case the global structures of both works, fragmentary and not committed to an easily decipherable overarching plotline, fall into a similar hybrid grouping as the graphic memoirs of Vanessa Davis, Aline Kominsky Crumb, and Lauren Weinstein. For all these cartoonists, the memoir text is composed of separate vignettes, which do not seamlessly lend themselves to narrative cohesion, collaged together to reflect a fractured sense of self. While most of the comics in Lasko-Gross's books are divided on the page into clear-cut panels, the breaks between individual stories, often marked by full splash pages, offer the reader a space to imagine and reimagine the links and gaps between different parts of the text or to assert her own imaginative authority. The reader's reception of separate stories across the pages of a single, longer work thus can be seen as somewhat analogous to what Scott McCloud, in speaking of reading over the gutter of individual panels on the same page, refers to as "closure" (63); in both cases the reader must actively piece together disjointed segments in order to imagine a more cohesive whole.

Though the plotline of *Escape from "Special"* somewhat improvisationally shuttles Melissa through various scenes and settings, what ties together the narrative slivers contained within is a consistently flat but intense drawing style reinforced by a thick and often heavy black line and expressive, handmade lettering. Drawn and shaded in densely colored blacks, whites, and grays, with starkly depicted figures on the page frequently accompanied by detailed and patterned backgrounds and shapes, the book juxtaposes resonances of the real and unreal, intimacy and distance, and, ultimately, past and present. In these and other ways, the memoir complexly conveys the uneasy relationship between images and memory.

What the reader witnesses on the page of an autobiographical work is always, of course, a mediated or translated version of that memory. In her 2011 study of narratives of childhood, *The Promise of Memory*, Lorna Martens issues a helpful analogy to describe that distance between memory and text: "Between the recollection and the product of the text there is a gap, similar to that between a dream and the account of the dream" (11). The various formal and stylistic elements that make up Lasko-Gross's memoir—in addition to the ones already mentioned, these include the simplistically exaggerated features of characters' bodies and expressions, framed in uneven, clearly hand-drawn panels—serve as constant, patent reminders of that gap, the subjectivity behind the text. The book exposes other gaps as well, and especially distinctions between the outward events, places, interactions, and objects that document Melissa's youth and her internal world, including the contours of her emotional experiences. If, as Martens writes, "the accuracy of a personal memory often counts far less than its emotional importance" (12), then this memoir is a testament to how affects can be strikingly and uniquely captured on the page through visual-verbal interactions and designs.

The very first story, entitled "Taxoplasmosis: My Earliest Memory," in its opening panel pictures the persona, Melissa, standing beside her mother's bed, grasping a Bert doll, one of the two featured Muppets characters from *Sesame Street* (1, figure 3.3). Melissa is drawn from an angle that disproportionately emphasizes her smallness in relation to her mother's more domineering figure, which is splayed in bed with closed eyes, puffy and swollen eyelids, and a rash covering part of her face. The child's thought bubble, drawn in the shape of a puff of smoke and positioned to the side of the page, reads, "Mom?" while her mother, head turned away, is unaware of the daughter watching her. Melissa's arms clutch her doll as she gazes at this semiconscious figure, whose only sign of life is a groan that emerges in white block letters on the next panel. Her inquiring look, in the opening panel, is reflected by the doll, who also stares with wide eyes at the unconscious mother—though the doll's "gaze" can be read as vaguely confident (if not glassy-eyed) rather than anxious. The distinction between Melissa's and her doll's outward appearances, emphasized by the shared angling of their faces, prefigures the disparity she experiences between her inner and outer worlds throughout the text, a discrepancy that intensifies as she encounters the world outside her home. While her doll represents what will become her public, somewhat nonplussed and frequently resigned visual, and verbal, exterior in times of stress or crisis, her own expressive, frowning visage more closely matches the distressed and uneasy affect suggested by the style of the comic as a whole; it is a mood that matches the sense of uneasiness and displacement she often feels later in the text, though she then tries hard to suppress it.

The inclusion of the depiction of this childhood object in a comic representing her "earliest memory" prefigures a common theme throughout the first half of Lasko-Gross's memoir (as well as Weinstein's memoir, *Girl Stories*), which is the importance of objects in the recollection of early life. In her book's introduction, Martens notes the significance of "the habitation of space (having one's places)" as well as the "possession of things" in the act of self-definition. As she writes, "They grant the comfort of a self-extension" (44).[7] As an extension of her self, the doll represents the parts of the persona's inner life that are not captured in

3.3 Miss Lasko-Gross, first two panels from "Toxoplasmosis: My Earliest Memory." In Escape from "Special," p. 1. Images copyright © Miss Lasko-Gross. Courtesy Fantagraphics Books.

the drawing of her own face and body; it suggests the more restrained, hidden, or forgotten side of Melissa's internal reflections, memories, and emotions. The inclusion of the doll in this first panel thus broadens the spectrum of Melissa's inner life, and especially its contradictions, as it is reflected on the page. Between her own visage and the doll's, the drawing conveys everything from Melissa's feelings of intense longing, uncertainty, and worry to her impassiveness, reserve, and even confidence. The childhood object, which appears in various forms, particularly throughout earlier parts of the memoir, serves as an additional vehicle for self-expression and reflection.

As another example, in a short comic pictured later in the memoir, titled "Meet the Band," Melissa receives a teddy bear from one of her mother's bandmates just before she is told that she will be joining them on their tour for the summer. In the final two oversized panels of the comic, which each take up half the page, a content Melissa sits in her bedroom at home, an intimate setting enclosed in a dark black background. She has come to replace her old bear with a new one, a gesture that marks an impending transition. In the final panel, her hand cast in front of her in a dominant, instructive gesture, she replaces her old bear with the one just given to her, telling it, "Don't be offended, I still love and honor you very much!" (41). In this comic, too, the dolls' faces portray human expressions that change, however subtly, over the course of the narrative. While the young Melissa looks generally cheerful and at ease, the teddy bear pictured beside her in most of the panels often wears vaguely anxious and frightened expressions, as does the old, replaced bear at the very end of the narrative. Childhood objects, such as the teddy bear or Bert doll, therefore increase the surface area, so to speak, of the alter ego's inner life as it appears on the comics page. Particularly throughout her early childhood, contrasting with the affect drawn into Melissa's body and face, inanimate objects convey a kind of affective self-exile that persists throughout the memoir and intensifies once she has left behind the comforts of the familiar. As Alison Bechdel writes of her teddy bear Mr. Beezum in the 2012 graphic memoir exploring her own childhood, *Are You My Mother?*: "He's not me, but he's not not-me, either" (115). Bechdel's second graphic memoir is similarly engaged in the question of the emergence of subjectivity, especially in relation to the family and, in particular, the mother. In one panel in her book, describing the comfort she found, as an adult, in sleeping with her "old Teddy Bear," and the subsequent embarrassment she experiences as an adult author sharing this detail, she writes: "But Mr. Beezum is not some mass-produced, button-eyed toy. His finely crafted gaze expresses a sublime and infinite compassion. It always calms me to look at him." Bechdel's persona's engagement with the doll as an object of affective transference parallels Melissa's interaction with her toys in these early scenes. In each case treasured, and sometimes no longer treasured, objects summon a tangible connection to the past even as they evoke the many disparate versions of that past existing in the mind of the memoirist.

In addition to calling attention to the past as a mediated translation, the first panel of the book additionally raises the problem of negotiating the central figure in the narrative of one's own life. As with Aline Kominsky Crumb's "Goldie," the history of Melissa's self begins with a documentation of the relationship between that self and others, and particularly with maternal figures. In this rendering of her earliest memory, her mother is featured as the central character, the person who, in addition to her doll, though even more fundamentally, serves as a proxy for her sense of self. Her horror here is based on seeing her mother lie dormant and silent; her corpselike appearance disorients Melissa from the outset of her remembered life, as she can only as yet define herself in relation to her mother. Notably, this comic, as with Aline Kominsky Crumb's mother-monster images, as well as "Goldie," narrowly envisions the mother from the point of view of the daughter and hence serves to essentially erase the mother's perspective.[8] Such a perceptibly limited point of view, highlighted here by the mother's unconscious state, reinforces the memoir as a series of partial fragments culled from a land-scape encompassing many other often unseen potential perspectives and rela-tional configurations; the visible and invisible scripts emerging from the past are continually and dynamically tied to one another, regardless of whether they are finally omitted or visualized on the page.

By exposing Melissa's early fear of alienation and isolation, this image thus serves as a forerunner to the relational question of identity explored throughout the book, a question that inevitably shifts outside of, or beyond, the family. In this scene Melissa's mother is depicted as almost a monster—a strange, sickly, and ghostlike presence whose resemblance to the real thing ("Mom?") increases the horror and anxiety captured in this visual. Even, or perhaps especially, this most "natural" of affiliations is also a site of potential distortion and surprise, a space where belonging, though it should feel most certain, is contradictorily most easily unmoored.

The story comic that follows this earliest memory in the book, another related to the persona's relationship with her mother, similarly foretells Melissa's unre-mitting search for identity and reveals it to be a journey with no clear starting point, even as it maintains its urgency in the memoir's "present." This comic, titled "Kidnapped," which takes up five full pages of the text, could arguably be viewed as part of the "Taxoplasmosis" comic, since there are no clear or definite beginnings and endings to each of the separate stories that make up the book. The easiest way to differentiate between "chapters" is in locating their titles, which are almost all drawn in noticeably diverse lettering—some in cursive, some in block letters, some accompanied by images, some bleeding out or drawn onto a separate panel, and some occupying a good deal of space on the page. In contrast, the remainder of the overall architectures, tones, and styles of the individual stories do not fluctuate considerably. The various, somewhat isolate lettering techniques heading each chapter can consequently be read as a reflection of the persona's desire to define herself by guardedly experimenting with different identities, a driving force behind many of the stories in the text as a whole. Moreover, this inconsistent lettering, which creates an uneasy indication of where one story ends and another begins, adds to the dreamlike quality of many of these chapters, which are based on memories that coalesce to form one long, phantasmagorical memory-text.

The title of what is arguably, then, the second story within the book is presented in a splash panel, a crowded and oversized image, which in this case takes up the entire page (2, figure 3.4). The letters composing the word *Kidnapped* are drawn in what looks like a collage of different cutouts, a design meant to mock the style of a ransom note. Mirroring this loosely splayed lettering on the bottom of the image, the upper portion features four female faces, a detail that foreshadows the importance female relationships will play in both of Lasko-Gross's memoirs. An oversized drawing of the persona's face, her eyes shut and a large set of "zzzz"s emerging from her head, is depicted at the top left corner. Below the sleeping figure is an image of Melissa's mother, Jacqui, who is recognizable from the opening panel, although in this depiction, while her eyes are still shut, her face does not have a rash and her torso is naked. With unnaturally long, sinewy arms, the mother grasps at yet another depiction of the persona, this time pictured with a look of terror on her face as she stretches her arms out toward an unknown figure off to the right of the page. Only the ends of the hands of this unknown figure are visible, and they seem to almost but not quite reach Melissa's hands. Finally, beside the mother stands another, older woman, her eyes shut as well, and her abnormally long arms and hands also reach for the persona's body.

As the next three pages of the comic unfold, in a pulsing series of smaller, similarly styled panels, five or six to a page, Melissa wakes in her bed, screaming from the dream ("Mom!"), and asks her mother, soon seated beside her, point-blank: "Jacqui, are you my *real* mother?" (3). Her mother comforts her with reassurances ("Well, I *was* there at your birth" and "Of *course* I am. You just had a nightmare"), but Melissa cannot believe what she does not remember, and she

3.4 *Miss Lasko-Gross, first page from "Kidnapped." In* Escape from "Special," *p. 2. Images copyright © Miss Lasko-Gross. Courtesy Fantagraphics Books.*

cannot understand why she cannot remember her birth (3–4). Throughout these panels the mother's face is almost always fully or partially hidden, as she is drawn looking in the opposite direction from Melissa, with closed eyes, or as a shadowy figure in the background. The story, which visualizes the horror of dreams when they cannot be differentiated from waking life, conveys a tension made comparable to the horror of not being able to differentiate between self and other, as between "reality," or "truth," and memory. If she cannot remember something, could it have really occurred? What happens when her mother's memories do not match her own? The full-paged opening panel of the comic, which includes two versions of the persona's face—the sleeping Melissa, with her eyes closed, and the running, moving Melissa, with her eyes open—reflects this fragile border between full consciousness and the dream state or, analogously, between real life and memory. By depicting these two disparate but always connected versions of herself, Melissa offers the possibility of various self-representations, and therefore perspectives, coexisting at the same moment in time. The fear of having been "kidnapped" points to this concern with maintaining a unified sense of self and ties it to the problem of communal belonging. Here Melissa is among a group of women stretching their hands toward her, prompting her to associate with them, to join them. She runs away from them, from this forced affiliation, but it is unclear to whom she is running, a pair of hands with no face or body attached. There is a sense of both horror and excitement, or possibility, at the prospect of being snatched away, of not belonging and of not having any determined outside presences with which to orient the self.

As the comic progresses, Melissa's mother leaves her alone in bed, musing about her consciousness and memory. Throughout the book, scenes that take place with Melissa alone in the privacy of her bedroom or in bed often result in moments of intense introspection. They contrast with the isolation she experiences when she is among other people, especially in groups, and suggest, as in Vanessa Davis's comics, that certain kinds of solitariness allow for carefree, imaginative freedom while others result in anxiety and despair. In this scene, once Melissa's mother has left the room, Melissa is pictured alone in her bed, from different angles. These diverse points of view, collected on the page, project an increased sense of urgency and emotional intensity, as a series of thoughts and questions about subjectivity and memory culminate with the sentence "I always want to know everything true" (5, figure 3.5). The panel depicting this thought pictures a close-up of Melissa's eye, with two drops pouring down her face. One of

3.5 Miss Lasko-Gross, *panel from fourth page of "Kidnapped." In* Escape from "Special," *p. 5. Images copyright © Miss Lasko-Gross. Courtesy Fantagraphics Books.*

the drops is obviously a tear, as it clearly emerges from the bottom of her eyelid. The other ambiguously located drop can be read as a tear, representing sadness, or as a drop of sweat, representing exhaustion or anxiety. The image presents the verbalized desire to remember, to "know everything true," as an aspiration closely entwined with the visual representation of various affects: to remember is a subjective act affiliated most strikingly with images, which in turn are filtered and shaped by emotions. In addition, the "I" wanting to remember "everything true" is represented by the drawing of a single eye, thereby reinforcing how memory is also always fashioned through an individual consciousness, the eye reflecting the "I." The panel can consequently be read as a testament to this impossible wish of the autobiographical artist to "know everything true." At the same time, the image captures the importance of the internal world—of consciousness, subjectivity, and especially emotions—as the keys to external representations of self, to what eventually gets inscribed on the page. While Melissa cannot remember everything "true," at the very least she can capture the remembered affects related to certain experiences and bring these to life on the page. The very subjectivity that motivates her search for "home," for a so-called true or objective representation of her individual self and memory, is also, therefore, paradoxically, what prohibits its completion.

Taken together, these two opening story-comics, "Toxoplasmosis" and "Kidnapped," align Melissa's desire to record the "truth" with her continued concern for belonging and/or not belonging. Such questions regarding the relationship between identity and subjectivity are interwoven throughout the memoir, tentative inquiries that remain unresolved even as they inform and provoke one another. As Melissa moves through her narrative of childhood and toward adolescence, general ontological inquiries—*who am I? where did I come from?*—fold into more specific questions of identity, especially in relation to other children in her peer group. She finds herself confronting not only what it means to have been born into a particular perspective but also the significance of acknowledging the manifold filiations and affiliations that continually shape and transform this perspective as its vista extends.

"I Really Am Alone"

In her book on adolescent literature, *Disturbing the Universe*, Roberta Seelinger Trites differentiates between childhood and adolescent literature by explaining that the former genre generally deals with conflicts in the protagonist's immediate environment, whereas the latter focuses on tensions between the individual and the social forces and institutions, including but not limited to the family, she encounters in her daily life.[9] As she states, "The chief characteristic that distinguishes adolescent literature from children's literature is the issue of how social power is deployed during the course of the narrative" (2). Trites sees the conclusions of works of children's literature to be generally comforting in that these books "often affirm[] the child's sense of Self and her or his personal power" (3). In contrast, adolescent literature is concerned with the ways in which adolescents "learn their place in the power structure . . . [and] learn to negotiate the many institutions that shape them" (x). Lasko-Gross's graphic memoir, which traverses memories from her early childhood through adolescence, generally confirms this trajectory. In the early childhood scenes depicted at the beginning of the book, despite her consistently anxious posture in relation to her place in the world, she ultimately displays a strong sense of confidence in her determined and emphatic inquiries and observations. Once Melissa enters school and encounters her peers, her sense of alienation, while correlated with depictions of this younger self, is manifestly amplified, and her confidence, or sense of personal power, seems to proportionately diminish. The transition from childhood to adolescence, as tracked in *Escape from "Special,"* thus reveals how Melissa's struggles and negotiations with "social power," as a young adult, are intricately tied to her senses of belonging/not belonging, which extend as far back as her conscious memory and her initial emergence as a subject. But, once Melissa is among her peers, what becomes newly visible is a reactive need for restraint from the ideas, thoughts, feelings, and insecurities that once shaped her remembered experiences. This increased preoccupation with control, and particularly with the suppression of traces of her inner world, emerges as she becomes more aware of her sense of self as relational.

Various comics throughout the first half of the book trace Melissa's introduction into new schools or other settings involving young adults and teachers; she is generally cast as an outsider almost right away, not only in her own mind but also in the ways that others treat and react to her (at least through her eyes). Her difference is often linked to how she thinks, looks, and behaves around both her peers and adults, and particularly her once authoritative insistence in questioning what is generally taken for granted or recognized as the status quo. This kind of questioning is no longer empowering or without consequence. Instead, it divides her from others. Situated early in the memoir, after several narratives picturing Melissa alone or solely in relation to her mother, the comic "The First Mindfuck," for example, features her sitting in art class with her classmates, who are all drawing pictures (12). Although this comic clearly takes place while Melissa is still a child—definitions of the time frames of childhood and adolescence vary considerably, but in this case she has clearly not even begun to enter puberty—I read it as an "adolescent" experience because of its focus on the ways that Melissa interacts outside the home, especially among those not in her immediate family.

In the opening, full-page image, she sits sandwiched between two classmates whose eyes are both closed, casting a confused, sidelong glance at one of them as her hands grope carelessly at the picture in front of her. From its outset, Melissa's time at school, ironically even in an art class, is marked by her sense of difference from those around her. On the following page her increased isolation is recorded in a series of smaller panels, six to the page, that feature her in a range of confused, shocked, and resentful postures. In the first, standing in front of the class, the teacher, colored in white and facing the reader, tells the group, "Ooooh, you're all doing great pictures!!" (13). Melissa is differentiated from those around her yet again, her body and hair shaded in solid black and her hand raised in isolation.

3.6 *Miss Lasko-Gross, final panel from "The First Mindfuck." In* Escape from "Special," *p. 15.*
Images copyright © Miss Lasko-Gross. Courtesy Fantagraphics Books.

"But they're all different so they can't *all* be great," she counteracts, and her speech dilates across the page in lettering that contrasts with the teacher's airier, loosely drawn words. In the following panels she is pictured as progressively set apart from the rest of the group and, unlike her initial, bold proclamation, over the course of the remainder of the page the only word she utters is *Really?* in response to her teacher's assertion that "no two people see things the same way." In the page's final panel she sits at a table, again set apart from the rest of the group, her hands propping her head up in a gloomy gesture. This resigned posture is mirrored two pages later, in the concluding panel of the comic, after an intense series of meditations that capture her increasing sense of difference from others, whose content, often easygoing semblances dramatically differ from her anxious and gloomy self (15, figure 3.6).

This closing image encapsulates the sense of seclusion and difference Melissa experiences throughout the rest of the story, as in many parts of the memoir, and it also reflects a resignation that contrasts with the determination of her earlier, questioning childhood self. Here she is pictured alone, and the words that appear in thick black capital letters above her head read, *I don't know anything for sure.* As with the "eye" panel from "Kidnapped," her reflections belong to an unacknowledged narrator, and they are represented not in a speech or thought bubble, but instead in a more ambiguous text box accompanying the image. The aimlessness of the heavy words pictured over her head visually reinforces the feelings of isolation and confusion she experiences after this, one of a series of moments of internal crisis recorded throughout the memoir. But her bearing in this case—head leaning on the table, hand cradling her head in an attempt to partially cover her face—differs from her earlier, more expressive and demanding stances. Even the wavy line surrounding this narrative text reflects a softer, more submissive thought process relative to the dramatic zigzagged creases surrounding Melissa's thoughts in bed. Despite its powerfully morose tone, then, in this image of Melissa at her desk her posture conveys a sense of restraint and a desire for concealment, as though being cast into the world of her peers also means leaving behind the very expressivity, the visible sweat and tears, that once helped affirm her sense of self and connected her internal and external worlds.

Melissa's separation from other students, especially in various classroom settings, persists throughout the book as she changes schools and ages into new grades and classrooms. Like many adolescents, she desires transformation, to be less like herself; it is a transformation that would ostensibly help her belong, even as it requires hiding the very attitudes and postures that once helped define her sense of self. The five-page comic "How It Seems," for example, records Melissa's desperate attempts to learn from and copy the social cues of her peers in an effort to erase her perceived differences from them and, by extension, find comfort in fitting into an established communal identity. In this story line she has once again started at a new school, a potential clean slate, but she quickly endures scenes of humiliation and shame as other children pick up on what they see as her behavioral anomalies. These differences, so visible to those around her, come as shocks and surprises to her, further reflecting the increased division between how she presents herself to the world and her internal perceptions and experiences. "How come you never look anyone in the eye?" one boy asks her, and another student soon tells her that she has the handwriting of a small child. Although she works hard to repair these apparent deviations, to smooth over the peculiarities that confuse and seclude her in order to limit the ways she is marked as "other," the difference stubbornly persists.

In the end, despite Melissa's frequent, sometimes frantic, and generally unsuccessful attempts to fit in, it is as a distanced, questioning observer—an identity encapsulated in being an artist—that she finally finds her place of belonging, a place that is paradoxically marked by her distance from others. At various points in the book she takes great pride in not being associated with others, in being set apart or "special." Significantly, these moments often coincide with, or relate to, occasions in which she references her Jewish identity. For example, the comic directly following "How It Seems" recounts Melissa's entry into Hebrew school, as the title, "Of Little Faith: Jew School," attests. "Hebrew school"—or "Jew school," as the narrator satirically references it—is the Jewish equivalent of "Sunday school." Generally taking place on Sundays or weeknights, this schooling, a supplement to secular education, focuses on Jewish history and culture and often involves the uses of religious texts and/or Hebrew language learning. In this two-page comic, as the teacher sits at the front of the classroom, Melissa's thought bubbles, large and bright, reflect her impatience with what she views as the enforced morality of the lecture. "How DARE they tell us how to live" (80), she thinks to herself while drops of sweat emerge from her head. Her visible affect here is strong, as she clenches both hands in front of her, but it goes unnoticed by other members of the class, whose division from her is emphasized not only in their bowed and engrossed postures but also in the gray coloring of their faces, which contrast with her bright white one.

In the following panels, alone with her mother on the car ride home, she feels free to more openly unleash her distaste for this additional, faith-based schooling. Her facial and bodily expressions in this scene recall the young Melissa, grappling with questions of "truth" in her bedroom as her mouth and hands contort, words expressively splayed across panels. "You never made me do any religious stuff before this year," she tells her mother, and the emphatically spoken words are emphasized by the thundering, zigzagged speech bubble that surrounds them. "You waited too long. I'm too old and too smart to fall for any of it" (81). Melissa's desire to assert her own independent thinking and rebel against authority emerges here—calling to mind that assured, younger self—because she has finally been cast into a classroom setting premised on the assumption that she belongs. She is immediately affiliated with others in the classroom because she is Jewish, a label attached to a particular set of expectations about what she and those others are supposed to believe and, presumably, how they are all supposed to act as a result of those beliefs. As opposed to her experiences in a "regular" (secular and public) classroom, it is this presumption of sameness that pushes her to openly resist, a rebellion that summons up a latent, affirming sense of self.

In *Reading Autobiography*, Sidonie Smith and Julia Watson describe the basic paradox of identity and affiliation: "identity as difference implies also identity as likeness" (38). As Eve Kosofsky Sedgwick, José Esteban Muñoz, and others have shown, to identify is always to partially disidentify or counteridentify.[10] In order to rebel, even internally, against her religious school teacher—and, consequently, to actively separate herself from others in the class—Melissa has to yield, if unconsciously, to the ties that bind: the Jewish thread that has led them all to "Jew school." This paradox is made even clearer in "Of Little Faith II," a related comic located almost forty pages later, in which Melissa is once again pictured in Hebrew school. The title of this sequel is drawn in a lettering style similar to that of the original, with the main difference being that in this case Melissa's incensed visage is drawn alongside the title lettering, marking her active dis-affiliation from the start (115, figure 3.7). Only a small part of her face is pictured: a quarter of it, including a single eye framed by a furrowed, devilish brow, an ear, and several chunks of hair. This portrayal of her face reveals two small Jewish stars drawn onto it, and instead of a pupil the center of her eye features a third Jewish star. The thought bubble over her head plainly reads, "Get me out of here." The remainder of this opening page of the comic then depicts Melissa conspiring with a friend in class who agrees with the absurdity of a lecture that literalizes the story of Noah and the flood. Her friend, who is notably also a young girl with long, dark hair, asserts, "As if the *whole* world could flood!" as Melissa looks on, happily agreeing and thinking to herself, "I'm not the only one." In a series of three panels following, however, each picturing Melissa at the center of the image with her friend no longer in the picture but for her word bubbles, Melissa is brought back into isolation as the friend asserts, from off the page, "But of *course* I believe in God!" In the third and final panel, which is also the last one on the page as a whole, Melissa is pictured in profile, morosely sitting at her desk with eyes closed and thinking, "I really am ALONE." In this portrayal she is drawn as if she were by herself, even though, as earlier panels reveal, she is seated beside a friend in the classroom. Her eyes are shut and her head hangs down heavily. An oval-shaped spotlight falls over her figure, as though to feature her isolation and sense of being cast out of a space where it seemed like she would finally fit in, if only because her internal rebellion had been externally acknowledged by a fellow student.

This sequel to "Of Little Faith" reflects Melissa's continued inability to fit in, even when it is by questioning the status quo that she attempts to assert her likeness to others. But the stars pictured on Melissa's face at the beginning of the comic also symbolize an active resistance folded into this otherwise distressing and isolating experience. The opening depiction, and particularly the mark of the

3.7 Miss Lasko-Gross, first page from "Of Little Faith II." In Escape from "Special, p. 115.
Images copyright © Miss Lasko-Gross. Courtesy Fantagraphics Books.

Jewish star, clearly designates Melissa's connection to others in the classroom, which in turn underlines the exertion of her internal rebellion. This visualized negotiation, between a mark of descent and a posture of consent, illustrates an active and relatively confident engagement with her surroundings. As Miss Lasko-Gross explained in an interview, accounting for her inclusion in the memoir of these religious-based upheavals from her past, "your identity is revealed to you in relation to your struggles with whomever or whatever you're coming up against" ("'A Portrait of the World'" 179).[11] Melissa's sense of self is affirmed most powerfully in scenes like this one, in which she is connected to a larger Jewish community; it is an association that prompts her to respond. These moments of dis-affiliation empower her, as she transforms from a passive and resigned outcast to a responsive and resistant one.

While the final image in "Of Little Faith II," with Melissa sitting isolated at her desk, thus seems on first glance to mirror the resignation she frequently feels among her peers, as in her early art school experience, a reading of the illustration in the context of the page as a whole casts the depiction as a moment, instead, of defiance. The spotlight surrounding Melissa in this panel additionally inflects the image with a sense of mediation, of the narrative "I" recalling this past moment from her singular perspective. What the reader witnesses here is not simply a testament to Melissa's early sense of isolation and difference; instead the portrayal potentially functions as a kind of portal to that incident, a space where its emotional impact can be opened up, prodded, and reoriented in relation to other occasions and reflections from the past.

The oval spotlight in this image, for example, visually connects it with an earlier, imposing, and memorable representation, a self-portrait of Melissa likewise sitting alone at a desk. The full-page illustration is the title panel of a comic, "(Special)," which traces Melissa's experiences in secular school when she is placed into a "special education" classroom, a move that once again distinguishes her from those around her. In the depiction, which is set against a black background, Melissa is pictured at the center of the page, sitting at a desk with a pencil in her left hand while her entire figure is engulfed in a large flame (82, figure 3.8). The portrayal of Melissa drawing at a desk is a representation that marks the cover of the book and winds its way through many of the pivotal moments in both Lasko-Gross's memoirs; it is a visual trope that binds the different themes and experiences traced throughout. The desk typically represents the institutions that confine the protagonist and attempt to normalize her. But the act of drawing, alluded to in this and other images not only by the pencil itself but also by the series of sketches visible in her notebook, conversely represents the possibility of freedom. With a pencil and notebook she can imagine a way out of the stifling pressure to conform that is otherwise so tied to the desk.

This self-portrait thus reflects not only the pain of Melissa's separation and estrangement, from others as well as from various versions of her self, but also the power and drive to repair this separation through a provocative and solitary engagement with art, however anxiety-driven that engagement (as the tapping of her pencil reflects). The underlying subject of *Escape from "Special,"* as of all the other texts explored in this book, is how self-representations can help revise or reconfigure feelings of being an outsider, which are often initially alluded to in childhood and reinforced or confirmed in adolescence. The personae explored in these diverse texts all actively claim their senses of not belonging by drawing their displacements. Each panel or page becomes a space in which to experience, simultaneously, home and not home. This aesthetic possibility is symbolized here by the flame surrounding Melissa's body. Her identity as an artist has the potential to free her. But what becomes apparent from this image too is that that identity also has the potential to engulf the more particular categories of difference through which she defines herself. Like her inexplicable, often unidentifiable differences from others, an otherness she has trouble verbalizing and consequently understanding or coming to terms with, her Jewishness is not directly visible here. Setting out to live, like Aline Kominsky Crumb's Goldie, "in [her] own style"—to define herself through an independent, self-fashioned temperament—also always means running the risk of assimilation, of dissolving other particular categories of difference. But ultimately, as the memoir as a whole reflects, the strength and promise Melissa derives from her art is closely allied with, and at least partially established by, her Jewish identity. It is, after all, in those moments of grappling with her Jewish identity that she establishes a secure and forceful sense of self from within the confines of being figured as different. These moments mark Jewishness in particular as an identity that has the potential to transform her from being a person who is objectified, humiliated, and acted upon, as she is in her "regular" school, into one who can see herself as a subject, who actively responds to the ways others make her feel through her own particularized rebellions.

The near disappearance of the question of what it means to identify as Jewish in Miss Lasko-Gross's second memoir, *A Mess of Everything*, mirrors Melissa's

3.8 *Miss Lasko-Gross, splash page from "(Special)." In* Escape from "Special," *p. 82. Images copyright © Miss Lasko-Gross. Courtesy Fantagraphics Books.*

general loss of interest in taking on many of the questions about truth and identity that preoccupy her in the first book. This thematic shift is related to Melissa's aging out of "Jew school"—the religious institution that marks almost all her engagements with her Jewish identity in *Escape from "Special."* There are several exceptions to this direct connection between Melissa's explorations of her Jewishness and her institutional ties, including the occasional trip to temple, that are recorded in the first memoir.[12] These include the comic "Summers in Exotic Atlantic City New Jersey" (49–53) in which she confronts her grandfather's racism and notes its injustice and hypocrisy, "especially since we get so upset when people hate *us* 'cause we're Jews," as she tells her parents (52). Another exception is the comic "The Gruswerk's Sabbath" (62–64), which pictures her attending a Sabbath dinner with her friend's family and acting out at the table while prayers are being recited. In the final panel, after being scolded by the father, she thinks to herself, "I'm glad my family isn't Orthodox and has a sense of humor" (64). In all these comics, including the ones about her experiences in "Jew school," Melissa's explorations of her Jewish identity are linked to her parents and family more generally. This is arguably a consequence of the basic affinity between religious affiliation and family. As Trites explains in her discussion of religion as it is addressed in adolescent literature, "Adolescent novels that deal with religion as an institution demonstrate how discursive institutions are and how inseparable religion is from adolescents' affiliation with their parents' identity politics" (38). In the second memoir, as Melissa moves her attention increasingly away from her parents and more completely toward the world of her peers, and as her activities slowly shift outside her parents' control and begin to reflect her own chosen affiliations and involvements, her interest in her religious identity begins to fade, though it never completely vanishes.

This turn from an emphasis on categorizations of identity does not occur in Lauren Weinstein's *Girl Stories*, a book in which Jewishness is more often than not presented through silences or omissions, rather than direct or indirect engagements. In Weinstein's graphic memoir, because religious identity is never tied to any particular institution, like school or synagogue, the association between Lauren's sense of being an outsider and her Jewish identity has to be extrapolated from what is presented in the text.[13] In this way *Girl Stories* proves to be a corollary text to *Escape from "Special."* Lauren's tenuous relationship to her Jewish identity, like Melissa's, holds the potential to empower her in her search for an affirming sense of self, but its often unconfirmed presence also means that her Jewish sense of self is continually at risk of erasure.

"Okay! Fine! You Can Read It!"

Initially published as a series of short comics on gURL.com, a teen website and online community founded in 1996, Lauren Weinstein's *Girl Stories* follows her persona, Lauren, as she finishes middle school and enters high school. Like *Escape from "Special,"* *Girl Stories* is composed as a series of vignettes. The various short autobiographical comics contained in the collection are differentiated from one another in a clearly marked index at the beginning of the book, and the coloring and style of each story—and particularly their often distinct backgrounds, many published on a set of distinguishing colored paper—also visibly differentiates them. In addition to their arrangement, the shape of the book, which is roughly 9 1/2 inches wide by 6 inches high, was in part guided by the way the comics were first constructed, as they were initially published on the Internet; the panoramic configuration was the easiest way to fit those images onto paper. As Weinstein explained in an interview in response to a question about the disparate sizes of her three published books, and particularly the thumbable *Girl Stories*, the book "seemed like [it] should be wide and thin and accessible" ("Thinking Panoramically" 185).[14]

Despite their parallel emphases on adolescence and identity, Weinstein's graphic memoir follows a different trajectory than that of Lasko-Gross's first book. *Escape from "Special"* opens with a preoccupation with filial ties and moves toward an engagement with affiliative registers, including encounters with friends, classmates, and, later, boyfriends. *Girl Stories*, on the contrary, which tracks an adolescent Lauren as she moves through eighth grade and into her first year of high school, settles in where Lasko-Gross's first memoir ends. From its opening, Lauren is already immersed in the world of her peers, although the introduction to the book, presented on two sides of the same page, somewhat misleadingly features school and family as dual focal points in her life. On the first page of this introduction, the narrator displays a panoramic scene from her school hallway, which evokes a carefully constructed chaos (5, figure 3.9). This bottom half of the page pictures a wide rectangular image bursting with brightly drawn, vibrant

3.9 *Lauren Weinstein, first page from Introduction. In* Girl Stories, *p. 5. From GIRL STORIES copyright © 2006 Lauren Weinstein. Reprinted by permission of Henry Holt and Company, LLC. All Rights Reserved.*

watercolors, including lime-green lockers bordering the background and animate characters doing everything from shuffling importantly with their coffee mugs (teachers) to chatting in clusters, rolling together on the floor, or passing by in coupled pairs (students). In the space over this bubbly, active illustration, whose contours are irregularly shaped through brushstrokes that bleed onto the surrounding white page, the narrator's shaky, inked writing is visible. Beginning with the word *Hello!*, captured in oversized and colored-in bright-red rounded letters, the textual introduction continues with a string of short statements, drawn in all-capital letters and often punctuated with exclamation marks. "And welcome to my life, which is currently like being in jail! I'm in eighth grade, and I've been going to the same stupid school with the same stupid fifty people since Kindergarten! That's nine years!!!!" (5).

Upon turning the page, the reader encounters matching handwriting, a brightly colored "Meanwhile" mirroring the opening "Hello!," and the narrator continues, "My parents are totally messed up. Like, my dad is addicted to playing 'The Legend of Zelda,' and my mom is always working to save the poor (which is really admirable, but she never rests!)" (6). In addition to this placement of the dual introductory image-texts on two sides of the same page, the word *meanwhile* suggests that the narrator's family life is a concurrent plotline unraveling alongside her school life. Two separate panels are depicted below this second introductory text, with Lauren featured, however peripherally, in both of them. In each she is pictured standing at home, behind a parent, asking for a favor and receiving an indifferent response. Her repeated presence in these portrayals of her parents contrasts with her absence from the panoramic school hallway drawing, as does the more muted verbal description of her life at home, in which she is relegated to a minor character. Despite their coexistence on the opening pages of the book, then, life at school, as opposed to life at home, is portrayed as bustling, explosive, and still somewhat unpredictable, a world that has yet to be fully explored or comprehended, but one that potentially has a space in it for Lauren. On the contrary, domestic life, exemplified by these mirroring interactions with her parents, who each face away from her as she talks to the backs of their heads, is boring, predictable, and characterized by Lauren's marginalized status in relation to her parents' obsessive and isolating preoccupations.

While the book builds on this split between Lauren's parallel lives, its primary focus is what happens to Lauren outside the realm of her family, in the larger, more mysterious, and infinitely more exciting world of her peers. It is a world in which, at least at its outset, she still has the potential to take center stage, or at least find a space of comfortable belonging. Her parents figure only several times throughout the remainder of the book, and in each case their appearances serve to amplify the distance between these two proximate but nevertheless distant spheres, the one representing possibility, the other characterized by a certain dogmatic certainty of her established, though peripheral, place in it.

Although family is not emphasized in the bulk of *Girl Stories*, this prefatory dual framework suggests that the book is interested, like Vanessa Davis's *Make Me a Woman* and Miss Lasko-Gross's *Escape from "Special,"* in the contrast between so-called private and public lives and identities. The memoir is structured as a private diary, a conceit introduced in the inside cover just prior to the introduction and a hand-drawn "Author's note" and "Table o' Contents." "This is the book of

3.10 *Lauren Weinstein, inside cover page. In* Girl Stories. *From GIRL STORIES copyright © 2006 Lauren Weinstein. Reprinted by permission of Henry Holt and Company, LLC. All Rights Reserved.*

Lauren R. Weinstein," the page reads in the same bright-red and bubbly handwriting found at the opening of the introduction (figure 3.10). As a diary composed in the "present" of adolescence, the book conveys an emotional urgency, as though Lauren does not know how events will turn out. "If found please don't read!" the inscription continues, although it concludes, "Okay! Fine! You can read it!" This opening prefigures a tension that winds through the memoir—the contrast between how Lauren presents herself to others in her real life and how she presents herself not only in private but also to the readers of her "private" diary. In other words, even the so-called nonpublic or intimate act of diary keeping becomes a performance, an operation colored by Lauren's overwhelming adolescent self-consciousness, which makes her feel inclined to share everything she thinks and does as a matter of course.

On the other end of the same page, with its bursting, psychedelic background illuminated in fluorescent coloring, a framed self-portrait of the author introduces the mix of humor, apprehension, and confessional fluency that characterizes the rest of the book, and particularly the way these elements will come together through the expressive drawings and verbal accompaniments of the diarist-narrator. Lauren is drawn here in a posture, coloring, and style relatively restrained in relation to the brighter, more lively, and expressive drawings of this persona throughout the text. She stands at an easel, sketching a still more subdued, even morose, version of herself, devoid of color or texture. Beside the image, which is a self-portrait incorporating another self-portrait in the making, both contained in the space of a single panel, large red arrows animatedly caption the otherwise calm scene, announcing, in separate white bubbles, "That's me!!!" "Big wrinkly forehead" "Bags under eyes" "Kind of fat." As this opening depiction suggests, the alter ego presented in the text is one version of many possible alter egos, and it is the framework of the diary, a kind of dialogic self-portrait, that allows Lauren to explore various and simultaneous accounts of self-knowledge and self-perception.

Crucially, and in contrast to Lasko-Gross's memoir structure, the diary construction of *Girl Stories* also inflects Weinstein's persona, Lauren, with a sense of agency, however qualified, from the very outset of the text, an outlook that might otherwise be more difficult to capture in this memoir similarly recording the pains of adolescence. Mary Pipher, clinical psychologist and author of the aforementioned *Reviving Ophelia*, endorses adolescent girls' diary keeping for just this reason. As she explains, "Girls this age love to write. Their journals are places where they can be honest and whole. In their writing, they can clarify, conceptualize and evaluate their experiences. Writing their thoughts and feelings strengthens their sense of self. Their journals are a place where their point of view on the universe matters" (255).[15] Because of the diary structure of her memoir, unlike Melissa in *Escape from "Special,"* Lauren is not a young girl winding in and out of moments of paralysis and resignation in the "present" tense of her past memories, searching for a potentially freeing sense of self and identity. She is instead an observing artist from the outset, even if those observations still emerge from a presumably adolescent mind, and this stance allows her a safe vantage point from which to record her humiliations, anxieties, and occasional triumphs.

This somewhat distanced posturing is evident in the opening pages of the book, after the framing prologue and introduction. In one of the stories, for example, a twelve-page comic titled "The Tub," Lauren recalls a humiliating incident that takes place in the eighth grade, after an event occurring earlier in the year already established her status as an outsider. The comic is drawn in various drab green tones, with a contrasted bubble gum pink background highlighting strips of verbal narration woven throughout the story. This distinction in coloring underscores the presence of the narrator—a diarist—as an intermediary in this otherwise candid recollection of a humiliating event. Besides the pink, the comic's narrow range of colors, with its unappealing palate of murky yellows and greens, additionally casts Lauren's depiction of this experience as closely tied to the very particular impression it left on her, an impression that has made an indelible mark even as she seeks to reimage it on the pages of her diary.

In the comic, as part of an effort to rejoin the clique that recently excluded her, Lauren volunteers herself in science class for an experiment relating to measuring water volume. In the classroom scene in which she raises her hand to assist, an act that will further divide her from her classmates, though she hopes it will do the opposite (presumably by getting her noticed), Lauren's appearance is nearly unrecognizable from many of its more usual iterations (39). As Weinstein has said of the process of drawing her characters expressionistically, exposing internal worlds with external representations, "I think morphing the way somebody looks—as long as you keep those big iconic markers—means you can make them look like anything" ("Thinking Panoramically" 191). Weinstein's sentiment here echoes that of Aline Kominsky Crumb, who in an interview described her drawing process as "coming out in the line" ("Interview," *Outside the Box* 96). As she further elaborated, relating her work to that of German expressionist artists as well as Frida Kahlo: "So the drawing isn't pretty or accurate; a lot of it has little to do with what reality looks like. It's an emotional reality." In the case of Weinstein's comic, Lauren's face is depicted as exaggeratedly rounded, yellow, and accented with worry lines; she trembles with an apprehensive, hopeful anxiety that contrasts with the placid, confident sneer of the classmate seated behind her. The shaky outline of her face, along with the restrained coloring of the image, correlates with her experience as one who, even in the process of volunteering in class—an act that supposedly demonstrates choice—is confined in her options; here she is a character who will inevitably be shamed, or acted upon, rather than one who will have any control over how she is perceived or treated by those around her, at least at the time of the event.

The scene concludes when, having submerged herself in front of the entire class in a "garbage can lined with a big, black garbage bag," Lauren walks away mortified. In the final image of the story, she is dressed in a swimsuit and surrounded by fully clothed classmates gathered around her in the middle of the "old boys' locker room," her hands covering her shivering body. In the background, olive green lockers line the room, recalling the lighter-colored lime green lockers pictured in the school hallway in the book's introduction and emphasizing how experience has changed Lauren's impression of the once cheerful and energetic spaces around her, full of possibility. One observing student in a line of students, his hands burrowed in his pockets, calmly declares, "Freak," as she passes by (45). Lauren's sense of estrangement is reinforced by the lack of narrative text on this concluding page, a near-silent configuration that fortifies the immediacy of the indignity she has just undergone. There is, at least for the moment, no interpretive voice to soften the force of the event.

But the memoir, as it is structured, does not claim this painful image as a conclusive one. Instead, upon turning the page, the reader is greeted by a panoramic, fantastical epilogue, a one-page comic whose title, "Freak!" directly connects it to the previous story line (46, figure 3.11). A set of ghostly but nonetheless inviting faces lines the top of the page, sketched and shaded in different colors against a bright yellow backdrop that contrasts with the generally gloomy, muted greens of the previous comic as well as of the one that follows. In this image *freak* is scribbled over and again on the page, in both filled-in red lettering and also sketchy, inked outlines. The word comes to stand for Lauren's lack of presence in the illustration, as it connects her, even in her absence, to a community of artists and musicians that presumably holds a place in it for her. "Well, I might be a freak, but at least I have my music and ART," the bright red words on the page read, and they are partly superimposed over the centered drawing of an androgynous-looking character playing a guitar. The figure is likely Morrissey, lead singer of the independent rock group, The Smiths, who is known not only for his biting and melancholy lyrics but also his often contrarian and enigmatic real-life persona. The title page of "Morrissey & Me," the following comic, which envisions an imaginary series of conversations between Lauren and the singer and is set against an equally morose sequence of drab green backdrops, faces this full-page image and reinforces the sense of connection Lauren experiences with other self-proclaimed outsiders. By depicting this cluster of outcasts, however imaginary the scene, Lauren transforms the experience she has just portrayed: a hostile epithet becomes a proud banner as a victim transforms into a puppet master. The diarist is the narrator of her own life.

3.11 *Lauren Weinstein, "Freak!" In* Girl Stories, *p. 46. From* GIRL STORIES *copyright © 2006 Lauren Weinstein. Reprinted by permission of Henry Holt and Company, LLC. All Rights Reserved.*

This representation, which can ironically be read as a kind of self-portrait, thus serves as Lauren's intervention into a scene of paralysis. Her focus here—in drawing other people, instead of herself—is on the ways she can manipulate or shape others through her art and writing, even if her ultimate objective is to reimagine herself so she can find a place of comfort and belonging. This approach differentiates her from Miss Lasko-Gross's protagonist, whose quest to fit in is most often directly tied to a desire to control her own outward self-expressions and whose search for an affirming sense of self, even among her peers, is therefore centered on a desire to negotiate between her inner and outer worlds. Lauren's search for belonging is instead largely cast as a struggle that begins and ends with how she is perceived and treated by others and how she can fashion their perception of her.

This pursuit aligns with the diary structure, which allows her to continually maintain a dialogue with an audience, albeit a presumably imaginary one.

Several comics early in the book that depict Lauren even before she has endured various school-related mortifications demonstrate her investment in establishing such an imaginary, pliable audience. These background narratives, which center on her creative engagements with Barbie dolls, take place in the private space of her bedroom, reflecting a comfort with both a place and objects that she must eventually leave behind. Viewed alongside later humiliating events recounted, such as "The Tub," these early scenes may be read as precursors to, or even analogies for, the very act of composing the diary. Through her Barbie play, Lauren is able to perform, in a safe, controlled environment, the very preoccupations with confession and shame that later unfold in her "real life." But what makes these early comics especially significant is how they divulge the pleasure she at times derives from not fitting in, provided she maintains some control over how this difference is framed.

The early seven-page comic "Barbies!" for example, opens as Lauren "admits" to playing with dolls. This confession is shameful because she is supposedly too old for such play. "I know, I'm thirteen and I still play with Barbies" (8), she professes, and the indiscretion of this declaration is emphasized visually as she is portrayed standing at the threshold of her room, a surreally sketched pile of dolls scattered across the floor behind her, like skeletons. Soon after, she additionally reveals that playing with Barbies is also and somewhat ironically considered a disdainful act because of its accordance with certain often-publicized problematic cultural norms and practices. As Jacqueline Reid-Walsh and Claudia Mitchell write in their essay on Barbie play, "in the culture of a feminist class Barbie is beyond the pale, so the simple admission of play is a transgression of the norm of the class" (179). As evidence of her awareness of this second transgression, in a kind of afterword to the Barbies comic, titled "A Letter to Myself," Lauren claims, "I am much less superficial than that, really" (15). Lauren's embarrassing admissions, followed by the statement positing her interactions with Barbies as an anomalous guilty pleasure, reflect her discomfort with violating accepted codes of behavior, with nonconformity, no matter the disparate contexts of the accepted norms. Yet, in carefully framing her self-awareness by disclosing and qualifying her offenses, she can take charge over the way these potentially embarrassing declarations are read and appraised.

In the following pages of the comic, Lauren similarly reframes these scenes of Barbie play by recording, in careful detail, what Erica Rand describes as "queering Barbie" (12), using the doll and her accessories in ways that are not endorsed by its seller, the Mattel company. Rand uses the term *queerness* to connote both what she describes as its "narrow sense"—gender—and also its "broader sense"—the "odd, irregular, and idiosyncratic" (11), though she recognizes that the two meanings of the terms are always "entangled." In this discussion I am particularly invested in the broader sense of the term, as it is Lauren's primary focus. As she writes on the following page of the comic, above a diagram mapping out her process, "Once a Barbie enters my realm she goes through at least three weeks of reconditioning" (9). She then conveys, through words and pictures, the stages of transformation she puts her dolls through, turning them into unsanctioned and unconventional Barbies, including an "Astrobabe," a "Punk," a "Fabulous Vampire Superstar," a "Cavegirl," and a "Mom" with blue hair and bags under her eyes (10). Lauren's

3.12 *Lauren Weinstein, final page from "Barbies." In* Girl Stories, *p. 13. From* GIRL STORIES *copyright © 2006 Lauren Weinstein. Reprinted by permission of Henry Holt and Company, LLC. All Rights Reserved.*

"queer" Barbie play foreshadows the many themes that take up the rest of the narrative, but especially the tension between the conventional and the unconventional, between wanting to fit in, even in two worlds that seem diametrically opposed, and taking pleasure in not fitting in, in rebellion. Her manipulation of these dolls also relates to the book's consistent engagement in the hazards and freedoms of self-fashioning: these games grant Lauren the power to shape the doll's appearances and, consequently, their identities, but the very involvement in play with such a popular toy excludes her. In a subsequent comic, for example, her Barbie play leads her to self-identify as a "loser" (15), a precursor to her later self-characterization as a "freak."

In the end, whatever pleasure Lauren derives from confessing to and exposing herself in these intimate scenes, these early comics finally reflect the limitations of her imagined audience. While shaping her own experiences on the page might lead to the pretense of feeling in control, these solitary ventures confirm her isolation and difference, as the final page of the comic reflects. Alone in her room, Lauren laments the absence of her friend, Diana, "The only person who I have ever met that was good at playing Barbies . . . who was my best friend until about two years ago, when she decided to be cool" (13, figure 3.12). This passage, included just pages before Lauren is finally pictured interacting in the school hall presented in her introduction, sets up the book to be a story about loss, or banishment, from a previous state of belonging, and the subsequent search for companionship, return. But, although the absence of Diana's character is framed as the source of Lauren's alienation, as the careful drawing of her bedroom reflects, it is also the empty, private, and once animate space of her room juxtaposed against the adolescent world of her peers—the spacious corridors of middle and high school—that prompts Lauren's heightened sense of alienation early in the book. This feeling of estrangement persists in the second half of the memoir, even though, in ninth grade, Lauren increasingly, and often uncomfortably, finds herself cast in the role of insider.

"And I Have A Bigger Nose"

Halfway through *Girl Stories*, Lauren transitions from eighth grade, a year of mortifications, to high school, a new and as yet unexplored world that once again seems to offer her a clean slate, the potential to find a place of belonging. This time, the exciting new sphere is introduced with a panoramic depiction spanning the entire width of the open book, two full pages about a foot and a half in diameter (104–5). This image, the splash panel of a comic titled "Whoa! It's High School!" pictures a much larger, more concentrated group of students gathered in a mass outside of several school buildings, as though the enormity of this new world, and the possibilities comprised within it, cannot be contained indoors. Peppered with adolescent male and female bodies of various shapes and sizes, the crowd represents many anonymous figures differentiated from one another through details—their body shapes, haircuts, facial features, and the colors and styles of their clothing. But these particularities somewhat blend together as they stand, packed, a collective presence extending across the expansive panorama.

Unlike her absence in the introductory image of her eighth grade hallway, Lauren is included here, on the left side of the page, her body somewhat separate from other students and her eyes shifting away from them, as if to bridge this new space with the one that came before it. Her lone figure is mirrored by the depiction of a smaller figure, standing even more alone in the background just over her shoulder. Like Lauren, this young woman is also dressed in blue, though her outfit is darker, her body slimmer, and her facial features are represented by black smudges. On the other side of the panorama, across the considerable crowd, stand two of Lauren's friends from grade school, including Diana, and one of them calls out to her, her exclamation the only speech visible on the two pages: "Hey, Lauren, over here!"

Lauren's physical presence in this image, as well as the calling out of her name, marked in a bright white bubble, delineates her place among her peers as interposed somewhere between complete alienation (like the lone peripheral figure in the background) and connection. As in earlier parts of the book tracking her eighth grade experience, her recorded high school quest will consist in trying to figure out where or how she fits in. And just as her presence could easily be missed in this depiction of youth loitering on school grounds as time ostensibly passes, the majority of students in the picture do not stand out as individuals. This representation of the beginning of Lauren's high school experience thus simultaneously emphasizes and downplays the importance of the individual body. The adolescent body is easily assimilated into the crowd, but it simultaneously prevails as a potential marker of individuality and difference.

Lauren's physical presence in this image also prefigures her increased preoccupation, throughout the second half of the book, with the (female) body as a site of adolescent anxiety, desire, and humiliation—the target of both longed for, and dreaded, changes. Despite the self-reflexive nature of the memoir, and the conscious attempts that Lauren makes, with line, color, style, form, and even narrative text, to control her own adolescent body, that body repeatedly surfaces as a problem. As Sidonie Smith argues, in memoir writing the body is often a potential site of simultaneous identification and disidentification. She describes it as a starting place for many memoirists, especially in their searches for a singular sense of identity, since "bodies seem to position us as demarcated subjects separate from others and to locate us in bounded temporalities and trajectories of identification. Thus the body seems to be the nearest, most central home we know" (267). However, Smith adds, the very closeness of the body and its unity, "temptingly stable and impermeable," is nothing more than a facade, disruptive as soon as we take into account its politics, or the differences that need to be stifled in order for us to consider it a reflection of a singular, categorizable, and unitary self. For this reason, along with its potential to "anchor" us, "the body is our most material site of potential homelessness."

Like memoir writers in general, many adolescents, in searching for a point of entry to understand or locate their identities, might also begin with the body. This is, in part, because "adolescence is a developmental moment of intense awareness of and preoccupation with the body" (Irvine 22). The adolescent body, subject to intense flux and growth, thus often becomes the starting point for experiments with various forms of identification or self-making. Lauren's preoccupations with her uncontrollable body ultimately serve as a metaphor for her inability to locate a comfortable space for herself on the map of adolescence, to experience an identity as home. Nevertheless, the very unwieldiness of the body, its steady presence also frequently a site of transgression and eruption, oddly enough marks it as a catalyst for rebellion, for the very dis-affiliatory creative and imaginative possibilities that finally reaffirm her as the narrator of her own life.

As the following two pages of the comic introducing high school reflect, Lauren's experience in ninth grade is strongly shaded by her related, increased interest in and awareness of her gender and sexuality. Her requited interest in one particular boy, John, transforms her, on the following page, from another anonymous member of the crowd to an individual. Her impending role as his girlfriend presents her, for the first time outside her fantasy life, with a confirmed insider position. However, like Melissa in *Escape from "Special,"* that identification also functions as the starting point for an affirming sense of self that is most powerfully established by her rejection of it. By finding herself tied to a specific role, belonging, particularly when, for Lauren, it is initiated in and through the visible body, prompts estrangement, the division of self from self.

The early recordings of Lauren's and John's courtship showcase the two of them up close, emphasizing the intensity of these initial interactions as well as the manner in which this conventional adolescent narrative casts the two of them as central rather than anonymous or peripheral characters. In "Skate Date," a three-page story tracking one of their first, planned interactions outside of school, all of the individuals on the page are depicted in the same vibrating, blue colors, which also shade the simplistically styled backgrounds of the outdoor scene. Only John's blond hair differentiates him from the pair of girls—Lauren and her friend Diana—who watch him as he skateboards and covertly discuss whether Lauren is interested in him. Throughout this comic for the first time her affiliation with her peers is visibly confirmed; in particular, her strong resemblance to Diana early on in the story line—the two huddle together in conversation, their shapes, coloring, features, and hair styles nearly identical—solidifies her connection to others, her sense of belonging.

Halfway through this short narrative, Lauren is finally distinguished from Diana, as she is pictured increasingly in relation to John or as part of a couple. On the final page of the comic, the two are featured alone in a series of six panels (118, figure 3.13). As the first three snapshots of the scene unfold, the awkwardness between them is punctuated by minimal word bubbles and a panel, the central one, reflecting silence, though there is no indication of how long that silence lasts. The blue hues consistently shading these images confirm the atmosphere of anticipation that accompanies Lauren's memory of their first kiss, including, crucially, the uncertain and uncomfortable moments leading up to it. Her thought bubbles add humor to the limited bits of conversation recorded between the two, hinting at the layers of unspoken and unpictured subjectivity that never make it to the page. The final three panels record the decisive event in the exchange, though again there is no sense of how long this interaction lasts or whether these final illustrations represent a time span somewhat equivalent to the previous three anticipatory ones. "Wow! We're kissing," Lauren thinks to herself in the central bottom panel, which is the second image depicting them kissing, and the words highlight the disparity between the calm, matter-of-fact illustrations of their two figures and the disbelief Lauren experiences internally. "And now we're Frenching," the next and final panel reads, the words reinforcing Lauren's continued need to narrate, especially when she feels out of place in her own body.

3.13 *Lauren Weinstein, final page from "Skate Date." In* Girl Stories, *p. 118. From GIRL STORIES copyright © 2006 Lauren Weinstein. Reprinted by permission of Henry Holt and Company. LLC All Rights Reserved.*

Beside the careful drawings of the couple, along with Lauren's accompanying thoughts, a crude close-up drawing of a pink mouth with a large tongue lodged in it finally interrupts the otherwise generally even tone of the scene. Its presence unsettles the relatively symmetrical architecture of the page, adding a final distorted shape to the series of three panels mirroring the ones pictured above. This sudden insertion of a gaping mouth at the end of "Skate Date"—an eruption on the page— transforms what is otherwise a conventional, relatively cliché narrative about a first date between two teenagers into a somewhat grotesque, transgressive recollection. By focusing in on the corporeal, the messy and unattractive shape, look, and, by extension, feel of the mouth on the inside as it is being kissed, the final image upsets the otherwise agreeable, normative story line of the young man pursuing the compliant young woman and sealing his conquest with a calculated kiss.

In their 2005 review essay, "Writing Back: Rereading Adolescent Girlhoods Through Women's Memoir," Elizabeth Marshall and Theresa Rogers argue that many contemporary memoirs written by women about adolescence offer counter-narratives to popular culture's notions about what their experiences are actually like. Reading four works in particular, including Marjane Satrapi's coming-of-age graphic memoir *Persepolis*, they assert that "women's retrospective constructions of adolescent girlhood provide alternative scripts about gender" (17). Throughout *Girl Stories*, portrayals of Lauren's body frequently interfere in scenes that might otherwise be read as part of a predictable adolescent narrative; these intrusions emphasize Lauren's subjectivity, foregrounding her point of view. By transforming the innocuous and somewhat disembodied representations leading up to the "first kiss" into a disproportionately magnified and unattractive anatomical image, the protruding mouth at the end of "Skate Date" empowers Lauren as storyteller by recording the reality of her otherwise "typical" adolescent experience from the perspective of a resistant female body. The image of the mouth visualizes the abject in what would otherwise be a detached and stereotypical representation.

In another interaction between the couple, recounted three pages later in the comic "John & I Go to the Movies . . . ," Lauren's experience of the situation is conveyed, in contrast, in a series of images depicting *only* her external body as it corresponds with his. But a close reading of this story line similarly confirms the power Lauren's narrating self can wield from within the space of conformity and belonging, provided she finds a way to distance herself from the scene. At first glance the representations of the two on a date seem to erase Lauren's individual subjectivity. The first page of the story features a sequence of small panels—eighteen in total—without a single word pictured besides the title, written in bubbled red letters at the top of the page (121, figure 3.14). The small panels look like photos from a photo booth, or individual panels from a filmstrip, a conceit that adds to the sense of performance of the occasion. The series opens from the point of view of a distanced observer, as Lauren and John sit beside each other, and their interaction of being on a first date at the movies recalls, in itself, a spectacle. The panels then zero in on their hands, as they inch together slowly, and these depictions are portrayed from the couple's vantage point. The point of view then shifts once again, and, as the comic goes on, somewhat repeatedly, picturing fragments of the two of them (arms and legs, mostly) from diverse angles, with Lauren's individual perspective sometimes interjecting to catch the profile of John's face. The last image on the page features a final close-up of the two, once

3.14 *Lauren Weinstein, opening page from "John & I Go to the Movies." In* Girl Stories, *p. 121.*
From GIRL STORIES copyright © 2006 Lauren Weinstein. Reprinted by permission of Henry Holt
and Company, LLC. All Rights Reserved.

again from the viewpoint of an unpictured third person, an imaginary observer, and this time they are holding hands with their heads slightly angled toward one another. This image resembles a drawing of a photograph, as the couple's eyes seem to be concentrated on an anonymous onlooker. Their stances look artificial, like the entire interaction was staged for the benefit of that observer.

The posed interactions portrayed within these panels draws attention to the couple's bodily postures as pretense. In this deconstruction of the event, their behaviors are conveyed as affectations based, presumably, on a mirroring of actions and behaviors learned and absorbed from the wider world, including the movie screen. The voyeuristic illustrations of these bodily interactions thus reinforce the performativity of Lauren's diary project as a whole. Her role as diarist, which compels her to direct and record the unfolding details of her life, complements her place as star of this adolescent plot, as she acts out the prescribed role of a teenager on her first real date. In each of these narrative portrayals of Lauren and John, first in "Skate Date" and later at the movies, whether by disruption or deconstruction, the off-center depictions reflect a consistent awareness of a potentially real or imagined audience. This mindfulness transforms Lauren from one passively undergoing these experiences to one actively shaping them. Each of these scenes therefore demonstrates how Lauren's capacity to develop a sustaining counternarrative to the experience of adolescence hinges on her ability to create distance between that experience and the telling of it. It is a possibility reflected in earlier parts of the book, particularly in scenes—like the eighth grade hallway or the "freak" self-portrait—where her absence from the image actually conveys her presence as storyteller. Lauren's capacity for self-definition and self-possession is therefore tied to her identity as an artist and writer, the composer of her own story. Nonetheless, many of her interactions with others, and particularly with her friend Diana, also powerfully expose the limitations of this affirming sense of self, mapping out the ways her self-representations are also always tied to how she sees herself in relation to others. In other words, her self-depictions, relational no matter their particular expressions, mark her body as a potential site of both locatedness and homelessness.

From the final page of the "Barbies" comic to the early interactions between John and Lauren, it is clear that Diana's absence, and presence, in various scenes throughout Lauren's adolescent life crucially affects her sense of fitting in. In many ways, throughout *Girl Stories*, Diana acts as a foil to Lauren, as Lauren often unsuccessfully searches for a space of belonging. A comic located toward the end of the book, and titled "Diana," exemplifies just how tied Lauren's self-definition is to her friend. The title panel of this comic is a full page, featuring Diana's name neatly scripted against a background of green trees with two disparately shaped noses poking through them, each drawn wildly out of scale (170, figure 3.15). The connecting page of the comic then introduces the friends with an image of the two of them standing next to each other. "This is my friend Diana," the narration reads. An arrow points to Diana's head, as if to single her out, even though she is the only other person in the illustration besides the narrator. "We are really great friends," the narration continues. "Look at how beautiful and special she is! And skinny too!" As both the visual and verbal cues on the page indicate, Lauren's identification with Diana is grounded in their similarities. Both have dark, wavy hair and almond brown eyes. But these similarities also crucially underline their

3.15 *Lauren Weinstein, opening page from "Diana." In* Girl Stories, *p. 170. From GIRL STORIES copyright © 2006 Lauren Weinstein. Reprinted by permission of Henry Holt and Company, LLC. All Rights Reserved.*

points of difference, and particularly the ways Lauren experiences certain bodily details (hinted at here by Lauren's mention of Diana's skinniness) as stubbornly distinguishing the two of them.

The following page breaks down the dual nature of the previous two pages, featuring a close-up of a partially illustrated, single face: two large brown eyes span the page, with colored blue and pink stars framing those eyes and adding a dreaminess to the otherwise innocuous figure (172, figure 3.16). Because the two adolescents "have many things in common," as Lauren explains of the depiction, the close-up, at first glance, could be of either girl. The illustration itself does not plainly attempt to distinguish between the two, and, in fact, the absence of the nose, so glaringly present in the comic's opening, compels the reader to imagine that either could be pictured here. The words written below the illustration, however, tell of their differences: "Except her hair is shinier, and she has this awesome widow's peak, which frames her larger more mysterious eyes. And I have a bigger nose."

WE HAVE MANY THINGS IN COMMON, LIKE WE BOTH HAVE BROWN CURLY HAIR AND BROWN EYES, AND WE ARE BOTH ABOUT THE SAME HEIGHT.

EXCEPT HER HAIR IS SHINIER, AND SHE HAS THIS AWESOME WIDOW'S PEAK, WHICH FRAMES HER LARGER, MORE MYSTERIOUS EYES. AND I HAVE A BIGGER NOSE.

3.16 *Lauren Weinstein, third page from "Diana." In* Girl Stories, *p. 172. From GIRL STORIES copyright © 2006 Lauren Weinstein. Reprinted by permission of Henry Holt and Company, LLC. All Rights Reserved.*

Introducing the widow's peak, shiny hair, and, most crucially, the nose into this comic as potential markers of difference disrupts the narrative, much like the drooling pink mouth violated the otherwise inoffensive portrayal of Lauren's first kiss. These seemingly trivial details come to stand as disproportionate indicators of Lauren's sense of otherness, hinting at a counternarrative to an otherwise conventional story of adolescent female friendship, with its many highs and lows. The exaggerated significance of such particular bodily features reflects how these body parts, especially the glaringly absent nose, function synecdochically to convey Lauren's more general and persistent sense of difference and alienation over the course of the book. The nose is ultimately what distinguishes Lauren from the friend whose existence regularly informs, and shapes, her sense of self.

The nose thus sets Lauren apart, but, particularly when read in the context of the memoir as a whole, its exaggerated importance here also symbolizes Lauren's self-fashioning as a means of empowerment. After all, Lauren's very feelings of displacement, of being a "freak," are what often compel her to actively map her life on the pages of her diary. The nose as an embellished sign of difference consequently reflects how shaping her unwieldy body on the page is actually a way of asserting control. A number of female autobiographical cartoonists in particular seem to utilize this very tactic in drawing images of their personae. Consider, for example, how cartoonist Phoebe Gloeckner, author of the semiautobiographical coming-of-age graphic narrative *The Diary of a Teenage Girl*, recently described the ways that autobiographical self-depictions, and specifically how one chooses to distinguish oneself on the page, can be a means of self-affirmation. Rather than presuming self-representations are always literally or directly correlated with the particular anxieties of an autobiographical cartoonist, with how she feels about her body in real life, Gloeckner suggested that such depictions can more powerfully be understood as reflections of the complex process of conscious self-fashioning. As she delineated in a conversation about the question, so often posed to female cartoonists (as we have seen with Aline Kominsky Crumb), of why they frequently draw themselves as ostensibly "uglier" than they are in real life: "Maybe it is not even always a question of ugly or beautiful. It is something else. You don't want to make your features so reduced to just bumps that it is not you. You just have to find your essence somehow. And it is beyond any kind of judgment" (Gloeckner et al. 103). As Gloeckner suggests here, and as Kominsky Crumb reveals in her self-representations, orienting the self with a single, reductive detail, however drawn out of scale, can be an act of defiance. In the context of a culture in which women's self-depictions are so often literalized, "leading" with the nose, something Kominsky Crumb admitted to on the same panel, becomes a means of resistance, a refusal to operate within the confines of conventional systems of calibration, of "space and scale."

Similarly, for Lauren, then, the glaring absence of the nose in this particular image from "Diana" can be read as an act of defiance. As their relationship throughout the book reflects, Diana's appearance, or disappearance, serves, at times, to stress Lauren's capacity for conformity and assimilation, while at other times it calls attention to Lauren's stubborn inability to fit in. The perceived contrast between the two women is what ultimately propels Lauren's need for self-definition. As a marker of her difference, the nose comes to stand as a characteristic that finally, and obstinately, resists the possibility of conformity, of assimilation. Its presence may signal Lauren's occasional shame in standing out, but it also represents the power that comes from designing your own narrative of alienation, from drawing your own displacements.

Although this protruding nose is never directly revealed to be a Jewish nose in particular, certain moments in the narrative point to that distinct and probable association. For instance, in one of the early Barbie comics, Lauren writes to the makers of Barbie, reporting four of her "frustrations with your product." One of these includes the fact that "I have never been able to find a pretty brown-haired, brown-eyed Barbie. All your Barbies look like Aryans!" The term *Aryan*, used often in the late nineteenth and twentieth centuries as a racial term meant to divide Jews, among other marginalized groups, from a supposed blue-eyed, blond-haired "master" race, establishes Lauren's annoyance here as prompted by her Jewish identity and her stereotypical "Jewish looks." Not coincidentally, Diana can be characterized by many of these same physical attributes, with her dark hair and eyes, suggesting that Lauren's repeated need to define herself in relation to this friend stems from a recognition of their joint Jewish heritage.

In an interview, Lauren Weinstein confirmed this reading of the nose in "Diana" as a Jewish nose, explaining of her depictions of this friend, "[She was l]ess Jewish looking. . . . Her nose [was] not as *schnozzy* as mine. That was definitely a real feeling I had" ("Thinking Panoramically" 191). For women growing up in the late twentieth and early twenty-first centuries, while the pressure to hide the "Jewish nose" is no longer as widespread or forceful as it was for Kominsky Crumb's postwar generation, it remains, in certain contexts, what Lisa Jervis has termed "the sign on my face," a marker of difference (67). As Jervis describes it in her 1998 essay, "My Jewish Nose," the pressure to change her nose mostly stemmed from "older Jewish female relatives" who had come of age at a time when *not* getting a nose job was nothing short of a "liability" (64, 65). Although the pressure was not as intense for Jervis, growing up in the late twentieth century, it still strongly informed her sense of self. In the case of Weinstein's narrative, if Lauren's exaggerated drawing is of the nose as a particularly Jewish nose, then her Jewish identity can be understood as a frame of reference established by her dis-affiliation from her friend, Diana. Like The Bunch, who actively claims pride in "keeping" her own Jewish nose, a decision that divides her from the Jewish Long Island community of her youth, the exaggeration of Lauren's Jewish nose as a marker of difference from her friend—an exaggeration paradoxically conveyed through its absence on the page—is a means of actively claiming her Jewish identity. As Sander Gilman argues, "It is in being visible in 'the body that betrays,' that the Jew is most uncomfortable" (*The Jew's Body* 193). Lauren here seeks out this discomfort, claiming her Jewish difference by highlighting its nonappearance.

Like Melissa, then, Lauren's Jewish identity, signified by the whopping presence and subsequent absence of her nose on three consecutive pages in "Diana," offers her a space of not belonging that ironically and powerfully fortifies her personal rebellions, her moments of potential imaginative revision. There are several other comics throughout the book that more directly address Lauren's Jewish identity, including the eleven-page comic titled "The Chanukah Blues."[16] This story, featured when Lauren is still in the eighth grade, between comics that more directly address her relationship with her peers at school, is telling not only for its content but also for its peculiarly slapstick and fantastical tone and style. Set against a light-pink background, the story opens with Lauren uncharacteristically addressing her Jewish identity directly, as she sits on Santa's lap and tells him that she doesn't want anything for Christmas because she is Jewish (64–74). The rest of the narrative reflects her continued sense of alienation in relation to her non-Jewish peers, a feeling that leads her to exaggerate her differences. As she relates, "In Kindergarten I was the one who told all the Christian kids that Santa didn't exist" (65). In the comic, Lauren is approached by Latke Boy, an oversized potato pancake, who tells her, "I help Jewish boys and girls everywhere get over the Chanukah Blues" (71). On the final page she stands beside an oversized menorah, her parents hugging her while she uncharacteristically smiles and accepts their embraces without a word.

"The Chanukah Blues" is an anomalous piece in relation to the rest of the memoir not only because in it Lauren addresses her Jewish identity directly, as well as relating comfortably to her parents, but also because of the way it is drawn. Each page of the caricatured comic presents a dramatically divergent image of Lauren, including a number of depictions of her younger self, but the emotional resonances of these depictions are difficult to interpret or collectively decipher. Additionally, many of the characters Lauren encounters throughout the plotline are nowhere to be found in the rest of *Girl Stories*, and the ones that are (like her parents) are almost unrecognizable. Latke Boy's incongruous nature in relation to the rest of the memoir reinforces Lauren's inability to grapple with her Jewish identity in any easy or direct manner. Instead, as its farcical tone reveals, such an unquestioned and direct relationship to Jewishness makes Lauren uncomfortable. Jewish identity is a site of potential connection and freedom, but only when established in a peripheral or oblique manner, one that reinforces Lauren as both the protagonist and director of her own story, however illusory those roles.

Self Visualization Activity

In a black-and-white cartoon collected in Lauren Weinstein's first collection, *Inside Vineyland*, published in 2003, she pictures a large, rectangular panel at the top of the page, which contains a carefully sketched rocky seascape and two ghostly outlines of people, with the words *you* and *other* etched inside of these figures (figure 3.17).[17] Below the image, a smaller rectangular box features a sampling of possible people and creatures that may be inserted into the blank space of "your companion." The list, with accompanying illustrations, reads: "(1) snail; (2) sea lion; (3) Cheryl; (4) proud Indian; (5) Smokey; (6) Mercenary; and (7) Jesus Christ." Each of these potential "others" is drawn in a shape that does not easily match the long, ghostly silhouette of the "other" figure posed by the sea. Finally, beside the title of the comic, simply written in large capital letters at the top of the page, a tiny sailor, standing with one leg crossed over the other and his hands at his side, is depicted looking off into the distance.

Despite its satiric and cryptic bent, in a single page this comedic "Self Visualization Activity" encompasses many of the features of Weinstein's and Lasko-Gross's memoirs. The self is always identified in relation to the other, and both are phantoms whose presences can potentially, though never comfortably, materialize to reflect a bafflingly particular individual presence. In other words, people, in life as well as on the page, are always situated somewhere between complete anonymity and particularity, between stereotype and antistereotype.

By listing certain identity labels in connection with names and figures that do not match in any discernible way, this cartoon questions the ease with which people are labeled and referenced in relation to one another. As Eve Kosofsky Sedgwick writes in *Epistemology of the Closet*, "People are different from each other" or "the sister or brother, the best friend, the classmate, the parent, the child, the lover, the ex-: our families, loves, and enmities alike, not to mention the strange relations of our work, play, and activism, prove that even people who share all or most of our own positionings along these crude axes may still be different enough from us, and from each other, to seem like all but different species" (22). Both *Escape from "Special"* and *Girl Stories* are works that question the ease with which identifications are imagined and framed. It is because Jewishness emerges at key moments in the texts—and all but disappears at other moments—that it maintains its significance as an unstable but potent marker of difference, a potential site of powerful rebellion.

SELF VISUALIZATION ACTIVITY

3.17 *Lauren Weinstein, "Self-Visualization Activity." In* Inside Vineyland, *n.p. Used by permission of Lauren Weinstein.*

In presenting such Jewish engagements in relation to more universalized accounts of the self as it moves through the transitional framework of adolescence, both memoirs resist easy categorization or genrefication, ultimately claiming Jewishness as a site of connection rather than isolation or dislocation. At one point in *Escape from "Special,"* in a series of panels conveying Melissa, at intervals, in both rebellious and resigned postures, she tells her childhood therapist, "I don't want people to know my identity" (70). "And what *is* your 'identity'?" the therapist asks in reply—a question that confounds her. Melissa can only respond, in turn, with another question, inquiring, "Is that a trick question?" Identity, as in the works of all the cartoonists examined in this book, is posited as a question, an inexplicable paradox. As with genre, categorizations of identity are points of departure for larger conversations about how and why such categorizations continue to exist. Jewish identity, in its many iterations, becomes a site of potential affiliation, even as it consistently reveals the ways in which our Jewish selves often disorient us, particularly in relation to other Jews, as "all but different species."

"But you don't live here, so what's the dilemma?"

Birthright and Accountability in the Geographics of Sarah Glidden and Miriam Libicki

hroughout this book I have been utilizing the language of exile and diaspora—words like *home, homelessness, belonging,* and *not belonging*—to discuss the approaches that contemporary Jewish American women cartoonists use to map their identities.[1] Jews have often been considered the "archetypal or prototypical diaspora people," *diaspora* being a term meaning "dispersion" that originated in the one of the original Greek translations of the bible (Zeitlin 1; Aviv and Shneer 3). Given the long-standing associations of Jews as travelers and wanderers, as well as the more recent employing of such concepts by scholars exploring Jewish identity, the application of these and related expressions by contemporary Jews to describe themselves seems inevitable. This terminology has also strongly informed the works of many cultural theorists, including those engaged in postcolonial discourse. Scholars such as Paul Gilroy and Edward Said openly acknowledge their "creative debts" to nineteenth-century Jewish intellectuals who "sought ways to account for the Jews' persistence over the long span of centuries in a variety of lands that were not their homeland" (Omer-Sherman 12, 3).

Despite these historical connections between Jews and concepts of diaspora, as many have recently pointed out, there is a danger in relying too heavily on such rhetoric to describe the situation of a group of people—however diverse and diversely located—whose place in the American landscape, as well as, generally speaking, most parts of the world, is no longer easily or directly related to a condition of literal exile. As Susan Stanford Friedman articulates in *Mappings*, "The metaphor of migrancy may well be the luxury of the housed and the relatively stationary" (102). To ruminate on one's sense of homelessness is to recognize the possibility of what it means to belong, to have a home. It is an act that, if carelessly executed, potentially and harmfully erases the realities of those who do not have that choice.

The problem of figurative diasporic discourse, and particularly the valorization of such states of being, is not limited to its potential to diminish the experiences of others. Such language, specifically when used in discussions about Israel, can also, and relatedly, evoke Jews in particular as impotent victims. This characterization leads to problematic justifications for illegitimate and otherwise indefensible actions, as comic book writer Harvey Pekar points out in his posthumously published 2012 graphic narrative illustrated by J. T. Waldman and titled *Not the Israel My Parents Promised Me*. Like some other liberal and secular Jews, Pekar draws the connection between the history of Jewish exile as caused by oppression and the resultant justifications made, by some, of certain actions in recent Israeli history. As he writes, "Being Jewish does not automatically absolve one of guilt. Despite the fact that Jews have such a long history of being oppressed, Israeli treatment of Palestinians eats at Jewish claims of fairness" (149). In a 2010 essay on the topic in the *New York Review of Books*, in an attempt to understand why so many young Jews have "checked their Zionism," Peter Beinart points to a similar discrepancy. As he explains, an "obsession with victimhood lies at the heart of why Zionism is dying among America's secular Jewish young. It simply bears no relationship to their lived experience, or what they have seen of Israel's."

Like many young, self-proclaimed left-wing North American Jews, the cartoonists under discussion in this chapter, Sarah Glidden and Miriam Libicki, reject a comfortable figuration of Jewish identity as easily rooted in diasporic conceptualizations. But in their graphic narratives, unlike the college students that Beinart attempts to understand in his essay who are supposedly indifferent about Israel, the personae of these texts plainly struggle with the ways such constructions affect their senses of what it means to be Jewish.[2] Glidden's 2010 graphic narrative, *How to Understand Israel in Sixty Days or Less*, and Libicki's comic series, *jobnik!* first collectively published in 2008 and ongoing, both struggle with the discomfort that accompanies "metaphoric articulations of identity issues" (Friedman 102), especially in the case of the relationship between North American Jews and Israel as the so-called Jewish homeland.[3] In their accounts of traveling to Israel as part of a tour group, in Glidden's case, and as a dual citizen and member of the Israeli Defense Forces, in Libicki's case, these authors' personae recognize the importance of moving beyond language as signifier and image as icon to confront the material and historic realities of identifications that are rooted in actual places and affect people as individual bodies. In addition, they acknowledge the impossibility of establishing closed linear narratives to unite and reflect those realities. Glidden and Libicki somewhat ironically employ the medium of comics, a language premised in large part on stereotype and shorthand, to convey the importance of researching and relaying detailed and individual histories in order to locate the self and, by extension, the other. Perhaps more than any of the other cartoonists discussed here, their texts reflect dis-affiliation as an ethical posture, a way of envisioning an ethics of accountability that recognizes self-representation as inextricably connected to the ways that others come to see and be seen.

Both these cartoonists' works can be categorized as travel narratives, a genre focused on the transitional as a way of examining and exposing the self. In his book, *Travel Writing*, Casey Blanton argues that "there exists in the journey pattern the possibility of a kind of narrative where inner and outer worlds collide" (3). It is the transitional moment—or movement—that educes such collisions, allowing an individual's inner and outer worlds to fully engage in a space that is somehow "safe" because it is neither here nor there; the self in transit remains unfixed and relatively free. In that sense, travel memoirs, which "dramatize[] an engagement between self and world" (Blanton xi), are texts, much like adolescent memoirs, in which questions of identity can be expansively attended to and explored. The dramatic engagements reflected in such works, where identity issues unfold primarily in relation to space, follow what Susan Stanford Friedman pinpoints as "the new geographics." According to Friedman's model, identity, "constantly on the move," is figured most aptly in spatial terms, which, as explained in my introduction, is what makes the relational language of comics such an interesting medium for its expression and analysis. Autobiographical comics focused on travel reinforce a perception of identity as, fundamentally, a function of space and movement, or of the individual's always shifting point of view; like all of the works examined in this book, these memoirs present a spatialized graphics that depicts the self, and subjectivity, as it unravels, or the self as process.

In their travel narratives, by calling attention to the self away from "home," the texts under discussion challenge the very notion of "home" as a fixed concept, an idea that, as Caryn Aviv and David Shneer point out in *New Jews*, presumes people—and, by extension, communities—to have locatable centers and peripheries. Aviv and Shneer question the notion of diaspora as a model for understanding contemporary Jewish identity because, for them, such a model "has discounted or overshadowed the extent to which people—as individuals and as groups—are creating new forms of home in a more mobile world" (18). They emphasize instead the possibility of a communal Jewish identity founded in transnational constructions of home that are based in a global world as well as in "the ways in which many Jews are remaking their sense of home and establishing new kinds of roots, not just to particular pieces of land but also to concepts, ideas, stories, and spaces" (20). *Israel* and *jobnik!* are books that establish travel, and the visualized narration of travel, as the in-between spaces where their central personae feel both most and least at home, as they too question that very concept. Through their visual-verbal experimentations with self-portraiture, these works interrogate not only the centrality of a specific locale or nationality in the establishment of a Jewish sense of self but also the very possibility of mapping out any and all spaces as home or not home. Instead, these graphic narratives reimagine home, and subsequently identity-as-home, in terms of movement rather than stasis or as expansive and elliptical in nature.

"We are A Little Bit 'There' Already"

Despite its origins as a minicomic tracking her two-week trip to Israel in 2007, Sarah Glidden's *Israel*, spanning 206 pages, is the most linearly structured of all the graphic narratives explored in this book.[4] At 6-by-9 inches, the majority of pages are divided into nine hand-drawn rectangular panels of almost identical size, with narrative remarks and speech bubbles fastidiously drawn and arranged. Glidden's book also stands out due to her careful and delicate use of watercolor, a now characteristic element of her comics that was originally her publisher's suggestion.[5] But in spite of what appears to be a straightforward story following the evolution of a series of events presented in sequential order, *Israel* stealthily traverses the boundaries of its own apparent linearity by presenting various, often unexpected, points of rupture within its pages.

The work is divided into seven discrete chapters, each tracing a leg of Sarah's journey on the guided Birthright Israel tour: "Orientation," "The Golan Heights," "The Kinneret," "Tel Aviv and Environs," "The Desert," "Jerusalem," and "Post-Birthright."[6] Although this arrangement conforms to the conventions of a general Birthright itinerary, Glidden's particular shaping of the layout of her trip is telling. She names five of the chapters in terms of places traversed, whereas the first and last chapters ("Orientation" and "Post-Birthright") disturb this arrangement. Instead of referring directly to places, these two titles point, instead, to more ambiguous figurations that simultaneously bookend and interrupt the place-as-time scheme encompassed by the structure of the memoir as a whole. In addition, in the five intermediate chapters locations are presented as comparable to one another, even though the places named represent regions with disparate geographies, topographies, and levels of historical and cultural significance. For example, the focus of an entire chapter is "The Desert," unspecified here in name but referring to Israel's Negev, which spans over half the country's land area. As one of five central chapters, it is made equivalent to the city of Jerusalem, the focus of another chapter, and the Kinneret, also known as the Sea of Galilee (Israel's largest freshwater lake) and the topic of yet another chapter. The structure of the book, which initially appears as a basic consecutive unfolding, therefore also subtly plays with notions of places as discrete, substitutable, and easily identifiable and classifiable units, a preoccupation that winds through the work as a whole.

The chapters also present travel, and especially planned travel, as an enterprise inevitably characterized by the unexpected. The titles are not presented together in a table of contents at the beginning of the book. Instead, they appear only within the span of the text itself, separate from the generally uniform multi-paneled pages. Each title page, encountered by the reader as the story unfolds, is structured as a map, with the name of the chapter etched into a box at the top left corner of the page. This box also sometimes functions as the map's legend. The individual maps are watercolor drawings, and they distinctly feature a somewhat limited variation of colors in order to foreground certain aspects of the pictured geographical locations over others. The varied depictions of the seven full-page maps incorporated into the text, which differ in the ways they illustrate the scope, scale, compass, and context of each particular place, draw attention to these representations as subjective constructions. While the maps in some ways match those of conventional Israeli tourisms, by drawing them in her own hand and style Sarah claims them as constructions connected to the experiences unfolding, from her particular point of view, in the attendant chapters.[7] So, for example, in the map of "Tel Aviv and Environs," the page is divided almost equally in two, with the Mediterranean Sea spanning the left side of the page and an intricate drawing of the streets of Tel Aviv traversing the right side (78, figure 4.1). The sea is colored pale blue, while Tel Aviv is drawn in combinations of faded oranges, browns, and pinks. The map features only five landmarks: Mike's Place (a bar), Hotel,

Rabin Square, Miri Aloni Square, and Independence Hall. Each of them indicates a place Sarah visits and a related event she recounts over the course of the chapter. By marking these sites on the page in illustrations that are slightly, but visibly, out of scale with the weblike grid of streets pictured, the image represents space as subjectively rendered by the individual mapmaker. The drawing of Tel Aviv is inflected as much by Sarah's sensorial experiences and the material indicators she encounters externally as by her internal, sometimes even imaginary, world. Furthermore, by featuring human-made structures, like streets and a hotel, in opposition to the relatively consistent and uninterrupted blue sea, the map, like the chapter it precedes, foregrounds the two kinds of interactions—with people and with the landscape—that inform the alter ego's journey and her subsequent understanding of Israel. As she comes to realize about the conflict in Israel in her chapter about Tel Aviv, "it seems that it's never really been about religion but about land" (87). This particular drawing of Tel Aviv, which visualizes the city as a piece of developed land, but also part of a larger geographical topography, calls attention to various characteristics of the area in time and over time. Tel Aviv is "prime real estate," a port city, and a tourist site with a "great view" (87). It serves all these functions, but it is not defined by any of them individually.

The map of Tel Aviv at the beginning of chapter 4 is also portrayed differently from other maps featured as chapter headings throughout the book, such as the one pictured two chapters earlier of the Golan Heights (30). This map includes a key, tacked just underneath the chapter title, and this key indicates what color lines represent the bus route, the highway, and the United Nations demilitarized zone. The maps pictured at the beginning of the "Orientation" and "The Desert" chapters similarly contain clear markers of the politically disputed and militarized boundaries within and around the country as well as the bus routes and highways that enable the persona's journey to, from, and around this particular area. Instead of the details of streets contrasted with the wide, empty stretch of the sea, the image introducing the Golan Heights features an amorphous expanse of land, colored pale yellow and delineated by various disruptive lines painted in reds, pinks, and black. The yellow area is simply labeled "Israel," with the bordered countries of Lebanon and Jordan rendered as white, or blank, spaces that bleed off the page. By emphasizing this part of the country as a geographical region marked by seemingly haphazard human-made boundaries and thoroughfares, but otherwise dislocated from individuals and communities, Sarah differentiates these areas, and the story lines that take place in them, from the ones, like Tel Aviv

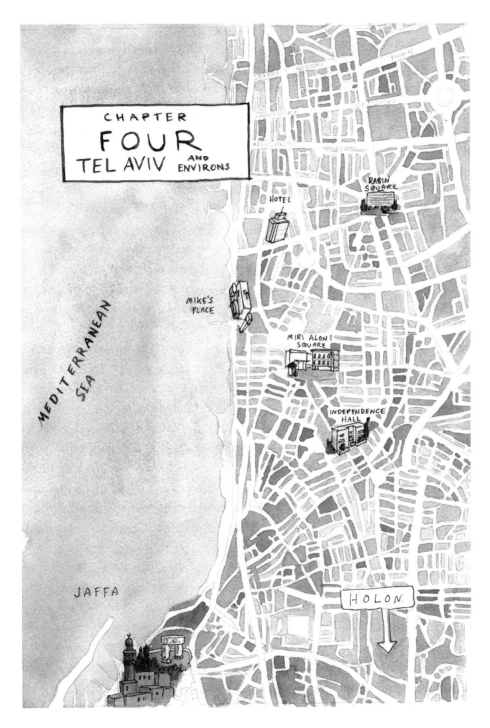

4.1 *Sarah Glidden, title page from chapter 4. In* How to Understand Israel in 60 Days or Less, *p. 78. Copyright © Sarah Glidden 2010.*

and Jerusalem, that are defined in large part in terms of her interpersonal interactions within those places. In these ways, not only is each representational map depicted as predicated on Sarah's subjectivity at particular moments of time—the moments when she encounters the place and the moments when she reflects on and draws that place—but each is also dependent on her experience of that area within the trajectory of the narrative as a whole. As her journey unfolds, Sarah's understanding of Israel—and especially of what, borrowing from common terminology about the subject, she terms "the situation"—transforms. Her understanding slowly and somewhat recursively shifts from the abstract and indirect, a knowledge based in large part on research and books studied from a distance, to the concrete, a knowledge based more directly on people and the personal stories they transmit. Although the transformation is never complete, as abstract knowledge has its place throughout the text, the basic movement of the book, and of Sarah's journey, is away from theoretical, secondhand knowledge and in search of material and firsthand ways of knowing and telling.

The opening chapter, "Orientation," presages those very gaps—between theoretical or secondhand information and direct experience—that Sarah will continue to negotiate over the course of her trip, and in particular the distinction between her expectations for the visit and her actual encounters. As mentioned, she travels with the guided tour known as Birthright. On its webpage, the organization, whose full name is Taglit-Birthright Israel, describes itself as one that "provides a gift of a peer group, educational trip to Israel for Jewish young adults ages 18 to 26 from around the world."[8] In a Fall 2011 essay in the *Jewish Review of Books* analyzing four works written about Birthright since 2008, including Glidden's *Israel*, Philip Getz argues that a central question surrounding the organization is whether or not "Birthright's main purpose is to encourage participants to make *aliya* (move to Israel), or at least become Zionist activists" (24). While Getz believes this tacit agenda is "a widespread misconception," Sarah, like many others, approaches her trip unsure of whether or not she will be offered something like an objective look at Israel. Although in the opening chapter she dutifully quotes Birthright materials that advertise the trip as one in which the group "will be exploring the history and politics of Israel in an open-minded and pluralistic manner" (9), she continually asks herself, especially at the beginning of her journey, whether or not "Birthright is trying to brainwash me" (27). This uncertain framing of the excursion is Sarah's way of challenging Birthright's packaged commodification of their so-called educational tours, which proclaim wide-spreading goals, generally to be achieved in the span of ten days. Many of these goals are premised on the presumption that ties to the Israeli state help establish one's Jewish identity. The "About Us" section of the aforementioned website, for example, includes the following pronouncement: "We believe that the experience of a trip to Israel is a building block of Jewish identity, and that by providing that gift to young Jews, we can strengthen bonds with the land and people of Israel and solidarity with Jewish communities worldwide." As Sarah shows, her education necessarily extends beyond what is officially sanctioned by Birthright and involves an experience not necessarily of "strengthening" but instead of questioning and negotiating her Jewish identity and its as yet unconfirmed connection to Israel.

Sarah's experience of travel is therefore not relegated to a clearly delineated time or place (i.e., the ten or so days that she spends in Israel). Rather, it is characterized by a more indeterminate sense of time mirrored by a polysemous grasp of Israel as a place. The full title of the book, *How to Understand Israel in Sixty Days or Less*, thus satirically refers not only to the time Sarah spends abroad with Birthright but also the days leading up to and extending beyond her trip. On the second page of the travelogue, just after the inclusion of an "orientation" map depicting a stretch of Israel, she tells her boyfriend, "I'm ready to go there and discover the truth behind this whole mess once and for all. It'll all be crystal clear by the time I come back!" (6). However, once at the airport, and only two pages later, this possibility is already called into question, as her notions of time and place—and therefore the potential of identifying a single, unifying "truth"—are disturbed. After mentioning her friend, Melissa, who accompanies her on the trip, she retrospectively recounts the effort she spent researching Israel even before she left. As she explains, "After the two of us decided to go on this trip I spent every moment reading about Israel, Palestine and the conflict" (11).[9] This element of her self-education is developed in various narrative panels that picture her walking around the airport, undergoing security checks, and eventually finding her seat on the plane. The starting point of her trip is consequently hazy. Although the title of the book suggests "sixty days or less" as the span of time in which she is focused on and visiting Israel, the unfolding of this opening chapter instead collapses time, as well as space, and suggests the pursuit of "understanding" Israel as endless and indeterminate.

An unsettling interaction with airport security further prefigures the ways that conventional impressions of time and place break down throughout Sarah's trip and influence representations of the experience in her travelogue. When she first checks in with her airline, the security clerk for El Al questions her about the reasons for her trip. He asks her to recall specific aspects of her Jewish background, such as the number of guests at her bat mitzvah and the name of her Torah portion, the weekly section of the Hebrew Bible read as part of the bat mitzvah ceremony. In response to his questions, Sarah pictures herself standing and looking isolated, shy, and scared in two consecutive panels (8, figures 4.2 and 4.3). In the first panel, drawn as the "present-day" Sarah, she is dressed in an olive-green button-down shirt and wearing a backpack, her hands clasped in front of her, and she fumbles her words in response. The next panel, which follows the first, though on a succeeding row on the page, similarly pictures her alone against a hazy mauve watercolor background; here she portrays herself as an adolescent, and she is wearing what was presumably her bat mitzvah dress. This dress matches, in color, the shirt she wears in the "present," another detail that connects the two temporalities. In this second panel her hands clutch at her waist and her eyes look to the ground as she, once again sheepish, tells the security officer, "We didn't have a DJ. We had a luncheon in my backyard with food and stuff." The shuffling between Sarah's "present" and younger selves in these consecutive panels suggests that the line of questioning about her Jewish identity and history affects the way she perceives herself in the text's present. Although the book opens with her confidently confronting a desire to know the "truth" about Israel, an ambition that she does not at first evidently link to her Jewish identity, the clerk's questions disorient this initial perception. As her Israel trip unfolds, she begins to recognize a connection between this tour and a much more expansive, lifelong journey of coming to terms with her Jewish identity.

Sarah's initial sense of disorientation is also evident from her early experiences at the airport, as she finds herself already submerged in a strange mix of the familiar and the unknown before she has even left the country. While in line for the security check, she depicts two men standing behind her, one of them dressed in traditional Hasidic garb (7).[10] This visual detail assumes prominence three pages later, as she passes another presumably Hasidic man, this one carrying a guitar case (10). In the first panel in which she encounters him, she looks over with a smile on her face while the narration box above her reads, "Heh! A rock n' roll black hat." In the following panels, the man, sweat pouring off his face, transforms from an amusing sight into a cultural progenitor, as he spies an unclaimed bag by his feet and frantically asks passersby if the bag belongs to them. The bag that is nearly invisible to Sarah in her initial encounter with the

4.2 *Sarah Glidden, panel from chapter 1.*
In How to Understand Israel in 60 Days or Less, *p. 8.*
Copyright © Sarah Glidden 2010.

4.3 *Sarah Glidden, panel from chapter 1.*
In How to Understand Israel in 60 Days or Less, *p. 8.*
Copyright © Sarah Glidden 2010.

"rock n' roll black hat" emerges as an important element symbolizing the fear of terrorism that permeates everyday life in the Middle East. Interestingly, it is pictured in all the panels in which she includes the Hasidic man, although its presence changes meaning only in retrospect, after the man panics. As Sarah reflects in a narrative box at the top of the following page, "So maybe even though I'm technically still in Newark, it does feel like we are a little bit 'there' already"

(11). As the language and visuals here reveal, Sarah's journey to Israel is premised from the beginning in a collapsed notion of time and place, a series of reflections that confuse the past and present, the here and there. Even before she has left the United States, she is forced to confront the complexity of a "situation" that she has underestimated: not only is she unlikely to discover the truth, as though it were a latent set of facts waiting to be unearthed, but her journey "there" inevitably forces her to confront the truth about her life "here" or the ways that her North American Jewish identity affects her perception of Israel, its inhabitants, and the region's politics more generally.

Once Sarah has landed in Israel, while she is still at the airport, she undergoes yet another encounter that forces her to confront the various constructions of "us" versus "them" that also challenge problematic distinctions between here versus there. She pulls her luggage off a carousel, and another Hasidic man standing beside her shifts away from her, presumably to avoid contact (13).[11] Soon after, upon being greeted by her cousin, Matt, she asks about whether "they are the same as Hasidim in New York?" As she asks this question, the man who pulled away from her is pictured on his cell phone, although there is no indication what language he is speaking or whether or not he is a native Israeli. The man's ambiguous nationality is an integral component of this encounter, as it deconstructs the easy association that could be made between religion and nationality. His observable affiliation as a religious Jew does not necessarily place him at home in Israel, even though his presence there is not unexpected but rather an ordinary part of everyday life. In an attempt to answer her question, Matt explains, "For the most part Israel is a pretty secular state. The orthodox cause a lot of controversy though." The possibility of Israel as a "secular Jewish state" is one of the paradoxes that Sarah, a secular American Jew, wrestles with throughout the memoir. Like all of the personae pictured in this book, her Jewish identity is not defined in any straightforward manner by her religious beliefs or even necessarily any particular cultural affiliation. Similarly, many Israelis, both Jewish and not Jewish, do not necessarily define themselves by their relationships to religion and Jewish culture, although other people's perceptions of them—as well as, presumably, their own self-perceptions—are inevitably affected by those historical elements. Sarah's many interactions throughout *Israel*, beginning at the airport, consequently reflect the difficulty of placing people into distinct categories based on nationality, religion, or other factors taken outside the context of a person's particular life story.

The Hasid's presence at Ben Gurion Airport in Tel Aviv also collapses Sarah's sense of the distinction between here versus there, not only because the backgrounds throughout these Tel Aviv airport scenes are visibly indistinguishable from the earlier Newark ones but also because her conversation with Matt reminds her of an interaction with a Hasidic man back in her Brooklyn neighborhood. When she first sees all the Hasidic Jews at the airport in Tel Aviv, her narrative thought box reads, "Wow, so many Hasidic Jews! It feels like we're in South Williamsburg!" (13). Her initial experience in Israel disrupts her feeling of being over "there" by reminding her almost immediately of home. The incident with the Hasidic man who avoids touching her as she manages her bag leads Sarah to flashback, on the following page, on an encounter she had in a Hasidic Jewish neighborhood in Brooklyn when she was in her early twenties (14). In a series of seven panels bookended on the page by her conversation in the "present" with Matt at the airport, she pictures a younger self with shorter, dyed-orange hair. Setting the scene, she describes graduating from art school and looking for a place to live in the "bohemian Williamsburg neighborhood." But she takes a wrong turn and ends up on the "ultra-Orthodox" side of town rather than the "ultra-hip" side. When a Hasidic man asks her to come help him turn on his lights because of the Sabbath, Sarah agrees to do so. In a panel picturing the two of them side by side, her hands pressing a switch in a fuse box, she lauds herself, in a thought bubble, for being a "good Samaritan" as the overt exchange between the two is both formal and friendly.[12] In the following panel, as Sarah faces him, he grasps her hand and says "Thank you!" as her thought bubble now expresses confusion at his willingness to touch her. In the third and final panel picturing the two of them together, the man attempts to put his hands down her shirt as she resists. Sarah recalls this incident—her violation by a man who presumably is not "supposed to touch women"—when she comes across the Hasidic man at the airport who purposefully avoids contact with her. Just after her cousin tells her about "the rift between the Hasidic and secular Jews in Israel," but before she pictures this flashback, she explains, "I can't help but feel satisfied as my own prejudices are validated" (14). Recalling this past incident alongside her experience at the airport, Sarah here identifies herself with secular Jews in Israel, if only in opposition to religious Jews. In that sense her impression of being a foreigner in Israel is immediately challenged, as she finds herself joined by others who share in her bias against a particular brand of Jewish identity. Her own prejudice against Jews therefore ironically ties her to other Jews, allowing her to identify with one communal sense of Jewishness only as she completely rejects another.

Throughout the first half or so of *Israel*, Sarah's Jewish identifications are most often pronounced, as in this case, when she distances herself from specific beliefs and behaviors about what it means to identify as Jewish. But, as the text develops, her interactions lead her to recognize how seemingly unwavering identifications and disidentifications break down and complicate as she meets and relates to people as individuals instead of types. Although in this case Sarah's view of the Hasidic man as stereotype remains unchallenged, as her journey continues she is induced to confront many of her other misperceptions, especially how she regards her own Jewish identity and, in turn, how she considers "the situation" in Israel.

"I Still Don't Really Know What that Point of View is Yet"

Sarah's early identification with secular Jews, framed in opposition to her encounters with certain religious ones, connects her to a wider imaginary community, though this affililation is continually limited and challenged. Indeed, her identifications throughout the book—as a woman, an artist, a skeptic of Israeli policies and politics, and the girlfriend of a non-Jew—often lead her to feel disconnected from this same imaginary transnational secular community, as though these other associations preclude her from ever fully identifying with any communal sense of Jewishness. From the beginning of her trip, for example, she is wary of identifying with others in her Birthright group, and she consistently pictures herself as separate or isolated from them.[13] In an early set of images on the tour bus, she draws herself in a panel, once again set apart against a translucent watercolor background. Leaning over the back of her seat with a hopeful look on her face, the rectangular narrative box above her head somewhat humorously reads, "I'm sure you are all interesting and wonderful people!" (16). In the following panel, her head slumps into the back of the seat and her eyebrows furrow as she wordlessly disbelieves her own statement. As this second, silent panel suggests, Sarah is incapable of fully elucidating her sense of alienation from the rest of the group, although it often seems related to her assumption that they are not as politically progressive as she is, and especially that they are not as readily distrustful of Israel and its politics. Her sense of being an outsider thus emerges at disparate moments that are uncharacteristically *not* followed by self-analysis about these encounters, but are accented, instead, by silence and visible isolation. In another instance, after watching a government film about the Golan Heights and consequently declaring the trip "a regional propaganda tour," Sarah is interrupted by an unnamed member of the group, who asks, "You guys thought it was propaganda?" (40). This woman continues the discussion with others watching and participating, while Sarah, looking on angrily, declares, "It wasn't balanced at all!" Instead of engaging in the discussion that now involves numerous Birthright participants, the conversation that Sarah started ends with her wordlessly observing and eventually even turning her head away from the group as the conversation continues (41, figure 4.4). Over the remainder of the page, she breaks from them and approaches one of the tour guides to discuss the film, thereby further distancing herself from the others. In these and similar incidents throughout the narrative, she portrays herself as feeling different, or set apart, from the rest of the Birthright participants, a state that prevents her from being able to imagine that they might be able to enlighten her in her quest for the "truth." This self-enforced isolation is, at least initially, generally portrayed in a positive light—she alone, it seems, is willing to face "the situation" head-on. In this particular way, Sarah is distinguished, at least in the first half of the book, from the other alter egos described in these graphic memoirs exploring Jewish identity, including The Bunch, Goldie, Vanessa, Melissa, and Lauren, who offer primarily disparaging, if comedic, self-portrayals of themselves as outsiders.

4.4 *Sarah Glidden, panel from chapter 2.*
In How to Understand Israel in 60 Days or Less, *p. 41.*
Copyright © Sarah Glidden 2010.

Despite this dissimilarity, like all of the other personae explored, Sarah's sense of self is often tied to her inability to conform, to find a space of belonging. Her singular status from the rest of the group emerges most strikingly through images that picture her by herself, as though at these moments she were traveling around the country free of anyone else's guidance. This isolation can be read as self-imposed: she sets herself apart from the group in order to decide for herself how she feels about Israel, to avoid the biases of others. As the bus travels to the Sea of Galilee, as an example, she is drawn on her own in numerous panels, looking out at the Israeli landscape. In a sequence of such self-portraits, the only panel that features the whole group on the bus still emphasizes her difference, as she alone is awake and looking out the window (48, figure 4.5). The narrative box pictured here reads, "Inside the bus are forty tired people who are much too exhausted to ask more questions." Although this sentence presumably includes her as part of the group, the image conversely singles her out as the lone member who, despite her exhaustion, tries to witness firsthand all she can. The chapter ends with Sarah waking up early at their rest stop near the Sea of Galilee and venturing out as soon as the first light hits (54). The final panel on this page, which brings the chapter to a close, pictures her silently looking out at a colorful landscape. In depicting Sarah alone with the land, this image mirrors most of the panels that feature her by herself throughout the text. In fact, many of the concluding panels of the chapters portray her on her own, as though to emphasize that this particular narrative

4.5 *Sarah Glidden, panel from chapter 2.*
In How to Understand Israel in 60 Days or Less, *p. 48.*
Copyright © Sarah Glidden 2010.

about Israel belongs only to her. These self-portraits suggest that the absence of others is at least partially what enables her to feel like she can experience the region—as symbolized by the land—directly, or without anyone else's ideological filters hindering her own vision. Setting herself apart is her way of striving to "understand" Israel, to see the land without anyone or anything else getting in the way.

Sarah's largely self-imposed sense of being different and isolated from others includes not only those on her trip but also Birthright alumni who have visited the country in the past. In this way, as with her general reflections about her Israel trip, her initial disidentifications are based on conflated senses of time and space. On the final page of the opening chapter, she describes having read "as many firsthand accounts of the Birthright experience as I could online" (29). In many of these accounts, she writes, the alumni described "a real connection" to Israel, and "a few even said they felt like they were 'finally home.'" In contrast to those quoted, in this early reflection Sarah directly contradicts this narrative of Israel as "home" for all Jews. In a series of four panels included at the end of the page, she provides her own very different analogy for her journey so far, recalling not a sense of intimacy, but one of distance. She writes, "To me, it's more like spotting a celebrity in a crowded street. / Someone whose crazy life has been splashed all over the tabloid pages for years. / And there they are . . . / . . . Right in front of you." Underneath the boxes conveying this Israel-as-home narrative, and her own tabloid counternarrative, she pictures herself as a tourist, holding a camera and taking pictures. An Israeli gas station is visible behind her, and the panels shift from this depiction to one of various unnamed people—many or all, presumably, part of her tour group—walking into the station, as well as standing and smoking in the area that surrounds it. The last two panels on the page return to capture Sarah alone, and this time she is holding a camera with the Israeli landscape, as well as an Israeli flag, drawn behind her. The final two images render her once again on her own: separated from the group that is proximately right beside her, she looks out over the landscape with her camera no longer visible. The words *right in front of you*, drawn in a narrative box in the final panel, emphasize her desire to relate to Israel not by way of a metaphoric or imaginary association but rather through a direct engagement; here she gazes directly ahead with her hands deep in her pockets, looking to connect with the land as surface, not as symbol. As the visual and textual unfolding over the course of the page reflects, she has to put down her camera—to dislocate herself from her touristic vantage point—in order to break from the imaginary and/or mediated relationship with Israel that she recognizes in others and from which she consequently tries to distance herself by continually setting herself apart.

Despite this desire to isolate herself, however, Sarah eventually recognizes that to achieve such objectivity is impossible, and that considering the points of view of those around her is a necessary precondition for approaching a more balanced understanding of the world around her. In other words, approaching a so-called unfiltered look at Israel requires not isolation but connection with others. Avoiding the biases of people around her is not enough; she must explore them as well as consider them in relation to her own biases. In this way *Israel* confronts some of the complexities related to composing travel memoirs in general, and especially travel memoirs that relate to journalistic projects. Glidden has explicitly stated that she does not "label myself a 'comics journalist,'" particularly since her work, especially as reflected in *Israel*, is so focused on "the relationship between myself and my subject" (personal communication, July 27, 2014).[14] Nevertheless, she admits, like Miriam Libicki, that her projects have been strongly influenced by those of comics journalist Joe Sacco and, further, that "the definition of journalism is . . . not fixed and the line between what is journalism and what is memoir or travelogue or an essay is a blurry one." In the case of both *Israel* and *jobnik!*, though these comics are not pieces of journalism in the conventional sense, the frameworks of both texts incorporate journalistic objectives and practices, particularly those related to keeping an accurate record of events and attempting to contribute to social justice using this record (Borden 49).[15] Both these memoirs additionally convey how experiences of travel oblige individuals to face themselves outside the very communities, institutions, and environments that generally allow them to construct somewhat consistent notions of identity. The individual at "home" does not have the same need to question herself, as well as her connections to others, as these connections and affiliations are taken for granted in everyday life, where they remain generally uninterrupted. Once an individual has left "home," however, these self-identifications are unsettled. Because an individual's sense of self is based on her relationships to others, the comfort of this sense of self fades, or at least weakens, once she has left the familiarity of daily life or once she is forced to confront other kinds of transitions (like the shift, as we have seen in chapter 3, from childhood to adolescence). In leaving home, then, the individual is in the best position to examine her own always shifting subjectivity, even as the traveling memoirist, and particularly one with some journalistic objectives, is confronted by the task of observing others. *Israel* is a book that examines how these two undertakings inevitably overlap, even though they seem to demand conflicting ambitions. As the text reflects, in order to delve into how the self has been constructed, it is necessary to investigate that self in relation to others, to decenter the self from within that narrative. And in order to record the lives of others with any kind of accuracy, one must recognize the role that individual subjectivity always plays in such chronicling.

In many ways, then, *Israel* is a work focused on bringing to the surface the malleable, fragmented, and biased journalist/memoirist's point of view. In another interview about the book, Glidden discussed how, particularly through her manipulation of the comics form, she tried to make visible what many journalists, in their attempt to remain "objective," often hide about themselves. As she explained, "I had to put mine [my biases] out there for everyone to see. . . . I wanted to show that as a human being, there's more to learning about a complex political situation than just analyzing facts. There are neuroses, prejudices and emotions involved" ("An Interview with Sarah Glidden"). These subjective and internal projections, including several outright fantasy scenes, are visualized in various ways throughout the book. Early on, for instance, Sarah portrays a courtroom that she imagines in her head, and the case under review is called "Birthright is trying to brainwash me vs. Birthright is actually pretty reasonable" (27). She depicts herself as all of the players in this courtroom: she is judge, prosecutor, defense, and members of the jury. Later in the book, about halfway through the trip, Sarah returns to this imaginary courtroom, and it is empty but for the judge and a court officer, both still drawn as versions of herself (107). What she comes to realize over the course of *Israel* is that she cannot fully confront her own biases without engaging with others. Identity is not figured in isolation; instead, it is a response to and reflection of real and imagined communities and interactions as well as the disparate subjectivities, including prejudices, that shape them.

This awareness is exemplified halfway through the book, when Sarah is pushed to associate with other members of her Birthright group and explore the relational contours of her Jewish identity. She realizes then that her lack of communication with others, stemming from her desire to fully reject a conception of Jewishness that feels foreign to her, has hindered her ability to approach a full understanding of the complexity of her identity and, by extension, of "the situation." Sarah's somewhat compulsory interaction with the group occurs roughly a third of the way through the narrative; it leads to her eventual dis-affiliation, a consequent partial affiliation, with her Jewish sense of self. She initially dreads the "bonding activity" scheduled for Friday evening, a night when the group cannot travel because of the Sabbath. The discussion centers on the individual participants' Jewish identities, a topic that immediately elicits a groan from Sarah (66). The members of the group are given a single prompt, "I am a Jew because . . . " and asked to complete the sentence. Despite her initial antipathy, as the participants begin to talk, revealing diversely ambivalent relationships to their Jewish identities, she becomes attentive, allowing, "the discussion starts to get interesting" (67). In a series of four panels that follows her eventual engagement with others, as well as the end of her unquestioned disidentification from the group, she pictures herself, in contrast to her earlier self-portrayals, as one who belongs (figure 4.6). Although there are a total of six panels making up this page, these four can also be read independently because of the ways that they visually mirror one another, each featuring a single speaker as the focal point of the image. In the first two panels Sarah depicts herself listening intently while others around her tell their stories, as though she is finally open to the possibility that other voices can influence her. The Birthright members talking in these first two panels articulate Jewish identities that are complicated, although they echo one another. One tells the group that she was "raised Christian in Ukraine" but eventually converted. Another describes herself as having a mother who converted and growing up in Arkansas, where "we were the only Jews around." These women relay unique backgrounds—they came from, and grew up in, very different communities—but they share important similarities too: a history of conversion and a sense of feeling at "home" as a Jew. The third panel shows Sarah telling her own narrative of her Jewish identity, which is also different from the ones described prior to hers. Having been raised in a self-identified Jewish family, she takes her Jewishness for granted or, as she puts it, primarily understands it as "inherited." In the final panel of the four, a drawing of another participant mirrors Sarah's own image, and his story similarly involves a Jewish identity that has been passed on to him by his family. Despite the resemblance to their backgrounds, however, Sarah and this young man also disclose important differences. The man mentions that he only "started getting to know non-Jews" after he left for college, whereas early in the book Sarah tells the reader that Melissa is one of her only Jewish friends. In addition, unlike the man, Sarah limits her identification as a Jew, emphasizing the fact that her family is culturally Jewish, rather than religious, and that she is interested in only "some" aspects of that cultural Jewishness, including "learning, eating and arguing."

4.6 *Sarah Glidden, four panels from chapter 3. In* How to Understand Israel in 60 Days or Less, *p. 67. Copyright © Sarah Glidden 2010.*

The four depictions here delineate Jewish identities by incorporating visual and verbal details that differentiate each individual from the other, reflecting the plurality of the subjects involved, even as these minutiae bind the stories together and reveal similarities between the individuals pictured. In the first panel Sarah is the only listener visible, whereas various group members surround the speaker in the second panel. In the third and fourth panels, Sarah and her male counterpart face one another, but the scales and shapes of their faces differ. Sarah's face is rounder than the man's oval-shaped one, and her hand, or possibly someone else's, is pictured in her storytelling panel, whereas his is not visible in the following one. Even the backgrounds of the images are shaded in slightly different tints of yellow. These minor differences, which accent what otherwise would be somewhat seamless visual parallels, convey the senses of difference within sameness that emerge from the shared stories of these Birthright participants. Each individual reveals a particular history of identifying as Jewish, and each is affirmed, by participating as part of the group, in her own version of this identification. In the end, through hearing the various ways other people both do and do not affiliate as Jews, Sarah finally feels comfortable both decentering her narrative "I" *and* considering herself part of the group, if only because the dissimilarities between individual members who all consider themselves "Jewish" are finally so conspicuous. At this moment in the text, she maps her Jewish identity, figuring it in relational terms, and consequently recognizes that such an interweaving does not invalidate her own subjectivity, but rather enriches it. Her story becomes one of many deeply personal and individualized narratives of Jewishness.

This group activity compels Sarah to engage more directly with questions about her Jewish identity, a pursuit that leads her to recognize that her notions of what it means to identify as Jewish inevitably affect her views about Israel. Soon after the group discussion, she wonders "how many other people on this trip I've completely misjudged" (71). By facing her presumptions about others, she is finally forced to reexamine her entire misdirected approach to her Israel mission. Instead of a purportedly objective search for the "truth," she must inevitably recognize her own preconceptions about Israel as deeply rooted in the way that she relates—or, more aptly, does not relate—to her Jewish identity. As the chapter closes, she finds herself discussing politics with Nadan, one of the Israeli tour guides. Incredibly, it is only here, for the first time in the book, that she explores outright the intersection between her Jewish identity and her political beliefs in relation to Israel. In two panels she relays the "confusing" contradiction that she suppressed up until then, having chosen to frame "the situation" as a set of events peripheral to her personal history. Now she makes the connection:

I'm Jewish so that means I'm supposed to support Israel no matter what, right?
But according to a lot of people, any support for the Palestinians means that you don't support Israel.

"But you don't live here, so what's the dilemma?"

At the same time, when it comes to politics, I'm left-wing and progressive. And if you're progressive, you're supposed to be anti-Israel . . . Any sympathy with Israel means that you don't support the Palestinians. So see? I'm stuck![16]

(77, figure 4.7)

With this monologue, Sarah finally delineates how her political and cultural identities have been constructed as oppositional. The way she emphasizes her political identity over the course of the text, and downplays her Jewish one, can be understood retrospectively as her effort to stifle the very contradiction she verbalizes in this scene.

In their introduction to *Wrestling with Zion*, one of the books Sarah reads in preparation for her trip, Tony Kushner and Alisa Solomon pinpoint the reasons such conflicting paradigms persevere. As they write, "a dangerous illusion persists that the Jewish-American community speaks with a single voice" (8). In this passage Sarah acknowledges her sense that her desire to criticize Israel is antithetical to the way she is "supposed" to think and behave as a Jew. As such, she suppresses her Jewish identifications and is made uncomfortable by them when they are brought up by others (as in her interaction with El Al security). Paradoxically,

4.7 *Sarah Glidden, two panels from chapter 3. In* How to Understand Israel in 60 Days or Less, *p. 77. Copyright © Sarah Glidden 2010.*

only in her recognition of this seemingly impossible positioning is she compelled to begin to accept, and, consequently, explore her Jewish identity, and to relate the way this sense of being Jewish affects how she has come to view Israel. Kushner and Solomon implore others to examine these very questions that *Israel* brings to the forefront, questions that, they argue, "increasingly—and dangerously—go unexamined." These questions include the following: "What is at the heart of the connection between Israel and American Jews? Why should we have a connection (or not)? What is Israel's role in shaping Jewish-American identities?" Glidden's narrative does not take any such associations for granted. If anything, up until this moment in the text, Sarah attempts to counter the construction of Jews as inevitably affiliated with Israel. Yet her interactions with other self-identified Jews who come from disparate backgrounds drive her to confront the power of her own assumptions. She begins to question why she feels compelled to define herself primarily in terms of her opposition to Israel, without recourse to her Jewish identity, as though a person could not self-identify as Jewish and simultaneously question Israeli policies or even the existence of Israel. In the end the narrative performs, through the experience of a North American Jew encountering Israel firsthand, the ways certain prejudices about identity are transformed and challenged. While a connection exists between Sarah's North American Jewish identity and her views about Israel, that connection is not inevitable; it necessitates continual investigation and self-reflection. As these two panels, set side by side, demonstrate, such self-analysis often unmasks the contradictions and complications that compel the individual to lead a kind of doubled existence. Sarah's face and upper torso, in both images, are pictured similarly but for the way they are angled. Her configuration on the page provides a visual analogy for how competing narratives of the self can be housed within the same body. What Sarah comes to recognize is that both these versions of herself can represent "truth."

Throughout the remainder of the book, instead of continuing to cling to a notion of herself as Jewish outsider, Sarah subsequently claims her Jewish identity by toying with the various ways she disidentifies but ultimately partially identifies with her Jewish self, her dis-affiliations. Her explorations are often reflected in the ways she portrays herself in relation to the people and places she has traveled to observe and "understand." In certain instances she goes so far as to try on the possibility of Israel as Jewish homeland, a configuration she forcefully rejects early on in the narrative when she compares her visit to Israel to spotting a celebrity on the street. In the chapter on Tel Aviv, for example, describing her walk through a crowd of people, she writes that she unexpectedly senses "something strange missing" (82). Comparing this trip to Israel with other journeys she has taken around the world, Sarah asserts that here she feels like "I could easily be one of these people" (83). In a series of images, she pictures herself as a traveler in various other countries, and in each of these depictions she stands out. In Paris, she explains, this happens because of her "complete lack of sophistication." In Guangzhou, China, and Övörkhangai, Mongolia, in contrast, Sarah explains that she cannot possibly fit in because of her physical differences from those around her.

This consideration of Israel as Sarah's "natural" homeland in contrast to these other foreign communities is, upon closer inspection, tenuously laid out. What, for instance, does it mean to "lack sophistication," and would she, based on this superficial assessment, really then stand out in Paris and not on the streets of Tel Aviv? Her overly simplistic identification with Israel and Israelis collapses easily when, at the end of the page, a man asks her in Hebrew what time the parade will start. At that point, she is forced to admit that she cannot easily or automatically belong, however much she wants to. In a single scene, then, Sarah explores, and subsequently deconstructs, the possibility of Israel as homeland through relational configurations. The sequence of the text, presented in neat boxes across and down the page, allows her to play with the ways she can superficially imagine herself in and across different spaces as an Israeli insider, even though such oversimplified external identifications—based primarily in her drawn body—ultimately collapse.

Over the course of the remainder of the book, as in this scene, Sarah's relationship to Israel remains unresolved as she continues to experiment with various ways of relating to Israeli life and politics. Later in the Tel Aviv chapter, she hears a speech detailing the history of Israel's declaration of itself as a state in 1948. The speech ends when the speaker tells the group, "you are here because the state of Israel belongs to the whole Jewish world" (99). Sarah finds herself accepting these words and consequently undergoing an emotional upheaval. "Are these our soldiers?" she wonders soon after, as she passes six young people dressed in uniform waiting, unarmed, by the side of the road. In the following panel, she exclaims to herself, "My God, they're so young." By claiming these soldiers as "our" soldiers, Sarah privileges Israel as her homeland once again, while she visualizes herself in ways that both engage and distance her from this assessment. In the first panel she draws the soldiers, "our" soldiers, without her own presence in the image. In the second panel she introduces her body as part of the illustration, but this time her words separate her from the Israelis by evoking the age differential between them, a difference visually emphasized with bold lettering. Her ability to maneuver herself on the page, as one who simultaneously observes and interacts, or as one who both does and does not belong, is what allows her to examine and challenge, from various angles, the concept of Israel as Jewish homeland. In experimenting with different ways of relating to and dissociating from the country and its citizens, she confronts the very identifications that she has, until now, unquestioningly rejected.

Sarah's persistent examination of her relationship to Israel, even in the face of admonitions from others (as well as from the cynical parts of herself), connects her with the personae represented in the works of the other Jewish American women cartoonists discussed here who seek to rebel against the authoritative voices that attempt to fix or determine the limits and boundaries of their individual senses of what it means to be Jewish. As the narrative progresses, her questions remain explored but unanswered. The common refrain that surfaces as she continues to persistently ask others questions about Israel and its politics is that the issue is "complicated." "We don't have to agree about this," Nadan, the Israeli tour guide, finally tells her after another conversation in which they disagree about politics (203). In this panel she is once again pictured alone, but the thought bubble floating over her head clearly belongs to another individual, reinforcing the way her sense of self is always connected to others. Her hands float in the air, somewhat aimlessly clutched in front of her, suggesting, perhaps, that the very narrative she will create with those hands is what could potentially tie these points of view together.

In response to Nadan's assertion, Sarah recognizes that she, too, has trouble responding to the very questions she came to Israel to answer. Her narrative box several panels later conveys this acknowledgment: "I still don't really know what [my] point of view is yet, and . . . maybe I never will." This conversation, and the realization it engenders, reinforces her position as an outsider, both among North American progressive liberal Jews at large and also among the group of Jews that surround her in Israel. Instead of locating herself on any "side" of the narrative, she stubbornly refuses to assign herself a simple outlook, conjuring for herself, instead, a liminal or dis-affiliatory stance. Such an awareness of her ambivalence could be read as a renunciation of her plan to find the "truth," a way of withdrawing from a difficult state of affairs by refusing to take sides. As Kushner and Solomon point out, one of the gravest "temptations" of those looking at the Middle East at a remove is that they will take the easy way out. This often happens, they explain, in two ways: either they leave the challenge of "rigorous analysis, studied, disciplined comprehension, and finally policy itself to the experts, the diplomats, the soldiers, and the leadership of the nations and would-be nations involved" or they "fall back on instinct, on tribal loyalties of various kinds—ethnic, religious, ideological" (1). *Israel* is a book about resisting such tribal loyalties, including the ones, like Sarah's progressive politics, that are presumably formed in the pursuit of justice and subsequently do not always get questioned. Throughout the text, she comes to realize that these political affiliations exert as much pressure on her to conform as her "inherited" ones. She experiments with various identifications and disidentifications by visualizing them on the page and recognizing, inevitably, that no single image (or narrative) can tell the whole story.

But, all the same, her refusal to take a clear position at the end of the text could be read as a way of giving in to the first of the temptations outlined by Kushner and Solomon—the desire to let others deal with "overwhelming" complications instead of facing them. The book, however, does not end with this conversation, one in which she refuses to offer a particular point of view. Instead, on the following three pages, she records her last night in Israel, her departure, and her arrival in Istanbul, where she has decided to stop over on her way home. In two full pages we witness her undergoing this journey away from Israel without a single word inscribed in any of the panels. These pages potentially reinforce a problematic silence, a refusal to take sides. But, on the final page of the book, she finally breaks that silence. Having arrived at a hostel in Istanbul, she finds a group of young people gathered in a communal space, and they invite her to tea. Surrounded by strangers, they begin to ask her questions: "Where are you coming from?" "Isn't it kind of a war zone?" Sarah, a cup of tea in her hands, begins to answer their questions: "No, no . . . it's not like that at all" (206).

In the final three panels of the book, one of the strangers asks, in a thought bubble that emerges from outside the image, "What's the deal with that place, anyway?" Sarah pictures herself alone in three consecutive panels (figure 4.8). In the first she is sipping her tea comfortably, presumably observing the person asking the question. In the second, her hand at her mouth, she looks confounded, as though unsure where to begin. This second panel represents her continued ambivalence about certain aspects of the situation, her refusal to take sides. The final panel, however, presents the beginning of Sarah's movement beyond this potentially paralyzing ambivalence. Although she still looks somewhat nonplussed, with eyebrows raised, her hands are positioned as if she were ready to launch into a response, and her thought bubble reinforces that gesture, as she begins, "Well- -." This concluding panel of the book visually reflects Sarah's refusal to stop thinking about or discussing "the situation," even in light of the many uncertainties, contradictions, and complications she faces in trying to understand it. The end of her journey to Israel is portrayed, instead, as a mere starting point, the beginning of conversations with others (and in other places), to be continued.

Israel concludes with a much less assured, and reassuring, Sarah than the one who opens the book. She closes her narrative in the midst of searching for the right words and, as her partially open hand reflects, the right images too, symbolizing the way in which her narrative circles back to the problems that opened the book. In fact, as the final illustration demonstrates, the very act of maintaining dialogue, of speaking or writing about a topic in the face of overwhelming uncertainties, is what bolsters Sarah's initial pursuit of knowledge of self and others. Here she begins to tell a story, and it is a story that has been translated from an idea, assembled at a distance, to a reality embedded in countless conflicting realities and histories. Yet, as these final panels indicate, this story's end is really just the beginning of the pursuit for "truth."

4.8 *Sarah Glidden, three panels from end of book. In* How to Understand Israel in 60 Days or Less, *p. 206. Copyright © Sarah Glidden 2010.*

"I Am Still Miriam Libicki"

Towards the end of *Israel*, when Sarah decides that she will not visit the West Bank after her Birthright tour as planned, she admits to her part in leaving having witnessed only one side of the story. Her decision not to go to Ramallah is based on her fear of traveling without a guide, a move she is told is too dangerous for her as a Jew and woman. "What can I say? I'm a big hypocrite, talking about how people need to move past their prejudices and fears but then I can't take a fifteen minute taxi trip without someone holding my hand" (200). Here Sarah recognizes how her outlook has been limited by the choices she has made, from her initial decision to go on Birthright to her choice not to take a taxi into the West Bank once the formal trip is over. But *Israel* is ultimately a testament to the relevance and importance of such one-sided narratives. The book is about the transformation of Sarah's subjectivity in the context of a small and distorted glimpse of Israel's history, geography, and culture. She shows in this case an awareness of the significance of her missed opportunity to visit the Palestinian territories, which are discussed often throughout the book, though always from a distance. Instead of silencing her narrative in light of such flagrant omissions, she calls the reader's attention to them, thereby highlighting her travel experience as one of many possible journeys and pointing to the importance of continued research, dialogue, and testimony from a variety of perspectives, even when those perspectives are limited.

Libicki similarly frames her series, which tracks her time in the Israeli army, as invested in recording her very narrow experience of what, as a North American–born Israeli soldier, was once unfamiliar to her. In a four-page comics pamphlet that she titles *"jobnik* manifesto" and includes with sales of her *jobnik!* comics, she calls her work "subjective & personal" and "as honest as possible" (3). This outlook, while part of her mission, also at times makes her feel "guilty that my comics don't try to go beyond my own experience" ("A Conversation" 244). In each case, by stressing the limited scope of their projects and foregrounding their individual, inevitably limited, perspectives, Glidden and Libicki attempt to distance themselves from the journalistic enterprise, at least in the conventional way such an endeavor might be framed and defined.

Despite these qualifications, however, both books are clearly invested in the task of accounting for outlooks and subjectivities that are not always readily perceptible and that bind the individual to other people's experiences and viewpoints. Through the stories they tell, and the ways they tell these stories, these cartoonists attempt to make visible the limitations and possibilities intrinsic in all narratives based on first-person reportage. This is an undertaking for which graphic narratives are especially suited. As Libicki notes of hearing Joe Sacco talk about the biased point of view in his own comics, "he said one of the best things about being a comic artist and not a reporter is that he didn't have the specter of 'balance' hanging over his work. He felt it was important to get in with one group of people, and tell their story, and tell what you see, as best as possible" ("A Conversation" 244).[17] This conspicuous awareness of the complexities of documenting what one sees through hand-drawn images and words characterizes one of the distinctive qualities of autobiographical comics in general. As a prime example, the body of a cartoonist, drawn repeatedly in autobiographical comics, emerges quite clearly as a depiction filtered through that particular artist's point of view. The drawn body alters, however subtly in some cases and dramatically in others, with each rendering—a shift that, though it may be happening, for example, to the "I" of a prose narrative, is simply not as obvious. This visual subjectivity extends to all that is drawn "from life." As Sacco writes in his preface to *Journalism*, a 2013 collection of his comics reportage, "Drawings are interpretive even when they are slavish renditions of photographs, which are generally perceived to capture a real moment literally. But there is nothing *literal* about a drawing" (xi). The journalistic genre's claims to objectivity and factuality, however qualified and cosmetic those claims, are not as easily proffered in comics as they are in prose or photography. In other words, nonfictional comics, however they are categorized, can make more blatant and visible the subjectivity that inevitably drives every reporting impulse—specifically the desire to record what one sees in an unbiased manner—and that shapes and colors its subsequent rendering and reception.

While Libicki's work is thus focused, like Glidden's, on the particular ways Miriam reflects on and explores her identity over the course of the narrative, and how such reflections connect her with larger questions about Israeli life and politics, in *jobnik!* Miriam begins with an overt recognition that she is already a subject in limbo and that, in a sense, she always has been and likely will continue to be.[18] The publication history of the ongoing series reflects this simultaneous sense of dislocation and possibility. Originally published as a serial comic, the earliest issue of *jobnik!* came out in 2003. The ten issues published so far recount Miriam's time in the army in the "present" of the narrative, but they also offer diversions from the main story that reference the past.[19] The first six issues have since been compiled into a thin, single book of about 10 inches by 6 1/2 inches, published in 2008 with a prelude, a glossary of terms, and author's notes included. Individual issues are still forthcoming, and Libicki has promised that the series will most likely account for her experiences "from enlistment to discharge" (personal communication, August 13, 2014). This open-ended publication history reflects a sense of such autobiographical storytelling as both boundless and fitful, subject to forces set apart from the narrative plot in itself.

Based in large part on her journals from the time, as well as letters and e-mails, *jobnik!* is a series that is also invested, like *Israel*, in preserving experiences that took place in real life by retelling them. It opens with Miriam already immersed in army life. Unlike the subsequent individual issues (or chapters) of the comic series, which generally limit the narrative voice holding the story together and instead allow the events, for the most part, to speak for themselves, the four-page prelude is composed as a journal entry. With the date, "Monday 11 September 2000," neatly scrawled at the top, the images on this opening page situate Miriam at rest in various beds, as though to convey her emotional and physical displacement from the narrative's very opening (4).[20] Like the series as a whole, the images are carefully drawn and shaded in pencil. This format suggests intimacy and simplicity—as though the reader is encountering a person's private sketchbook, not intended to be shown to an audience. But the exhaustive detail apparent in the penciling and the unique architecture of each page, which does not generally follow a particular pattern, also convey the careful construction that has gone into the composition of the work. At the bottom of this first prelude page, snapshots depicting Miriam engaged in sexual acts are arranged, scattered across a dark surface. The drawings of photographs included here suggest a contrast similar to that of the penciling: the intimacy illustrated in the photographs makes looking at them feel like a violation, as though the reader has "caught" Miriam in the midst of these private acts. However, because the images are drawn as photographs, with dates carefully documented at the bottom of each drawn Polaroid, there is also the possibility that these confessions were calculated from the start, intended to be shared with others.

As with *Israel*, a muddled sense of time and space carries through *jobnik!*, reflecting in this case how the daily routines of army life, including especially its inevitable proximity to violence, have impaired the persona's ability to "find" herself. Indeed, even though a date is so evidently attributed to the opening of the narrative, various other dates, written on the drawn photographs, preempt any linear unfolding of the story line on this opening page and predict the often confused ways time and space will be portrayed. The narrator here is pictured in beds and rooms that all look somewhat different, but there is also the potential that these are three varying perspectives of the same space. Additionally, the opening lines of the prelude, sprawled across the page in a series of short but neat handwritten fragments, complicate the time frame by beginning in the middle of the story line. "It's been over a year since I've written in this," the first line reads. "I am still Miriam Libicki, I am a citizen of the United States and Israel, and a soldier in the Israel Defense Force" (4). These words contextualize the comics that make up *jobnik!* and anticipate a narrative that will trace Miriam's subjectivity in light of the three chief markers of her identity: her name (and, by extension, the self she attempts to portray on the page), her nationalities, and her decision to enlist in the Israeli military. By including the adverb *still* in this introductory sentence, Miriam reveals how, at the moment she is writing in her journal, her identity is already open to potential disruptions and transformations. The story becomes one, oddly enough, of attempting to track her own dislocations.

From its opening, the comic series accordingly privileges Miriam's search for identity over and above any other potential journeys to be imparted over the course of the narrative. Even if the book provides a glimpse at what is generally inaccessible territory—that is, the day-to-day life of an Israeli soldier—it is always clearly through the eyes of a somewhat naive young woman as she comes of age. The preface to the book nevertheless anticipates readings of the narrative as cultural translation by including Hebrew words transliterated into English as well as the definitions of these words and phrases included at the bottom of the pages. These translations situate Miriam as between cultures over the course of her time in the army. As a woman who was born and raised in America but is a dual citizen living in Israel at the time the narrative takes place, she positions herself not as visitor or even tourist. Instead, she presents herself as someone embedded in Israeli life and culture, even if she is unable to ever fully assimilate.

As the narrative reflects from its outset, Miriam's identity is premised in a desire to connect with others. Her sense of herself as an outsider is, along these lines, based in her failure to establish meaningful relationships, especially with the men around her. This alienated sense of self contrasts with her self-proclaimed allegiance to Israel, a configuration based in a concept of Israel as metaphorical homeland to all Jews. Throughout the comics, these personal and political narratives fade in and out. Only in a flashback mosaic included on a page in issue 3, for example, does Miriam begin to fully express her complex relationship to the

Israeli state—a plotline that seems particularly crucial given that it drove her to enlist in the army in the first place. This final page of the issue is presented just after Miriam portrays herself at a military gathering on the fifth anniversary of Itzhak Rabin's assassination. The commemoration is depicted in a singular, full-page spread featuring a female soldier singing to a group of soldiers, the Israeli flag waving beside her as the crowd stands at attention (72). Libicki's *jobnik!* comics in general can be described as carefully focused on people's bodies, particularly the ways these bodies, through their stances and facial expressions in particular, inhabit the spaces around them. In this image, the soldiers all stand generally attentive, and the details of their hairstyles and faces, when visible, are the central features that distinguish them. The singer's eyes are closed, but her raised eyebrows and solemn posture reflect the strong emotions behind her words, which tie all the individuals in the scene together.

In contrast to this tailored, full-page image, in which the soldiers all seem, for the most part, united, a coherent group experiencing or at least attending to the emotions conveyed by that central figure, the flashback is conveyed in fragments, a page outline that reflects the splintering of Miriam's individual, subjective experience (73, figure 4.9). The page is broken up into ten differently sized, curved panels that fit together like puzzle pieces, though with small white gaps of space dividing each of them. At the top left corner of the page, in a series of five smaller panels, the Israeli landscape is pictured as it pans out from another line of soldiers commemorating Rabin's death on a local Israeli army base (as Miriam notes, the first commemoration she observed in Israel) to the Israeli state as situated within the Middle East and, finally, to Israel as a small dot on the earth drawn as a globe.

The bottom half of the page extends outward with larger panels featuring individuals caught in particular moments of time, a scope and scale that contrasts with the topographical illustrations connected above it. We see a series of close-up images labeled by year (from left to right, 2000, 1998, 1995, 1998, 1998), and each traces a moment in time that in some way informs Miriam's relationship to those places pictured at the top of the page. These bottom panels almost all feature Miriam, as though to emphasize how her perspective has shifted over time with regard to these different spaces and perspectives. For example, in a panel that connects this flashback montage with the previous page, as it is labeled "2000," Miriam stands at attention with a group of soldiers behind her. She observes: "I don't belong *in* Israel as much as I belong to Israel. Every year on rabin's yahrzeit I know it's not even a choice."[21] This narrative of Israel as home is written into an illustration that transforms the previous depiction of the group commemoration into a representation where she is featured as protagonist, standing front and center with a few other soldiers pictured around her. Yet, read alongside the other close-up images on the page, which present her, or others, in regular clothes and engaged in more intimate conversations and activities, it still suggests a disconnection from the commemoration scene around her. This visual sense of isolation is ironically located in the space of her verbalized ultimate connection, her declaration of belonging. In addition, the framing of Israel as Miriam's homeland is complicated by her assessment of herself not as belonging "in" Israel, but rather belonging "to" Israel. By emphasizing a distinction between the two, the words, in addition to the images, dispel the certainty that one's appointed home is the place where one necessarily comes to feel at home.

The related close-up images at the bottom of the page, each tracking different moments that have informed Miriam's "present"-day subjectivity at the commemoration ceremony, similarly unsettle any simple notion of belonging. For example, in a panel depicting her mother standing alone at prayer, she narrates her love of Rabin—a connection that ostensibly binds Miriam, too, to this Israeli political figure and all that he represents. As she relates of her mother, "She was afraid for him, for what he was trying to do" (73). In linking the story of her own journey to Israel with her mother's love of Rabin and, by extension, Israel, Miriam situates herself as being tied to the country and its politics through a kind of inheritance. But, by leaving herself out of the image, she also conveys a distance between herself and her mother, carrier of this inheritance. That gap is reinforced by her mother's conservative dress, which contrasts with her own. Indeed, in chapter 5 of the story, she points to her inability to dress conservatively as something that sets her apart from others in her religious community. Although she implicates her mother in this problem of fitting in, admitting that "neither my mother nor i could ever get the hang of dressing me right," the depictions of her mother emphasize that the clothing issue belongs to Miriam alone (100). While Miriam's clothing often seems to cling to her, revealing the shape and outline of her body, her mother's conservative dress, in this prayer image as in other illustrations of her in the series, conceals her form. The illustration of her mother at prayer thus reflects Miriam's simultaneous sense of connection to and distance from someone who largely influences her attachment to Israel as a metaphorical homeland. This figurative and inherited connection, translated on the page through a web of disjointed though related images, figures here as unsettled and precarious.

4.9   Miriam Libicki, final page from chapter 3. In jobnik!, p. 73. Copyright © Miriam Libicki.

Through this network of images, Miriam's personal history is visualized as driven largely by forces outside herself even as these forces link back, in very particular ways, to her individual story. The book is invested, from its outset, in this reciprocal exchange. The day-to-day challenges that surface in Miriam's dealings with other individuals in the army often mirror a more general sense of displacement that she experiences from the spaces around her, including her adopted country. For example, as a voluntary soldier in what is a recognizably male-dominated environment, Miriam is subject to a series of humiliations that are often based on her interactions with men. From the beginning of her time in the army, she is labeled an outsider by the male psychologist who interviews her. She depicts this event on the second page of the prologue (5, figure 4.10). The military officer lists her so-called abnormalities: "Overly emotional, disconnected from reality, possessed of anxieties (especially social), unable to form interpersonal bonds, sexually conflicted . . . " The page in which Miriam illustrates this diagnosis is split in two. The bottom shows her sitting silently, arms folded, across a desk from the officer as she is given her diagnosis and asked, "Sure you haven't considered suicide a *little* bit?" The word bubbles that stem from this officer bleed onto the top of the page, which depicts various ink blots, arranged much like the Polaroid photographs in the opening to the prelude. Miriam is pictured alone in the bottom right corner of this part of the page, drawing on a piece of paper. Her figure is out of scale not only with the officer's word bubbles, which press in her direction, but also with the ink blots that loom in her midst, overwhelming her sense of self. It is unclear whether this depiction is meant to reflect her participation in the mental evaluation process or is instead a solitary moment from the same time period in which she is drawing on her own, perhaps as a means of coping or reflecting. But, in any case, this self-portrait links Miriam's abnormal diagnosis, and her isolation more generally, with her artistic personality. Her art potentially offers her the key to independence, to creating her own self-identifications, though it also links to the narrative of difference that comes to shape her sense of self throughout her time in the army. While she rarely seems to utilize art as a means of agency in the "present" as it is recorded in the issues of *jobnik!* that have been published so far, as reflected by this image, the potential is always there, latent. In fact, in addition to the prologue, depicted as a journal entry, each story line opens with a date scrawled at the top corner of the page. This formal detail links the unfolding narrative to the diary that shaped it, hinting at the possibility for self-representation exposed in this specific

4.10 Miriam Libicki, third page from the prologue. In jobnik!, p. 5. Copyright © Miriam Libicki.

image and also connecting that possibility to the eventual project of composing the autobiographical *jobnik!* series itself.

As the story unfolds, the reader learns that because of these strongly gendered classifications of Miriam's mental state, as well as her limited Hebrew speaking skills, she is prevented from being assigned a high rank in the army and is instead given the "extremely unskilled job of secretary of the infirmary" (6). In a sense, it is, ironically, her very desire to volunteer in the army—an action that symbolizes her unquestioning belief in Israel as Jewish homeland—that immediately casts her as outsider. In an interview about *jobnik!* and her time in the army, Libicki conveyed this paradox. As she explained, "I . . . think it was a bit of the catch-22: it's sane to pretend you're insane in order to get out of military service, but if you are volunteering for army service, odds are that you are insane" ("A Conversation" 248). As a woman and an American, Miriam is not expected to want to participate in what so many others around her view as an inescapable duty. Her decision to join the army and her notion of this act as compulsory, as part of her destiny, marks her, indelibly, as an outsider.

Miriam's daily presence in the army consequently comes to stand for a submissiveness and naïveté that native-born Israeli soldiers, as they are depicted in *jobnik!*, lack. In another image presented early on in the narrative, about halfway through the first issue, Miriam's difference from others is visualized on another carefully rendered, fragmented page that stylistically reflects disparate points of view as they coalesce in a moment of time. The image depicts her going about her daily work, which involves carrying an oversized bag of documents. She has been assigned to burn these because the base cannot afford a shredder—a minor detail that nevertheless emphasizes her expendability (16, figure 4.11). In contrast to her trivialized presence, mirrored by the formless bag of trash hanging limply behind her, she walks in earnest, her eyes downcast and two arms strongly gripping behind her. A series of small panels pictured underneath her form reflect various Israeli soldiers conversing casually with one another, even as she silently passes by on the page. The others pictured in these small, rectangular panels banter or flirt and tease each other, their casual and animate presences contrasting with Miriam's downcast, serious, and lonely presence. This superimposed illustration captures both the distance and proximity between Miriam and these soldiers, brought together on this army base. For the Israelis, being in the army is an inevitable fact of life. Their identities as soldiers are, by necessity, integrated into their identities as young people socializing with one another. For Miriam, who grew up in Ohio, being in

"But you don't live here, so what's the dilemma?"

4.11 *Miriam Libicki, half a page from chapter 1. In* jobnik!, *p. 16. Copyright © Miriam Libicki.*

the Israeli army is a significant *act*. It represents a sacrifice she has chosen to make, however much she wants to frame that decision as predetermined.

Miriam's unquestioning affiliation to Israel and the Israeli army therefore actually distances her from those around her. Her blind faith gets translated by others as a kind of willful obedience. This submissiveness extends not only to the tasks she takes on as a soldier, but also to the ways she interacts with men, as she is repeatedly portrayed as sexually submissive and naive. In addition, the first few issues in the series in particular establish a correlation between Miriam's loss of sexual innocence and her gradual introduction to political violence and terror as a part of daily life. These two areas of army life inevitably intersect and reinforce Miriam's sense of dislocation, as her so-called private life gets continually intruded upon by the political terrors around her.

In the second chapter, for example, Miriam records her budding relationship with a fellow soldier, Shahar. This is the first of many confusing relationships with men in the army. Their initial friendship is slow moving. In a series of panels depicted on two adjoining pages and reminiscent of Lauren's movie date in *Girl Stories*, the couple is pictured, somewhat innocently, sharing a bus ride together (28–29). Miriam is often drawn in *jobnik!* sitting on the bus as she rides to and from her army base. These illustrations almost always feature a series of words on the page reflecting radio broadcasts that transmit current events, and especially stories of violence in and around Israel. In these two pages, however, only a conversation between the couple fills the spaces between them, and the last four panels depict the two of them in total silence (29, figure 4.12). The images focus, instead, on the couple's bodies as they weave through sleep and consciousness, eventually collapsing together between the two seats. Miriam's large, expressive eyes in the first and final panels here additionally hint at the emotional upheaval—her excitement, perhaps, or anticipation—that remains otherwise undisclosed. Thus her budding romantic relationship is portrayed, in this initial encounter, as separate from her awareness of Israeli political life or as powerful enough to detach her from it, at least temporarily.

This disconnect does not, however, last. Several pages later the couple is pictured once again on the bus together. This time, the panel that depicts them is crowded in by words emerging from a news broadcast discussing army policy (31, figure 4.13). In this illustration the couple appears divided from one another. The radio broadcast takes up a large part of the image, and Miriam looks out the window gloomily as Shahar holds onto headphones that presumably block him from the sound of the broadcast as well as from her. The distance between the two is enhanced in the following scene, which recounts Shahar's declaration that "I really don't think I can have a girlfriend right now," followed by a sexual advance that depicts Miriam being groped by him, his head invisible to the reader, as she looks wide-eyed up at the sky (33). Miriam's loss of sexual innocence unravels alongside her slow but steady reintroduction into political turmoil, and its attendant violence, as an unavoidable part of daily life. Her isolated configuration in the depiction of her sexual encounter with Shahar, which pictures her as detached from the event, is representative of the many disempowering sexual and political experiences that she undergoes throughout the narrative. She seems to have as much of an inability to control her interpersonal relationships as she does the bloodshed occurring around her.

"But you don't live here, so what's the dilemma?"

4.12 *Miriam Libicki, four panels in chapter 2. In* jobnik!, *p. 29. Copyright © Miriam Libicki.*

Over time, then, as in this chapter's story line, Miriam's gradual dissociation from the daily military violence that surrounds her runs parallel to a passivity in relation to her sexual interactions. This disengagement is figured, throughout *jobnik!*, in images that convey her increasing confusion and defeat in relation to the spaces around her. In a powerful full-page drawing positioned toward the end of this second chapter, Miriam looks up at a sky full of stars and military jets (45, figure 4.14).[22] She is illustrated as a tiny and faceless figure at the bottom of

4.13 *Miriam Libicki, panel in chapter 2 In* jobnik!, *p. 31. Copyright © Miriam Libicki.*

the page as the brightness overwhelms her and she thinks to herself, "Dear god, where am I?" For Miriam, the sense of displacement she experiences in relation to her peers, locally, extends to her global surroundings. Her inability to feel at home among other Israeli soldiers is mirrored in her discomfort as witness to daily political life and violence in Israel. The physical disorientation illustrated in this image mirrors the many other disorientations hinted at over the course of the series, which she experiences in relation to her identities as a woman, an American, an Israeli, a soldier, and a religious Jew, as much as the very narrative of Israel as Jewish homeland that has transported her across the globe. While, at times, she might attempt to highlight this tie to Israel as inherited, her powerfully visualized sense of displacement throughout *jobnik!* continually unsettles that presumed automatic connection.

"I'm Mostly an Outsider Who Can't Really Understand"

Miriam's dislocations throughout *jobnik!* recall Sarah's confused sense of time and place in *Israel*, as each persona's account demonstrates the wide gap between her ideas about Israel and the realities she faces over the course of her time there. In a sense *jobnik!* can be read as a narrative that maps a journey counter to what is presented in *Israel*. Miriam's consideration of herself as

4.14 *Miriam Libicki, page in chapter 2.* In jobnik!, *p. 45. Copyright © Miriam Libicki.*

innately belonging to Israel contrasts strongly with Sarah's sense, especially at the beginning of *Israel*, that, just because she is a Jew, she does not necessarily identify with Israel or feel as if she belongs there. Sarah thus opens with a strong disidentification with being Jewish and with what she initially views as a subsequent disidentification with Israel. By the end of her narrative, she recognizes the inaccuracy of her unquestioned connection between the two. In contrast, Miriam presumes an Israeli affiliation from the beginning of her comic series, an association related to her (and her mother's) religious beliefs and, consequently, to her Jewish roots.

Yet, unlike Sarah, over the course of the narrative Miriam never voices (at least thus far in the series) a revelation regarding the ways that her identifications do not match up in reality. Even though her daily experiences in the army reflect her isolation, she does not overtly question her presumed connection, and obligation, to the country. This lack of self-consciousness about the meaning behind her sense of alienation is, in part, a function of the way *jobnik!* is presented. As a memoir connected, through dated sections, to a real diary, the series tracks the narrator's subjectivity in the "present" of her time in the army. In contrast, written as a travelogue, *Israel* is presumably a book composed after Sarah returns from her trip and assesses the meanings behind her journey. In each case the framework of the text reinforces the way the alter ego's subjectivity undergoes its transformations. For Miriam, the shift in her personal point of view is presented as a slow process that deepens over the course of several years of daily life in the army, even if in reality the series is being composed by a cartoonist looking back in time; for Sarah, her transforming subjectivity is something that can be portrayed as playing out over her ten-day trip, but also bleeding outside of that particular time frame. The structures of both texts, then, however disparate, reinforce the idea that the formation of a person's subjectivity is a lifelong process. While that process is often easier to scrutinize during the transitional phases of an individual's life, its conversions and effects can never be seamlessly pinned down.

Even though the transformation of Miriam's viewpoint is never made explicit in the ten issues of *jobnik!* that have been published so far, Miriam Libicki has written several visual autobiographical essays that calculatedly explore the very questions that her persona avoids explicitly asking herself throughout the series. As stated, Libicki started work on *jobnik!* as early as 2003, though her time in the army took place from August 2000 to May 2002. The autobiographical essays she has written, which she has described as "reveries," overlap, in time, with her composition of the comic series (personal communication, August 13, 2014). In a sense these shorter pieces may be considered countertexts or texts that potentially intersect with, broaden, and overtly challenge some of the issues of identity laid out in *jobnik!*

In 2005 Libicki published the short visual essay, *Towards a Hot Jew: The Israeli Soldier as Fetish Object*; in 2006, she published the travelogue *Ceasefire*, about the second war in Lebanon; in 2008, she published the essay, *Fierce Ease*, subtitled *Portraits of Israel*; and, most recently, in 2012, she published *Strangers,* an essay about Israel composed "long-distance."[23] In each of these works Miriam presents herself more certainly in the role of journalist, as she seeks to ask, sort out, and visualize some of the very questions left unanswered in *jobnik!* without foregrounding her own presence. Yet these corollary texts also proffer continued insights into Libicki's ever changing subjectivity, a limited but pronounced self-consciousness that is perhaps what differentiates these works from *jobnik!* over and above anything else and ultimately frames them as conjuring a dis-affiliatory outlook.

The cover of *Towards a Hot Jew,* a twelve-page-long pamphlet sketched in pencil and sized at about 8 1/2 by 11 inches, pictures seven Israeli soldiers lined up in uniform, their bodies and clothing drawn in watercolors against a white background. The people represented present as male and female, and they encompass the various ethnicities that, Libicki writes, in part explains why members of the Israeli army are so often fetishized. "Israeli Jews are more multiethnic than North American Jews, ingathering the exiles from Europe, North Africa, Ethiopia, the former Soviet Union, India, etc.," she writes. "Being more varied, they are more exotic and less like the kids you grew up with."[24] With these words, Libicki presumes her reader (and fetishizer) to be a North American Jew. The aim of her essay is to convey—as well as deconstruct—the stereotypical visions that North American Jews have presumably constructed about Israeli soldiers. From its onset, then, this picture essay is an exploration of an idea about Israel and its people that is too often left unarticulated. It investigates the metaphorical depiction of Israel as homeland by considering one of many possible threads that emerges from such an ideational outlook. In this way the essay takes up one of the many tacit associations between North Americans and Israelis as they are proposed in *jobnik!*

On each page of this essay, beside narrative text conveying Libicki's assessment of an Israeli soldier stereotype, a North American Jew stereotype, or quotes from often academic sources related to the topic, Libicki includes images of Israeli soldiers in various settings.[25] As she explained in a 2012 interview, these are mostly drawings of photographs that she took over the course of her time in the army and on "research trips" afterward ("Miriam Libicki Talks Comics"). In one image a couple in uniform kisses as the male soldier carries a duffel bag over his arm, an M-16 slung across his other shoulder. In another, a young soldier in uniform listens to music on earphones while staring at a cell phone clasped in her hand (figure 4.15). These early scenes humanize the soldiers, isolating their experiences and capturing, however partially, their subjectivities. Nevertheless, several portrayals at the end of the essay picture Israeli soldiers in relation to Palestinian civilians, and these images disorient readings of the earlier, innocent ones. On these final three pages, set beside civilians, the soldiers loom large. These images emphasize their prowess in relation to the powerless, including a blindfolded man, a child, and several unarmed men and women. In one full-page illustration, a young boy stands with a silhouette of an older woman behind him, her head covered in a hijab and her face tilted downward and hence not visible. He holds his backpack open as one soldier looms over him with a large gun and another crouches in front of him, searching the bag (figure 4.16). The young boy and crouching soldier eye each other, the end of the gun hanging threateningly between them. As in all the visual depictions in *Towards a Hot Jew,* there are no speech or thought bubbles. The reader must figure out what the individuals are thinking or feeling based mainly on these visual cues as well as the ways that the drawing interacts with the words that surround it. In this illustration the words ironically penciled in at the top of the page read, "By the quirks of history, propaganda, and the voyeuristic urge, we have arrived at the New Jew: an adorable oppressor for every persuasion." The scorching words included reinforce the sense of violence, inequity, and injustice conveyed in the illustration, collapsing any potential misreading of silence as compliance.

Taken as a whole, Libicki's essay is interested in the disparate ways various communities of Jews have come to be represented, particularly in the eyes of other Jews. She explores stereotypes of North American Jews and how they differ from and influence the ways Israeli soldiers are stereotyped as well. By revealing that each group of people constructs or is constructed by others, the essay explores the link between Israeli and North American Jews without presuming an automatic or inherited connection. In fact, if anything, in *Towards a Hot Jew* Libicki responds to the very assumptions Miriam takes for granted throughout *jobnik!* revealing their bases in historical movements and discussions. The image of the strong or "muscular" Jew, for example, is linked to contemporary figurations of Israeli

"The Jewish woman is represented through her body, which is at once exceptionally passive and highly adorned. She simultaneously lacks sexual desire ... and lavishes attention on beautifying herself." (Riv-Ellen Prell)

The term Jewish American Princess ("JAP") gained currency in the '70s. I don't know if there's a Canadian equivalent.

a joke:
"The scene is in bed.
He: can I do anything?
She: sure, as long as you don't touch my hair." (ibid)

4.15 Miriam Libicki, page in "Towards a Hot Jew," n.p. Copyright © Miriam Libicki.

By the quirks of history, propaganda, and the voyeuristic urge, we have arrived at the New Jew: an adorable oppressor for every persuasion.

4.16 Miriam Libicki, page in "Towards a Hot Jew," n.p. Copyright © Miriam Libicki.

military aggression and tactical "success." In contrast, as she notes, North American Jews are often depicted in American media as emasculated (the men) and passive though excessive (the women). By reading stereotypes of American and Israeli Jews in dialogue with one another, and with respect to Israeli-Palestinian interactions, Libicki shows the very real and violent implications and ramifications of underexplored Jewish identifications.

The essay ends by invoking Israel as the "ultimate post-colonial/neo-colonial villain," and, as we have seen, the images included here, involving representations of Israeli soldiers interacting with Palestinians, reinforce this conception. These soldiers are pictured in positions of power, illustrations that dispel whatever sense of seclusion, and consequent blamelessness, the earlier images conveyed. Taken in conjunction with the complex exchange of how representations of and notions about North American Jews and Israelis have unfolded over time, the essay links together disparate regions as well as groups of people to reflect on the way in which the story, the "truth," is always bigger than any single representation of it. In other words, introducing the Israeli soldier as a potential villain, rather than a definite victim, establishes a counternarrative, or counter-representation, to the "obsession with victimhood" that Beinart's young college students find so alienating. But this counter-representation is also presented here as part of a larger, more complex story that implicates even those outside the picture—and in this case, North American Jews, including Libicki herself. Just as ties between different groups of people cannot be automatically assumed, absolute rejections of those connections are equally problematic and damaging.

Published two years later, *Fierce Ease* is composed of watercolor drawings in which Libicki continues to scrutinize the relationship between North American Jews and Israelis, reflecting, once again, her dis-affiliation from the notion of Israel as Jewish homeland. This essay, however, is based in the project of recording the voices of Israelis, rather than examining static depictions of what Israelis look like to North Americans. By exploring the mind-set of various people who live in Israel, Libicki presents herself, in *Fierce Ease,* as an outsider looking into a world now foreign to her. Although her narrative ties the many individual stories of Israelis together, the essay is presented, first and foremost, not as a way of "understanding" Israel, but rather as a way of looking at the actuality of the lives lived there, of listening to, and recording, individual stories. Like Joe Sacco, Libicki here allows the words of the people she interviews to speak for themselves, although she is clearly the one who frames this narrative of Israeli life and politics.

The people Libicki interviews are all revealed to have some kind of associa-tion with her, and she makes these affiliations clear as she introduces them. For example, her first interview is with Ronnen, "a good friend" from when she was an Israeli citizen. Another interviewee is "Lisa, a Canadian-Israeli reporter and a newer friend." In each case, she draws on her connections with others in order to contextualize her narrative, which is framed more generally as an attempt to figure out what has changed since she was living in Israel from 1998–2002. "Are things much worse here now than they were two years ago?" she asks. She struc-tures her journalistic mission in a way that relates to her personally; the time frame is based on the last time she lived in Israel, and in that way her essay is meant to help fill in her own personal gaps. The project, in more general terms, is invested in what it means to transform from one reporting on Israel from the inside to one reporting from the outside. A visiting reporter, Libicki's essay seems to argue, is not allowed to form definitive conclusions on anything but her own relationship to the story. The images depicting Israelis in *Fierce Ease* are conse-quently accompanied by oversized speech bubbles that display the words of the person pictured, with little text from the narrator or outside sources included in the images. Unlike in *Towards a Hot Jew,* in this later essay Libicki allows Israelis to speak for themselves.

Despite her increased attention to what Israelis have to say, in *Fierce Ease* Libicki continues to present herself as both an insider and outsider Israeli, as she inevitably does in all of her works, however implicitly. Even as she confronts the sense Israelis have that the climate of the country is much worse than the last time she visited, that "everyone just feels hopeless," she also recognizes the limitations of her own reflections on what is happening. As she explains of the transforma-tion since her last visit, in which she witnessed and wrote about the second war in Lebanon: "During the war, all eyes were upon Israel as it apparently plunged the Middle East into the beginnings of World War III, but visiting, life here seemed its usual abnormal-normal. In the meantime, the world has moved on as if the small summer war never happened, while Israeli society is quaking from the impact." Libicki here implicates herself as part of the "world" that has "moved on" and for-gotten about Israel, even as she has returned as a way to confront this ignorance. Her early affiliation with Israel is what makes this narrative possible—since she is interviewing people she met through her time in the army—although it is also what highlights the fact that she never "belonged" to or in Israel in the first place. As Libicki states, at the very end of the essay, "The only conclusion I have is that

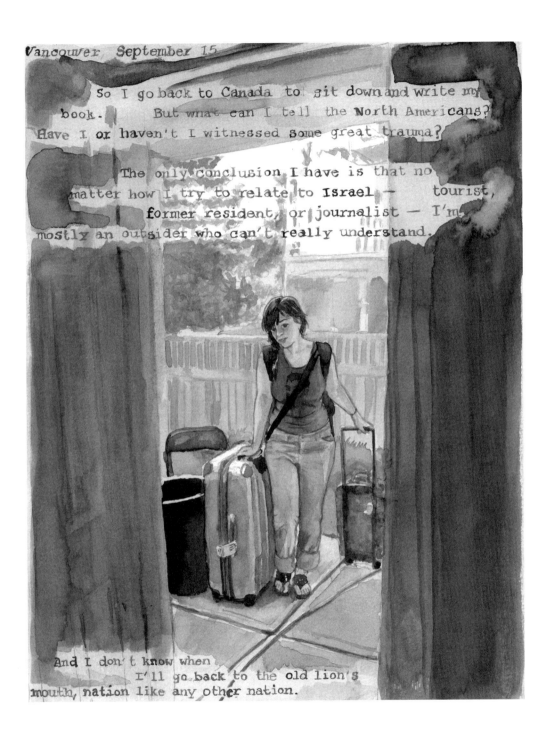

Vancouver September 15

So I go back to Canada to sit down and write my book. But what can I tell the North Americans? Have I or haven't I witnessed some great trauma?

The only conclusion I have is that no matter how I try to relate to Israel — tourist, former resident, or journalist — I'm mostly an outsider who can't really understand.

And I don't know when I'll go back to the old lion's mouth, nation like any other nation.

4.17 *Miriam Libicki, page in "Fierce Ease," n.p. Copyright © Miriam Libicki.*

no matter how I try to relate to Israel—tourist, former resident, or journalist—I'm mostly an outsider who can't really understand" (figure 4.17). Libicki ends her narrative by proclaiming a disidentification with Israel. But it is this very disidentification that allows her to maintain a connection—that paints the backdrop for her dis-affiliatory sensibility, one that in the end connects her with events that have unfolded and are still unfolding across the world.

Below this statement, in this final image, she pictures herself standing in a doorway, with several suitcases resting beside her and a backpack strapped on her back. It is unclear, based on this shimmering watercolor drawing, if Libicki is leaving or returning from her trip, and in this way she emphasizes how travel has informed her sense of home. While she admits that "I don't know when I'll go back," her posture and the baggage set beside her suggest that she is always, somehow, situated between various worlds—her past as an American, her time as an Israeli, and her current life as a Canadian. By ending her visit to Israel picturing herself in this in-between state, she reflects a continually shifting perspective. Here, as this illustration reflects, she assumes the transitional as home.

"But You Don't Live Here, So What's The Dilemma?"

Strangers is Miriam Libicki's most recently published essay, and she subtitles it, *A Long Distance View of Israel.*[26] The essay explores the influx of Sudanese into Israel (and mostly into southern Tel Aviv) between 2005 to 2012, the racist attacks that followed in the wake of these migrations, and the recent policies implemented to cast these refugees out of Israel. In this watercolor visual essay, only two pages in, Libicki depicts herself sitting, with a baby on her lap, in front of a computer, as she explains that she is "home with my first baby now, she's a couple weeks old." Here she shows herself firmly at a distance from the "situation" in Israel, observing from the comfort of her home in Canada. On the following pages, as the story line painfully unfolds, recapping news stories and events from a variety of perspectives, she also pictures drawings of computer screens displaying written posts on various sites on the Internet, including the popular social media sites Facebook and Twitter, as well as her e-mail inbox on gmail. With these images, as well as with her drawings of photographs of protests and other events related to the topic, Libicki pieces together a fragmented picture clearly assembled from afar. Her essay thus represents the impossibility of capturing a linear, straightforward narrative of the events being portrayed, while it also conveys a culture of connect-edness that has allowed her to feel somewhat involved, if only as a distant witness, in events unfolding across the globe.

In "Strangers," Libicki exposes a transnational online community that is bound to the goings on of a particular place—Israel—although it is housed in the spaceless realm of the "world wide web." In this way, the essay, like her others, continues to counter the conception of place (real or metaphorical) as a straight-forward marker of identity, favoring, instead, indeterminate and transitional spaces as the ultimate hallmark of postmodern contemporary identities, includ-ing Jewish ones. Libicki's assessment of the treatment of the Sudanese refugees further leads her to ruminate on her own identity as an outsider who finds herself continually invested in Israeli life and politics. On the final page of the essay she pictures herself, once again at her computer. Her hair is much shorter now and the once tiny baby has plumped up, reflecting the time passed since she initially started digging into this particular "situation." At the top of the page, but also bleeding into the space between her body and the computer, the words, composed in careful black handwritten lettering, in part read:

> I left a life of luxury in Israel for a life of even more luxury in Canada. My Israeli passport is burning a hole in my purse. These "infiltrators" walked half a conti-nent for the privilege of living in a dirty city, taking under-the-table jobs if they find jobs at all, sending their children to schools upstanding citizens sometimes throw molotov cocktails through, but some have lived there eight years, and now they hang up posters to try to convince the citizenry to let them stay.
>
> Who's the Israeli here?
>
> Who is the stranger?[27]

Here Libicki connects her own conflicted relationship to Israel with the often unquestioned declarations that people make to place, referencing Israelis and Jews who pronounce Israel as their birthright to the exclusion of unwanted others. How can one claim a place, Libicki wonders, from afar? How can an identity based on a metaphorical conception hold up in the real world?

Despite her recognition, however, that she is a "stranger" to and in Israel, she nevertheless continues to involve herself in its life and politics, attempting to understand, for example, the "horrifying irony" of events recorded in recent Israeli history such as those related to the Sudanese refugees. Her connection to

Israel is based on a series of complex questions and contradictions reflecting a desire to counter the tenuous construction of Israel as "Jewish homeland" and to begin to imagine, instead, new ways of relating to Israel and its politics as a North American Jew. In *Israel* Sarah is asked a question by an Israeli that undoubtedly surfaces for many Jews, like Libicki, who have spent a great deal, if not all, of their lives living outside Israel. "But you don't live here, so what's the dilemma?" (*Israel* 77). Rather than quietly assent to the implication of that question—that one is responsible only for the goings-on in one's immediate environment— Libicki's and Glidden's works challenge that conception, reinforcing the notion that "home" and "not home" are not clear-cut places or ideas. In their works these cartoonists struggle to reflect an ethics of accountability rooted in visualizations that unsettle, that decenter conventional notions of the self in relation to the world around it. Even if the authors of these texts and their personae do not fully understand "the situation" in Israel, or feel at "home" there, each takes responsibility for the real and imagined places and spaces that have both directly and indirectly shaped their identities.

Conclusion—"Where are they now?"

Translation and Renewal in Liana Finck's A Bintel Brief

"I was born, I have lived, and I have been made over." So begins the introduction to Mary Antin's famous autobiography of her immigration from Belarus to Boston, *The Promised Land*, first published in 1912. Antin continues, "I am just as much out of the way as if I were dead, for I am absolutely other than the person whose story I have to tell. . . . My life I have still to live; her life ended when mine began" (1). While Antin's memoir has often been cast as a narrative of easy assimilation, the seamless integration of a brave new self into a brave new world, these words reference the cost of that journey. Throughout *The Promised Land*, despite this initial, bold proclamation Antin's past self is in fact a persistent, however umbral, presence. As many who have approached the book, particularly from a late-twentieth century perspective, now recognize, the melancholy of immigration inevitably and relentlessly seeps into Antin's recollections.[1]

For example, in Eva Hoffman's *Lost in Translation*, an account of her mid-twentieth-century experience of immigration from Cracow to Canada, published in 1989, the author finds herself feeling "a particular affection" for Antin's memoir, even as she uncomfortably notes the author's insistence on "seeing her life as a fable of pure success" (162, 163).[2] Hoffman reads between the lines in an effort to unearth what is beneath this narrative "of triumphant progress," and she finds what she is looking for toward the very end of Antin's introduction. She points to a telling passage: "It is painful to be consciously of two worlds. The wandering Jew in me seeks forgetfulness. I am not afraid to live on and on, if only I do not have to remember too much" (3).[3] Remembering, for Antin as for Hoffman, is an exercise that painfully yields the fragmentary and problematic nature of the experience of assuming a new identity.

But, as Hoffman recognizes, while remembering often causes paralyzing pain, it can also be a redeeming and even liberating force. Looking back, maintaining ties to the past through language, culture, and storytelling, for example, can be a way of orienting the self, of tracing a trajectory, however muddled its path, in order to anchor the present self to its particular version of home. After all, it is in reading Antin's narrative alongside her own that Hoffman recognizes how much "I am a creature of my time—as she, in her adaptations, was a creature of hers" (162). In returning to this earlier narrative, which is one way of remembering the past, Hoffman excavates otherwise shadowy elements of her own story to reframe her sense of identity as an immigrant, a woman, and a Jew.

Liana Finck's postassimilationist graphic narrative, *A Bintel Brief: Love and Longing in Old New York*, published in 2014, is another text that, like Hoffman's, looks to the past to demonstrate how remembering can be a means of empowerment, of orientation. Composed not as a clear-cut autobiography but rather as an experimental mosaic that straddles the line between fiction and nonfiction, *A Bintel Brief* additionally reflects the ways graphic narratives can prompt expansive self-explorations through palimpsestic renderings that bridge together past and present versions of a self alongside the real and imagined communities that influence that ever changing self. In other words, what a reading of this graphic narrative suggests is how the medium can open up relational considerations of identity by visualizing the manifold, entangled layers that inform a person's sense of self, and in this case one's intersectional Jewish, American, and female identities. Concluding with a brief look at Finck's unusual graphic exploration offers a glimpse of where mapping one's dis-affiliations can potentially lead us, particularly when we venture into a world in which the semiautobiographical and the historic meet the fictional and fantastic.

Drawn in a sometimes gothic, sometimes magical realist style, this slim, unpaginated volume is framed by the first-person narrative of its contemporary, unnamed protagonist.[4] Her perspective bridges the various assemblies contained in the book: bits of a personal history cast alongside the fancies of an imaginary figure brought back from the past, a collective story molded through an individual outlook, and a text translated from Yiddish to English and adapted from prose to word-image. Through the narrator's eyes we experience a communal account that has been shaped by a sorting through and selection that conceals as much as it reveals of an early twentieth-century immigrant community. Unlike Hoffman, this narrator's look back is driven by a metaphorical, rather than literal, sense of herself as an immigrant. Nevertheless, she too is directed to the past by her need for guidance in the present, her desire to figure out where she fits within her own world and particularly what being Jewish in the twenty-first century means to her.

Our unnamed guide begins by describing a book of newspaper clippings passed on to her by her grandmother. Although she cannot read the content of these clippings, since the Hebrew lettering drawn across the cover of the volume eludes her, this does not pose much of a problem, as a spectral presence leaps out of the pages of the old notebook the second she opens it (figure C.1). The ghostly figure is none other than a wiry Abraham Cahan, the Lithuanian-born Jewish American man of letters who founded a socialist Yiddish newspaper, the *Jewish Daily Forward*, in 1897, serving as editor (with a couple of early bumps in the road) from its outset until his death in 1951.[5] As the narrator comes to discover, *Bintel Brief*, translated as "bundle of letters," was a popular feature of the paper, started in 1906, that included letters from readers, many of whom were immigrants, who would pour their hearts out about their personal lives in the hopes of seeing those stories published and accompanied by a reply from the editor. The replies were anonymous, in the sense that no particular name or person was attached to them, and they were originally published in a different typeface from the letters (Nakhimovsky 161). These characteristics of the exchange distanced *Forward* readers from their respondent, allowing them to imagine this figure as what Seth Lipsky has called a "sympathetic, seasoned voice, an enlightened cousin who had been in America just that much longer and could serve as a guide to the country's strange ways" (85). Unlike Mary Antin, whose best-selling memoir was aimed at an American audience and originally appeared in installments in the *Atlantic Monthly*, Abraham Cahan established *Bintel Brief* as a kind of interactive platform for, by, and about a close-knit Jewish immigrant community, however imaginary that community. It is this sense of connection and affiliation that our narrator, another "wandering Jew," seeks out with her supernatural creation; she too is in search of a guide to tether her to this otherwise indistinct and shadowy identity.

In Finck's text the ghostly Abe Cahan is a familiar, friendly, and often even sweet presence who fishes for pickles and kugel in the narrator's refrigerator, even as he remains a distant and untouchable "otherworldly" figure—a heart-shaped symbol of the past with a hat floating over his head like an intellectual's halo. He introduces the narrator to a city she has not seen before, describing, as they walk

I had time to notice that it was pasted full of newspaper clippings in a foreign language— before something <u>very</u> <u>unusual</u> happened.

Sholem aleykhem!

C.1 *Liana Finck, panel from introduction. A Bintel Brief, n.p. A BINTEL BRIEF: LOVE AND LONGING IN OLD NEW YORK by LIANA FINCK. Copyright © 2014 by Liana Finck. Reprinted courtesy of HarperCollins Publishers.*

around, landmarks from his day: "the dancehalls, the cafes where Yiddish poets gathered, the sweatshops." Our ever dislocated narrator notes how after a while "the year 1906 started to seem more real to me than my own time."

Indeed, this observation is especially telling considering how little we learn about her life, or her "own time," over the course of the book. The details that emerge are sparse: where she lives—a small, minimally furnished apartment—

her love of sushi take-out, and, above all, her thirst for the stories Cahan translates for her.[6] She comes to life as she listens to these old stories, all of them half-tales or beginnings. "What happened?" she repeatedly asks of the characters she learns about through these letters. "Where are they now?" The narrator's curiosity grows throughout the text, even as it remains repeatedly unsatisfied. Similarly, readers of Finck's *A Bintel Brief* come to crave more information about this mysterious narrator, although those cravings too remain unfulfilled.

The few historical details we gather about the narrator, like those we grasp about *Bintel Brief* writers more generally, furnish us with a powerful sketch of her past that neither fills in the gaps nor suggests where that past might lead. For example, early in the book, when the imaginary Abe Cahan starts to read to her, he licks a "transparent" finger to turn a page of the notebook. This gesture reminds her of her own grandfather, and in the following panel he is pictured sitting beside her, reading the children's picture book *Goodnight Moon* (figure C.2). The notebook itself, we discover in an epilogue to the book, was put together by her great-grandfather, a "paper hoarder" who wanted to pass on his archive of daily newspapers to his daughter, but selected his favorite clippings at his wife's insistence, so as not to "drown" this daughter in his paper archive.

These bits of information—particular moments from the narrator's history that do not necessarily or easily piece together—are disclosed in snippets throughout the text. Together they paint a picture of a person whose life is lived most intensely in fantasy and memory and whose outlook seems most powerfully shaped by the texts passed on to her: picture books, a notebook, the remnants of an archive. Other than a fictional Abe Cahan and her grandmother (who shows up in the epilogue), we never see her interact with anyone from her present life. In some ways she is everything Antin tries to suppress in her own narrative: a self who lives by and through remembering, who remembers perhaps too much, as Antin struggled not to do. Yet, it is this very remembering, this ability to be moved by stories from the past, that suggests the potential for artistry and transformation that shapes the book, a potential that persistently returns this narrator, as well as her readers, confidently into the present of her own creations.

In eleven chapters interwoven between the present-day fantasy story, the narrator is powerfully moved and impressed by selected stories from *Bintel Brief*. Within these diversely designed story lines, each cast in a slightly different style, format, and color scheme, we witness tales of people, all, to borrow from Antin's whispered words, painfully conscious of two worlds. This consciousness takes the

C.2 *Liana Finck, panel from introduction.* A Bintel Brief, *n.p.* A BINTEL BRIEF: LOVE AND LONGING
IN OLD NEW YORK *by LIANA FINCK. Copyright © 2014 by Liana Finck.*
Reprinted courtesy of HarperCollins Publishers.

form of emotional and material "hungers," as Anzia Yezierska, another famous
turn-of-the-century Jewish immigrant writer, termed them. While so many details
of the letter writers' lives—including their fates—are absent from these letters,
we still glean an overwhelming sense of a community steeped in poverty, illness,
shame, and loneliness. The unfulfilled needs and desires of these writers emerge
more potently perhaps *because* of the fragmentary nature of these stories without endings. The original *Bintel Brief* provided its readers with a chance, however
short-lived, to voice their hungers, even if those hungers often would never be
satisfied. Finck's *A Bintel Brief* generates an afterlife for those voices. As readers,
we simply but powerfully witness them, our own still unfolding stories, like our
narrator's, imbricated in these ancestral half-lives.

She leads the way. Cahan reads the first letter to her, involving a stolen watch, a stealthy neighbor, and a family on the verge of hunger. After presenting the editor's relatively formulaic response to the letter writer, composed in a polished typeface that contrasts with the letter's expressive graphic translation, we return to the story of our narrator and the ghostly Cahan. In a moving panel we see large tears running down her face as she admits, "I feel like she was speaking just to me" (figure C.3). Our narrator's emotional receptivity somehow becomes the central story, a state that, over the course of the text, includes everything from a sense of connection and excitability to disturbance and ennui; despite its continual modifications, this powerful emotional presence is perceptible in every line inscribed in the book. Indeed, as we experience her reactions to these letters, they come to inform the way we read the letters themselves. It becomes impossible to separate our guide from the world that she has drawn, and drawn us into. The narrative framework bleeds into the very story it seeks to enclose.

C.3 *Liana Finck, panel from final page of chapter 1.* A Bintel Brief, *n.p.* A BINTEL BRIEF: LOVE AND LONGING IN OLD NEW YORK *by* LIANA FINCK. *Copyright © 2014 by Liana Finck. Reprinted courtesy of HarperCollins Publishers.*

Perhaps the most moving section of the text comes late, when the narrator, who has begun to lose her imaginary, now assimilating Cahan to the "modern world," sets out on her own to look at original issues of the *Forward*. Perusing microfilm at the New York Public Library, what she finds herself most drawn to, in large part because she cannot read the Yiddish, is a series of photographs, termed "The Gallery of Missing Husbands." As she explains, "I found out later that the pictures were of men who had abandoned their families or disappeared. So many women were writing to the Bintel Brief with pictures of their delinquent husbands and notes pleading with them to come home that 'A Gallery of Missing Husbands' spun off and became its own newspaper feature." In Finck's *A Bintel Brief* the narrative is suddenly ruptured when we are presented, in its own unnumbered chapter, with ten black-and-white etchings based on photographs from this gallery feature. Each sketch depicts the close-up of a man cast against a shadowy background, with a first name and age carefully drawn at the corner of each image (figure C.4). As Finck described the "very physical process" of creating these etchings: "It's very labor intensive. I felt intense emotions while I was making them because it involved scratching" (personal communication, September 27, 2013). These recastings of photographs from the gallery become the author/narrator's way of inscribing herself into the past. In a sense, by reshaping these documents and inserting them into this contemporary story of a young Jewish woman's search for identity and belonging, suppressed and otherwise invisible experiences from the past suddenly become perceptible. With these etchings, though we are looking at the faces of the missing husbands, we feel the loss and pain of the women who sent these material pleas to the paper in the first place. This is no small feat, considering how marginalized women's voices often were in that early twentieth-century Jewish immigrant community.[7]

Ultimately, Finck's narrator too emerges as another one of these abandoned women, as her imaginary Cahan fades out. She relates this loss of her imaginary friend with an inability to connect with her Jewish identity. As she narrates in a significant passage included toward the end of the book, after the fantastical Cahan has mysteriously disappeared just as quickly as he once appeared: "Editor, my spirit has left me and I don't know who I am anymore. I need your advice." She then searches for the ghostly Cahan in what she terms "the most unlikely places," including an "abandoned Jewish deli," an "abandoned pickle factory," an "abandoned synagogue." These settings reveal how her journey, and more generally her turn to and investment in the past, is primarily driven by the search for

CHAYIM, 35

C.4 Liana Finck, page from "The Gallery of Missing Husbands." A Bintel Brief, n.p. A BINTEL BRIEF: LOVE AND LONGING IN OLD NEW YORK by LIANA FINCK. Copyright © 2014 by Liana Finck. Reprinted courtesy of HarperCollins Publishers.

a Jewish sense of self. When she is unsuccessful in finding Cahan, she narrates, "I joined a synagogue, / started learning Yiddish at the Workmen's Circle, / and even danced the hora when I got the chance." Such gestures reflect a self groping for a connection, a sense of identity, that is as elusive as it is urgent. But while she does not locate Cahan, the search itself puts her in touch with a community of lost souls who, like her, just want the opportunity to be seen and heard.

In the end, the narrator of Finck's *A Bintel Brief* dis-affiliates from the very past that she revises, trying to find a space for herself, and for shadowy others like her, in her reconstructions. Over the course of the text, the past is made over, but never completely anew. In "The Task of the Translator" Walter Benjamin describes a translated text as part of the original work's "afterlife": translation involves both "a transformation and a renewal of something living" (73). Paradoxically, as he explains, in its afterlife "the original undergoes a change." In *A Bintel Brief* we can see not only the ways that the past, through many different kinds of translations, can figure into the present but also the ways that the present transforms that past. For Finck's narrator, as for all the personae addressed in this book, visually mapping the self, even an illusory or preliminary one, is a process of translation. In transcribing the self on the page and exposing the limitations and possibilities tied to one's sense of location and dislocation, of home and not home, that self, and the spaces it seeks to inhabit, is transformed. Revisiting and revising the past in the present is a way for Jewish women to create spaces in which to dwell.

Notes

Introduction

1. See Biale, Galchinsky, and Heschel's introduction to *Insider/Outsider*, in which they discuss Jews as a "liminal border case." Scholars including Brodkin have described Jewish women as constituting a doubly "liminal border case." They are situated not only inside/outside North American culture, but also inside/outside Jewish culture, which, in many of its religious and cultural iterations, is premised on a patriarchal model of obligation and piety.

2. I ascribe to the term *postassimilation* many of the qualifications that Hirsch assigns to her notion of "postmemory," a concept that has strongly affected my readings of all these women's works. I have been especially influenced by Hirsch's attention to the visual, and often to the visual collage, as a productive site of inquiry into the connections between different generations, into how the past gets read in the present. For more on Hirsch's conception of postmemory, which she first developed in a paper published in the early 1990s on Art Spiegelman's *Maus*, see *The Generation of Postmemory*.

3. This is, of course, only one thread of the story of contemporary Jewish American literary history as it relates to immigration. For example, a generation of writers and artists born in the Soviet Union have formed what Senderovich, in a 2014 review essay published in *Tablet*, calls a "full-fledged literary subgenre" of Jewish American immigration. The books, written by those born in the 1970s who were transplanted to North America, tell a new story of Jewish American immigration and assimilation. Senderovich traces this literary genealogy back to Gary Shteyngart's *The Russian Debutante's Handbook* (2002). Anya Ulinich's fictional work, *Lena Finkle's Magic Barrel* (2014), joins this generational cluster, and as a graphic novel it deftly engages with both the poetics and aesthetics of the Jewish American immigrant experience.

4. As a response to such omissions, the Ladydrawers Comics Collective, founded by Moore, is a group of cartoonists and researchers who work "to research, perform, and publish comics and texts about how economics, race, sexuality, and gender impact the comics

industry, other media, and our culture at large." See http://anneelizabethmoore.com/ladydrawers/ The cartoonist MariNaomi, driven by a similar desire to diversify visibility in the comics world, recently developed an online Cartoonists of Color Database. See http://marinaomi.com/poc/cocindex.html.

5. Another famous second-wave feminist who somewhat belatedly contemplated her Jewish roots was Betty Friedan in her 2000 memoir *Life So Far*. For more on the feminist ambivalence toward Jewishness and Judaism from both women who do and do not identify as secular, see Gubar's "Eating the Bread of Affliction," Miller's "Hadassah Arms," and Prell's "Terrifying Tales of Jewish Womanhood." See also Levitt's *Jews and Feminism*, Pinsky's *Jewish Feminists*, Plaskow's *Standing Again at Sinai*, and Pogrebin's *Deborah, Golda, and Me*.

6. See Hollinger's *Postethnic America* and Magid's *American Post-Judaism* for more on the postethnic.

7. Howe's famous *World of Our Fathers*, for example, first published in 1976, is a more traditional history focused on Jews as a veritable independent entity. Recently, historians, including Jacobson and Brodkin, have attempted to view constructions of Jewish American identity as always inevitably intertwined with constructions of other (particularly racial and ethnic) identities. They argue that being Jewish in the early part of the twentieth century meant something very different from what it has meant since the Second World War and the passing of the G.I. Bill in 1944, which essentially converted Jews' statuses in America to privileged and "white"—or at least able to pass. See Brodkin's *How Jews Became White Folks* and Jacobson's *Whiteness of a Different Color*, as well as chapter 7 of Sander Gilman's *The Jew's Body*, "The Jewish Nose: Are Jews White? or, The History of the Nose." Gilman argues that, beginning at the end of the nineteenth century, the nose came to signify, more than anything else, the Western Jew's difference from the "other"—especially in light of the shifting categorization of Jews from "non-white" to "white" (181). Although their time lines slightly differ, Jacobson, Brodkin, and Gilman have all contributed to an understanding of Jewishness as, inevitably, entwined in a more encompassing narrative of shifting American identities.

8. For more on representations of Jewish women's bodies, see Kleeblatt's edited collection, *Too Jewish?* and especially Prell's "Why Jewish Princesses Don't Sweat" and Lieberman's "Jewish Barbie." See also Mock's *Jewish Women on Stage, Film, and Television*. A 2012 special issue of the journal *Nashim*, edited by Harris, was recently devoted to questions of "The Jewish Woman and Her Body." Finally, in *Jewish Identities in American Feminist Art*, Bloom addresses these questions from the standpoint of the ways that Jewish feminist artists from the 1970s on have or (perhaps even more often) have not responded to visual representations of Jewish American women.

9. Philip Roth's treatment of women in his literature—in particular, his tendency to stereotype his female characters—is a problematic element of many of the male writers who compose the so-called Jewish American literary canon, including Herman Wouk, Bernard Malamud, and Saul Bellow. For more on Wouk and Roth, see chapters 4 and 5

of Antler's *You Never Call! You Never Write!* Over the past several years, claims have been made that Roth's literature in particular has "evolved" away from its misogynistic tilt—or that his works have been misconstrued to begin with as antiwomen. This argument is at the premise of a 2012 special issue of *Philip Roth Studies,* "Roth and Women," edited by David Gooblar.

10. In addition to Antler's *You Never Call! You Never Write!* other books that address stereotypes of Jewish American women include her edited collection, *Talking Back,* and Prell's *Fighting to Become Americans.*

11. See, for example, Bulkin's "Hard Ground" (1984), as well as Beck's "The Politics of Jewish Invisibility" (1988), for reactions to such problematic assumptions. See also Anne Roiphe's more recent account of a panel she was on at a meeting of Artists and Writers for Peace in the Mideast sometime around Rabin's assassination in the mid-1990s, included in a piece published on *Tablet* in October 2014 and titled "My Jewish Feminism: A Memoir." In addition, Furman addresses Roiphe's earlier fictional representations of Israel and its politics in chapter 8 of *Israel Through the Jewish-American Imagination.*

12. See Silberstein's anthology, *Mapping Jewish Identities.* For critical texts that have employed such postmodern redefinitions of Jewish identity through readings of contemporary Jewish literature and culture, see, as examples, Berger and Cronin's *Jewish American and Holocaust Literature,* Brook's *You Should See Yourself,* Eichler-Levine's *Suffer the Little Children,* Franco's *Race, Rights, and Recognition,* Freedman's *Klezmer America,* Levinson's *Exiles on Main Street,* Meyers's *Identity Papers,* and Wirth-Nesher's *Call It English.*

13. For more on Rich's Jewish background, see her 1982 essay, "Split at the Root."

14. Woolf famously peppers *Three Guineas* with a series of photographs, inviting her (male) reader to "see then whether when we look at the same photographs we feel the same things" (10). Photographs become a common space for Woolf and her readers, a visual place that she hopes will evoke a sense of collectivity, empathy, and perhaps even a call to action. Cixous imagines that through writing she is similarly working "against the decree of blindness" (3). Like Woolf, visual imagining is a form of rebelling against the institutions that have oppressed her and others: "I will never finish fashioning the graven image for myself," she asserts (3). Rich, too, recognizes the "spiritual power" of symbols and images, how they can link together our histories alongside our everyday realities and experiences: "The Jewish star on my neck must serve me both for reminder and as a goad to continuing and changing responsibility" (227). The symbol, the icon, the graven image—these visual frameworks appear frequently in contemporary feminist women's literature, a literature engaged in a politics that foregrounds a visualized relationality as the key to thinking through identity and difference.

15. Comics scholar McCloud writes about this relationship between comics, time, and space in *Understanding Comics,* likening the division of panels on a page to the beating of time in a musical composition. See chapter 4 of *Understanding Comics,* "Time Frames." Art Spiegelman has also frequently expressed this sentiment, as in his book-length

interview with Chute, *MetaMaus,* in which he describes comics as "an essentialized form of diagramming a narrative movement through time" (168).

16. See the introduction to Pratt and Rosner's anthology on transnational feminisms, *The Global and the Intimate,* in which they argue that "pairing . . . the intimate and the global extends a longstanding feminist tradition of challenging gender-based oppositions by upending hierarchies of space and scale" (1).

17. Founded by Dan Nadel, Patrick Smith, and Tim Hodler, *The Ganzfeld* was a series of books and objects containing art and art criticism, most of it related to cartooning and comics, published by PictureBox Books. Weinstein's map was published in 2008, in its seventh and final issue.

18. *Understanding Comics* is often regarded as a text that helped establish a common vocabulary for such theoretical discussions of comics. McCloud owes many of his ideas and explanations about comics, and especially the interactions between words and images, to Will Eisner's *Comics and Sequential Art,* which he acknowledges in his introduction. See also Thierry Groensteen's *The System of Comics,* and particularly his introduction.

19. Cartoons generally refer to single-panel drawn images, which often include captions instead of thought bubbles, and they were the primary format of early political satire as epitomized in the infamous British magazine, *Punch.* McCloud more generally differentiates between cartoons and comics by emphasizing one, cartooning, as an "approach," and the other as a "medium which often employs that approach" (21). Theorists including Harvey have taken issue with this distinction, finding "verbal content" to be "the essential characteristic of 'comics'" (25). For Spiegelman, the essential difference between the two is that a cartoon is meant to "emblematize" or to "find[] a representation for many moments in one image," whereas a comic is about "creating individual moments that add up to having some overarching meaning beyond the individual moments" (*MetaMaus* 185). The widespread use of the term *cartoonist* to talk about practitioners of the form reveals how murky the division between the two can be.

20. See also Barry's *What It Is* (2008) and *Syllabus* (2014).

21. As critics have pointed out, the recent increased interest in Jews and comics is very likely at least in part related to the publication of Michael Chabon's Pulitzer prize-winning book, *The Amazing Adventures of Kavalier and Clay* (2000), a novel that conveys the interwoven history of Jews and comics. Books about Jews and comics, and specifically, Jews and superhero comics, include several written for mainstream audiences, such as Fingeroth's *Disguised as Clark Kent* (2008) and Weinstein's *Up, Up, and Oy Vey* (2009). Additionally, among various others, the nonacademic *Jews and American Comics* (2008), edited by Buhle, provides a short but lively history of the influence of Jews in American comics. The recently published *Yiddishkeit* (2011), edited by Pekar and Buhle, also calls attention to the link between comics and the vernacular—in this case, the link between comics and Yiddish language and culture, and Tabachnick's *The Quest for Jewish Belief and Identity in the Graphic Novel* (2014) provides a survey of Jewish-themed works. Within many of these studies, the role of women is downplayed, and most only

nod at the influence women cartoonists have had on the creation and implementation of the art form. This trend is slowly being reversed. Strömberg's nonacademic *Jewish Images in the Comics* (2012) includes examinations of works by a number of the Jewish American women discussed in this project, as does the anthology, *The Jewish Graphic Novel* (2010), edited by Baskind and Omer-Sherman. A recent exhibition, Graphic Details: Confessional Comics by Jewish Women, co-curated by Sarah Lightman and Michael Kaminer, showcased the works of international cartoonists. Lightman's edited anthology, *Graphic Details* (2014), was published based on the exhibit. The anthology is an excellent resource for those interested in learning about a range of Jewish women cartoonists, and it features essays about and interviews with some of them, including interviews that I conducted with Lauren Weinstein and Miss Lasko-Gross. Those interested in Jewish women cartoonists might also look into the works of Julia Alekseyeva, Joyce Brabner, Roz Chast, Leela Corman, Sophie Crumb, Debbie Dreschler, Bernice Eisenstein, Miriam Engelberg, Miriam Katin, Keren Katz, Amy Kurzweil, Sarah Lazarovic, Sarah Leavitt, Rutu Modan, Diane Noomin, Corinne Pearlman, Phoebe Potts, Trina Robbins, Rebecca Roher, Racheli Rottner, Sharon Rudahl, Laurie Sandell, Ariel Schrag, Tania Schrag, Karen Sneider, Emily Steinberg, Alissa Torres, Anya Ulinich, and Ilana Zeffren. This list is by no means comprehensive.

1. *"My Independent Jewish Monster Temperament"*

1. Kominsky was the name that Kominsky Crumb acquired from her first husband, and not her maiden name. Interestingly, some of the ways she has been referred to in various interviews and articles include Ms. Crumb, Aline Kominsky, and Aline Kominsky-Crumb. Given the importance of naming in her works, and for the sake of consistency, in this book I use the arrangement she uses (Aline Kominsky Crumb) to sign her name to entries on the blog *Crumb Newsletter,* http://rcrumb.blogspot.com/, which is also the way her name is written on the cover of her memoir.

2. *Shiksa* is a Yiddish and Polish word that means non-Jewish female and was initially coined as a derogatory term. In its more recent North American application, it is a term generally, though not always, used satirically.

3. These descriptions of her work often come from Kominsky Crumb herself, as in this interview with Kristen Schilt that took place in 2012.

4. In addition to Chute, several other people have recently engaged with Kominsky Crumb's comics: Gardner includes a short discussion of Kominsky Crumb in his article "Autobiography's Biography" (2008) and in his chapter on autobiographical comics in his more recent *Projections* (2012); Gilman refers to "Nose Job" in his book, *Making the Body Beautiful* (2001); and Most briefly discusses Kominsky Crumb's work in her essay, "Re-Imagining the Jew's Body" (2006). More recently, two articles that examine Jewishness in Kominsky Crumb's comics include my article, "Visualizing the Jewish

Body in Aline Kominsky Crumb's *Need More Love"* (2010), which is an earlier version of segments from this chapter; and Clementi's "The *JAP*, the *Yenta*, and the *Mume* in Aline Kominsky Crumb's Graphic Imagination" (2012).

5. Diane Noomin can also be considered a leading figure in the world of contemporary North American Jewish women's comics. Like Kominsky Crumb, Noomin's Jewish dis-affiliations take place through her evocations of Jewish and female stereotypes, and particularly as epitomized in her fictional character, Didi Glitz. Her Glitz comics were anthologized in 2012 in *Glitz-2-Go.* Noomin also edited two influential anthologies of women's comics, which featured the works of many artists who have come to be recognized as key figures in the comics world, including Kominsky Crumb, Mary Fleener, Carol Lay, Carol Tyler, and Julie Doucet. Many of the cartoonists I discuss in this volume have mentioned *Twisted Sisters: A Collection of Bad Girl Art* (1991), edited by Noomin, and *Twisted Sisters 2: Drawing the Line* (1995), edited by Lay and Noomin, as early influences.

6. The collaborative comics of Kominsky Crumb and her husband—and sometimes their daughter, Sophie—were collected in a 2012 volume, *Drawn Together.*

7. Only three pages of this comic are republished in chapter 3 of *Need More Love.* Many of the republished comics in *Need More Love* have been excerpted, and some, like this one, do not include a title page. The inclusion of just parts of certain comics throughout *Need More Love* adds to the fragmentary design of the text. Since I am examining these comics in the context of the memoir as a whole, I have included page numbers indicating where the images can be found in the memoir and not in the original publications.

8. Other critics have attempted their own word-image taxonomies. A useful summary of these formalist definitions can be found in El Refaie's *Autobiographical Comics,* especially 22–24. Many contemporary comics theorists have built on scholarship of image-text interactions based in other media, including photography and film. Some of the most well regarded of such theories include those outlined by Barthes, especially in his collection of essays, *Image-Text-Music,* as well as visual theorist Mitchell's *Iconology.* Many of Berger's works similarly address formal and theoretical concerns regarding the structural principles of image-texts. See, for instance, *Ways of Seeing* and *About Looking.*

9. Photography has been theorized in many now well-known texts, including (but certainly not limited to) Barthes's *Camera Lucida,* Sontag's *On Photography* and her palinode *Regarding the Pain of Others,* and many works written by Berger (including those mentioned previously). For more on the intersection between photography and autobiography, see especially Adams's *Light Writing and Life Writing,* Rugg's *Picturing Ourselves,* and Willis's edited anthology, *Picturing Us.*

10. For more on issues regarding contemporary receptions of autobiography, both in and out of comics, see Miller's "The Entangled Self."

11. Notably, Kominsky Crumb considers *Need More Love* to be a "guerrilla art statement" (quoted in Chute, *Graphic Women* 226). In fact, the night the book was released, the

publisher went out of business, and she has since declined opportunities to bring the book back into publication (225–26).

12. Green's work is generally considered to be the first full-length autobiographical comic by a North American underground cartoonist, and his book influenced countless other cartoonists, including Kominsky Crumb. See Chute's *Graphic Women* 17–20.

13. For more on the relationship between comics and the archive, and a brief history of scholarship on the subject, see Chute's "Comics as Archives."

14. The first known published comic drawn and written by women only was *It Ain't Me Babe: Women's Liberation* (1970), co-produced by a collective of women including Trina Robbins. Two years later, *Wimmin's Comix* put out their first issue. In publication from 1972–1992, *Wimmen's Comix* has featured many of the most well-known underground women cartoonists, among them Phoebe Gloeckner, Dori Seda, and Roberta Gregory. For a history of women's underground comics, see the introduction to Chute's *Graphic Women*, as well as several articles written by Samantha Meier on the topic for the *Hooded Utilitarian*: http://www.hoodedutilitarian.com/author/samantha-meier/. Trina Robbins has written various overview histories of women and comics, including *From Girls to Grrlz*, *The Great Women Cartoonists*, and *Pretty in Ink*.

15. Comedian Danny Thomas, best known for his role in the mid-twentieth-century sitcom, *Make Room for Daddy*, had a "distinguished" nose. As a *New York Times* reporter described him in a profile in 1991, when he was seventy-seven years old: "He reaches up to adjust the black-rimmed eyeglasses that somewhat disguise his trademark large hook nose, a nose that three movie producers—Jack Warner, Louis B. Mayer and Harry Cohn—could not persuade him to change" (Rothstein). Marlo Thomas, his daughter, also became an actress; she is best known for her role in the television sitcom, *That Girl*.

16. This character is often, but not always, referred to as The Bunch, rather than just Bunch.

17. For a social history of Jews and plastic surgery in contemporary times (including, as mentioned, a brief discussion of Kominsky Crumb's "Nose Job"), see chapter 6 of Gilman's *Making the Body Beautiful*. See also Lipton's 2014 article in the *New York Review of Books*, "The Invention of the Jewish Nose," and her related 2014 book on Jewish iconography from the Middle Ages, *Dark Mirror*.

18. This comic also lists their daughter, Sophie Crumb, as the third collaborator. The part of the comic that I am looking at involves only her parents.

19. For more on the ethics of collaborative life writing, see chapter 3 of Couser's *Vulnerable Subjects:* "Making, Taking, and Faking Lives: Voice and Vulnerability in Collaborative Life Writing." Although Couser is writing about prose memoirs, his discussion on possible exploitations involved in collaborative life writing could also readily apply to collaborative comics.

20. Interestingly, Ronnen's review in the *Jerusalem Post* of a 2005 German biography of Frida Kahlo's father, Guillermo Kahlo, points to claims that have insubstantiated his Jewish background. Ronnen argues that "Frida herself was probably the source of the

claims to her Jewish connection. . . . My guess is that German connections during the Nazi era were an embarrassment to her."

21. The American pop icon Madonna, well recognized for her own experimentations with self-fashioning and branding, is also referenced in this image, along with her ethnic heritage, in another speech bubble: "Look my eyebrows are like Madonnas'. Now do I look Italian?"

22. See Bloom's *Jewish Identities in American Feminist Art*. Bloom here is writing about the ways that certain Jewish women artists "reconfigure Jewish stereotypes . . . through a parodic rendering of these images" (3). Bloom focuses primarily on the works of Judy Chicago, Eleanor Antin, Mierle Laderman Ukeles, and Martha Rosler.

23. This definition can be found under "temperament, n. " in the *OED* Online.

2. "What Would Make Me the Most 'Myself'"

1. I use the phrase *narrative comics* to describe the often previously published comics that Davis includes in the text. I use this term to differentiate these from Davis's diary comics, which are generally marked with dates, and her one- or two-page sketches, which do not include any text.

2. Unlike in Kominsky Crumb's comics, the personae in Davis's comics share the same name as the author, Vanessa Davis. In order to distinguish between the two, I will refer, throughout this chapter, to Davis's alter ego on the page as Vanessa, while Davis or Vanessa Davis will refer to the cartoonist herself.

3. Buenaventura Press was a well-respected publisher of independent comics and anthologies. The press closed down in 2010 because of financial difficulties.

4. The history behind the creation and publication of Anne Frank's diary has been an especially enlightening case that highlights the difficulty of ever truly unraveling the transition between the original work and its later manifestations, especially when that work has passed through many hands on its way to publication. See Bunkers's "Whose Diary Is It Anyway?" and Lejeune's "How Anne Frank Rewrote the Diary of Anne Frank."

5. Genette divides his conception of the paratext into the peritext, elements inside the covers of a book, and the epitext, elements outside the book but somehow related to the book (like interviews or reviews).

6. See also Cardell's *Dear World*, a book that looks at contemporary diary practices in order, in part, to dispel the notion of diaries as private and unconstructed documents.

7. For more on the paratactic format of diaries, see Hogan's "Engendered Autobiographies" (103).

8. In this passage I invite an oversimplified reading of images in opposition to words, as though Davis's beautifully hand-drawn letters could not also be read as images in and of themselves.

9. Cates provides a striking example of this occurrence in his essay, "The Diary Comic," which focuses on the works of cartoonist James Kochalka, who published a daily diary online for over fourteen years. See http://www.americanelf.com/. Cates writes about Kochalka's comic from September 10, 2001, which, he explains, "preserves a moment of easy innocence before terrible events rang in a new national temper" (213). This ability to depict innocence without "self consciousness about that innocence" is what Cates argues distinguishes the diary, and especially the daily diary, from the autobiographical narrative.

10. For more, see McCloud's "A Word About Color" in *Understanding Comics*.

11. See also Garb, who describes Neel's portraiture generally as a "means of . . . rebellion" and her self-portrait in particular as "revolutionary" (31, 30). As she notes, "Very few precedents for naked female self-portraits exist" (30).

12. In an interview about her father's posthumously published book of photographs, *Strange Stories*, Davis attributed her interest in color to "him," Gerald Davis. See "Affectionate yet Arch" for her take on the book, which was edited by Todd Oldham.

13. The exception is an image on the page succeeding the short comic "Make Me a Woman," and preceding the slightly longer comic "Big Fun," of a young woman wearing a Hard Rock Café T-shirt and doing sit-ups. Since the subsequent comic is about Vanessa's experiences at "Fat Camp," the image could be read as prefiguring the narrative that follows.

14. Davis's interest in fashion, and her understanding of it as a political tool, comes across in the narrative comic "Money Can't Buy Jappiness," in which she traces the history of Vanessa's slow coming into consciousness about the politics of fashion and consumerism. In a recent interview Davis described her introduction, as a teenager, to the world of thrift shopping as "a change in perspective" ("Affectionate yet Arch"). She is also the illustrator of a 2010 book written by Leora Tanenbaum, entitled *Bad Shoes and the Women Who Love Them*, about the history of shoe fashions for women. The book is an attempt at recording and recognizing the political significance of such a history, as well as an effort to persuade those who wear uncomfortable shoes to think about the physical consequences. As Tanenbaum explains in her introduction, "My fervent hope is that when you finish reading this book, you will choose to reduce the amount of time you spend standing and walking in them. . . . Be smart about how often you wear them and for how long. If you wear them too much, you will end up with disfigured feet" (7).

15. These full-colored diary entries were originally included in the 2006 comics anthology *Kramers Ergot #6*, also published by Buenaventura Press and edited by Buenaventura and Harkham. Their incorporation in this anthology, which showcases mostly full-colored comics, might also explain why these particular diary comics were so carefully colored.

16. For a meditation on home, or, in Hebrew, *bayit*, specifically in relation to Jewish religious practices and beliefs over various historical time periods, see chapter 5 of Mann's *Space and Place in Jewish Studies*. Mann's work more generally engages in textual

readings that examine "spaces that often mark, or are marked by, Jewishness in relation to difference" (2).

17. Her comic, "Talkin' 'bout my Generation," included toward the end of the book, reflects the ways in which Vanessa experiences many of the same conflicted feelings about the works of Robert Crumb and how they have influenced her as a female cartoonist.

18. Gornick brought attention to the problematic depictions of women culled by these Jewish male writers in a 1976 article published in the *Village Voice*, "Why Do These Men Hate Women?" Her 2008 book, *The Men in My Life*, revisits this question, particularly chapter 6, "Saul Bellow, Philip Roth, and the End of the Jew as Metaphor." See also Gooblar's introduction to the "Roth and Women" special issue.

19. For a compelling recent historical study on the topic, see McGinity's *Still Jewish*. See also Fishman's *Double or Nothing?* which includes a discussion of representations of intermarriage in popular culture.

20. These include, for example, early twentieth-century writer Anzia Yezierska, as well as more contemporary writers like Allegra Goodman, Erica Jong, Cynthia Ozick, Grace Paley, Susan Fromberg Schaeffer, and Lore Segal.

21. For a "survey of Jewish-American literature on Israel, 1928–1995," see Furman's *Israel Through the Jewish-American Imagination*.

22. Trevor Alixopulos is a cartoonist whose work can be viewed at http://www.alixopulos .com/.

23. Davis and Alixopulos did publish a collaborative comic in O'Leary's anthology, *The Big Feminist But*. Titled "Pillowtalk," the two-page work, also documenting their two personae in bed, involved each cartoonist drawing roughly half the panels on the page, rather than sharing individual panel space as Kominsky Crumb and Crumb do in their collaborative works.

3. "I Always Want to Know Everything True"

1. Sendak's sentiment is echoed by Cart in chapter 8 of *Young Adult Literature*, "So, How Adult Is Young Adult? The Crossover Conundrum."

2. For a history of comics and youth culture in twentieth-century America, see Wright's *Comic Book Nation*.

3. Hatfield also references Peter Schjeldahl's October 17, 2005 article for the *New Yorker*, "Words and Pictures: Graphic Novels Come of Age," which reinforces many of McGrath's mistaken notions of comics as a medium most suited for young people. For more on this issue, see Baetens's and Frey's *The Graphic Novel*, particularly chapter 4, "'Not Just for Kids': Clever Comics and the New Graphic Novels."

4. For the sake of simplicity, I do not differentiate between the concepts of "children," "young adults," "teenagers," and "adolescents" throughout this chapter. For a detailed history of these terms, see Cart, chapter 1, "From Sue Barton to the Sixties: What's in a

Name? and Other Uncertainties." See also Driscoll's introduction to *Girls,* in which she points out how the concept of adolescence has often been "gendered and sexed" (6).

5. A fifty-four-page collection of Miss Lasko-Gross's "rarely seen short stories," *Miss Lasko-Gross, 1994–2014,* is also available on the digital comics platform www.comixology.com.

6. As Miss Lasko-Gross explains in interviews, while her given name is Melissa, she generally goes by the name Miss with everyone besides her immediate family. Any reference to Melissa throughout this chapter refers to her persona, while Miss Lasko-Gross or Lasko-Gross refers to the author of the text.

7. Martens discusses how the roles of places and objects in human development have generally been slighted, although she cites two well-known sources that have engaged the topic: Winnicot's *Playing and Reality* and Brown's edited anthology *Things.*

8. For more on the subjectivity of the mother, see especially Benjamin's "The Omnipotent Mother" as well as Kaplan's *Motherhood and Representation.*

9. For more on the distinction between childhood and adolescent literature, as well as a discussion of how these genres relate to and overlap with other categories of literature, including the *Entwicklungsroman* and the *Bildungsroman,* see chapter 1 in Trites, *Disturbing the Universe,* "'Do I dare disturb the universe?': Adolescent Literature in the Postmodern Era."

10. See Sedgwick's *Epistemology of the Closet* and Muñoz's *Disidentifications.*

11. Lasko-Gross's interest in questions of conformity and rebellion, particularly in relation to institutionalized religion, is also evident in her most recent work, *Henni,* a mythical coming-of-age adventure story. For more, see her interview, "The Unintentional Rebel."

12. In "Psychosomatic Refusal," for example, Melissa's aversion to attending synagogue with her parents culminates in an episode in which she vomits in the parking lot and is allowed to wait in the car (54–56). Brauner discusses this and other "visceral" reactions conveying what he describes as Melissa's "hostility toward Judaism" in his article, "The Turd That Won't Flush" (136).

13. Weinstein's persona has the same name as the author, so, for the purposes of clarification, Lauren refers to the persona in the book, whereas Weinstein or Lauren Weinstein refers to the author.

14. Weinstein is currently at work on a sequel to *Girl Stories,* tentatively titled "Calamity." She has also published *The Goddess of War* (2008), a 9-by-15 1/2-inch science fiction epic, and *Inside Vineyland* (2003), a thin, roughly 6-by-8-inch collection of one-page comics, many of which were originally published in Seattle's alternative newspaper, the *Stranger.*

15. For more on girls' diaries, see also Bunkers's introduction to *Diaries of Girls and Women.*

16. In another comic, "The Dysfunctional Family Thanksgiving," Lauren's cousin introduces his girlfriend at the dining room table, and his mother responds, "She's not Jewish, is she?" (138). This overt reference to Jewishness in the context of a romantic affiliation reinforces the way in which the theme of intermarriage is often the space, in contemporary American literature, where anxieties related to Jewishness surface.

Similarly, the name of a character in the memoir, Glenn Schwartz, suggests a Jewish identity, although in an interview Weinstein admitted that this character was "an amalgam of people and maybe some of those people were Jewish and some were not" ("Thinking Panoramically" 190).

17. Many of the singe-page cartoons from *Inside Vineyland* can be viewed on Weinstein's website: http://www.laurenweinstein.com/. This site also features Weinstein's more recent works, including humorous and insightful reflections on being a parent as well as the moving five-part web comic series "Carriers," which was first published on *Nautilus* and powerfully recounts the experience of being tested as a carrier for cystic fibrosis during early pregnancy.

4. *"But you don't live here, so what's the dilemma?"*

1. For a discussion of the distinctive historical uses of the terms *exile* and *diaspora,* see Wettstein's introduction to his edited anthology, *Diasporas and Exiles* and Zeitlin's *Jews.*

2. Beinart points to polls conducted by Frank Luntz, as well as separate studies conducted by Steven M. Cohen and Ari Y. Kelman, purportedly reflecting that a large majority of young Jewish college students, and particularly those who are not religiously affiliated, have little interest in discussing Israel. See, for example, Cohen and Kelman's 2007 report for the Jewish Identity Project of Reboot, available on the Berman Jewish Policy Archive website: http://www.bjpa.org/Publications/details.cfm?PublicationID=326.

3. For the sake of brevity, the full title of Glidden's book, *How to Understand Israel in Sixty Days or Less*, will hereafter be referred to as *Israel.*

4. Glidden's self-published minicomic won the Ignatz Award for Promising New Talent at the Small Press Expo in Bethesda, Maryland in 2008. In several interviews, she recounts the experience of being approached by an editor from DC Comics at a New York indie comics festival, the MoCCA Arts Festival, and soon after signing with Vertigo, an imprint of DC Comics, for a book-length version of the minicomic. See Glidden's interview with Alex Dueben on *Comic Book Resources.*

5. As Glidden noted, "when [Vertigo] asked me to do the book with them, they told me they would prefer it if I would do it in full-color. I hadn't really ever done color comics before and wasn't sure if I could do it, but I figured I would just say 'yes' and figure out how to do it later on" (personal communication, July 27, 2014).

6. Sarah refers to the author's persona throughout *Israel*, whereas Glidden or Sarah Glidden refers to the author of the text.

7. As chapter headings, these could be considered part of the paratext as well as of the text. For the sake of simplicity, I attribute them here to the persona of the book, rather than the author of the book or both author and persona.

8. See the Birthright Israel website, accessed May 4, 2015: http://www.birthrightisrael .com/visitingisrael/Pages/default.aspx.

9. The bibliography at the end of the book lists nine sources in all, including, for example, *The Masada Myth*, by Nachman Ben-Yehuda, the collection of essays and reflections *Wrestling with Zion: Progressive Jewish-American Responses to the Israeli-Palestinian Conflict*, edited by Tony Kushner and Alisa Solomon, and *A History of the Israeli-Palestinian Conflict*, by Mark A. Tessler.

10. Within the Hasidic world, there are various styles of dress. For the purposes of this discussion, I am collapsing such distinctions and using Hasidim to refer generally to the men that Sarah pictures on her trip who are dressed in dark suits and black hats and either wear traditional earlocks (*peyes* in Yiddish) or have long, uncut sideburns.

11. Often, observant Jews who follow the laws of modesty, or *shomer negia*, refrain from purposefully touching members of the opposite sex. Levels of observance vary, but strict Jews might try not to even stand or sit next to a member of the opposite sex in order to avoid accidental contact.

12. The Sabbath, or *Shabbat*, is the Jewish day of rest and, as such, a range of activities that are considered "work" are prohibited, including cooking and lighting a fire (or pressing or flipping a light switch). An observant Jew might ask someone she presumes or knows to be nonobservant or not Jewish to turn on her light for her on the Sabbath if she has forgotten to leave it on.

13. Although at times she identifies with her friend, Melissa, whom she invited on the trip, she generally singles herself out as different from everyone else in the group, including Melissa.

14. Glidden added that her new project, *Rolling Blackouts*, which is forthcoming from Drawn and Quarterly in 2016, would be different despite some "surface similarities" to *Israel*. *Rolling Blackouts* is a book in which she follows journalists, in 2010, on a reporting trip to Turkey, Iraq, Syria, and Lebanon. As she explained, while both books are told from her perspective and follow trips to the Middle East, "This time, my own feelings about [the journey] aren't really part of the story."

15. As Borden explains in *Journalism as Practice*, a definition of journalism is difficult to pin down, but a "framework" that connects "the practice's product and purpose" might include these five factors: "a link to human flourishing, commitment to the common good, reporting as the defining activity of journalism, a desire to make a difference, and a way to make a living" (49).

16. For a compelling delineation of this argument by another self-identified left-wing progressive, see Willis's "Is There Still a Jewish Question?" Willis argues that the apparent inconsistencies in her own political beliefs, and in particular her approach to Israel, stem from her "struggling to make sense of a situation that has multiple and at times contradictory dimensions" (227). Her essay was first published in the *Wrestling with Zion* collection.

17. See also Libicki's essay, published in 2008 in *The Jewish Graphic Novel*, "Jewish Memoir Goes Pow! Zap! Oy!" In it she links her brand of comics journalism to a Hunter S. Thompson-style "gonzo ethics," which she argues is a genre, in its iteration as comics,

that was "almost certainly established more recently by a handful of Jews and Jew-sympathizers" (254).

18. The full title of the book is *jobnik! an american girl's adventures in the israeli army*. Miriam refers to the author's persona throughout *jobnik!*, whereas Libicki or Miriam Libicki refers to the author of the text.

19. At the time this chapter was written, the tenth issue was the most recent publication, released in December 2012. All Libicki's works have been self-published by Real Gone Girl Studios: www.realgonegirl.com.

20. Any page references included hereafter for *jobnik!* will refer to the collected book.

21. *Yahrzeit*, which Miriam describes on the page as a "death anniversary," is the Yiddish-word for the commemoration of the death of a loved one (usually in one's immediate family) on the day of the year that she has died. Yitzhak Rabin was assassinated by a right-wing Israeli conservative in 1995 while at a rally in support of a peace initiative, between the Israeli government and the Palestine Liberation Organization, called the Oslo Accords.

22. Libicki has attributed her inspiration for this image to the Zionist illustrator Ephraim Moses Lilien's 1908 drawing "The Covenant of Abraham" (Hajdu 50).

23. *Strangers* was recently republished in the *Ilanot Review*'s Winter 2015 issue: https://ilanot.wordpress.com/strangers/. Libicki is currently at work on what she called a "mess of a 44-page memoir/cultural theory/humanist philosophy tract" about "Jew-ishness and Black Jews, in the U.S. and Israel" (personal communication, August 22, 2014). The essay will appear in the *Journal of Jewish Identities* in 2016.

24. Libicki's essays do not include page numbers.

25. She cites a variety of sources. These include academics Riv-Ellen Prell and Maurice Berger, cartoonist Joe Sacco, an Israel trip participant, a blog called *Peacepalestine*, and an Israeli online message board.

26. I thank Naomi Kramer for first making me aware of this comics essay.

27. Libicki here is referring to an incident that occurred in Israel, during which a Molotov cocktail was thrown into the front courtyard of a day care center housing African asylum seekers.

Conclusion—"Where are they now?"

1. Over the last few years, a number of critics have focused on this "rereading" of Antin's work. See, for example, Dayton-Wood's "The Limits of Language," Sillin's "Heroine, Reformer, Citizen," and Winter's "Mary Antin and Assimilation."

2. See Kellman's "Lost in the Promised Land" for a reading of Hoffman as a revision of Antin.

3. These two lines from Antin are only part of a longer passage that Hoffman quotes in her book (163).

4. Finck has attributed some of her stylistic influences for the book to the works of Marc Chagall, old Yiddish illustrations and prints, Molly Picon films, and the 1937 Yiddish classic *The Dybbuk* (personal communication, September 27, 2013).

5. See Nakhimovsky's "The Moral Evolution of the Russian-Yiddish-English Writer Abraham Cahan" for an early history of *Bintel Brief*, particularly Cahan's role in it. See also Cassedy's "A *Bintel brief*," which discusses, in part, its precursors in women's advice columns; as well as Greenberg and Greenberg's "'A Bintel Brief'"; and pp. 91–95 in Lipsky's biography of Cahan.

6. Finck's process of putting the book together involved selecting already translated letters from Isaac Metzker's *A Bintel Brief* and then finding the original letters and having them translated from Yiddish and back to English again (personal communication, September 27, 2013).

7. See, for example, Baskin's *Women of the Word* for examinations of Jewish women writers' marginalized status in the late nineteenth and early twentieth centuries. As Pratt writes of Yiddish women writers of that time period, "[they] were considered by literary critics to be rare phenomena" (119–20). Cassedy relatedly writes about the *Bintel Brief*'s editor's "implicit acceptance of a traditional role for women" on the pages of the *Forward*. Leela Corman's fictional graphic narrative *Unterzakhn* (2012) is another text that looks back in order to reimagine and recapture some of the lost histories of women from the time. See my "Not a word for little girls!"

Bibliography

Adams, Timothy Dow. *Light Writing and Life Writing: Photography in Autobiography*. Chapel Hill: University of North Carolina Press, 2000.

Alixopulos, Trevor, and Vanessa Davis. "Pillowtalk." In *The Big Feminist But: Comics About Women, Men and the Ifs, Ands and Buts of Feminism*, ed. Shannon O'Leary and Joan Reilly, 9–10. Gainesville: Alternative Comics, 2014.

Antin, Mary. *The Promised Land*. New York: Penguin, 1997.

Antler, Joyce, ed. *Talking Back: Images of Jewish Women in American Popular Culture*. Hanover: University Press of New England, 1998.

——. *You Never Call! You Never Write!: A History of the Jewish Mother*. Oxford: Oxford University Press, 2007.

Aviv, Caryn, and David Shneer. *New Jews: The End of the Jewish Diaspora*. New York: New York University Press, 2005.

Baetens, Jan, and Hugo Frey. *The Graphic Novel: An Introduction*. New York: Cambridge University Press, 2015.

Barry, Lynda. *Naked Ladies! Naked Ladies! Coloring Book*. Seattle: Real Comet, 1984.

——. *Picture This: The Near-Sighted Monkey Book*. Montreal: Drawn and Quarterly, 2010.

——. *Syllabus: Notes from an Accidental Professor*. Montreal: Drawn and Quarterly, 2014.

——. *What It Is*. Montreal: Drawn and Quarterly, 2008.

Barthes, Roland. *Camera Lucida: Reflections of Photography*. Trans. Richard Howard. New York: Hill and Wang, 1982.

——. *Image-Text-Music*. Trans. Stephen Heath. New York: Hill and Wang, 1977.

Baskin, Judith. *Women of the Word: Jewish Women and Jewish Writing*. Detroit: Wayne State University Press, 1994.

Baskind, Samantha, and Ranen Omer-Sherman, eds. *The Jewish Graphic Novel: Critical Approaches*. New Brunswick, NJ: Rutgers University Press, 2010.

Bauer, Denise. "Alice Neel's Female Nudes." *Woman's Art Journal* 15, no. 2 (Autumn 1994— Winter 1995): 21–26.

Bauman, Zygmunt. "From Pilgrim to Tourist—or a Short History of Identity." In *Questions of Cultural Identity*, ed. Stuart Hall and Paul du Gay, 18–36. London: SAGE, 1996.

——. *Identity Conversations with Benedetto Vecchi*. Cambridge: Polity, 2004.

Bechdel, Alison. *Are You My Mother?: A Comic Drama*. New York: Houghton Mifflin, 2012.

——. *Fun Home: A Family Tragicomic*. New York: Mariner, 2006.

Beck, Evelyn Torton. "The Politics of Jewish Invisibility." *NWSA Journal* 1, no. 1 (1988): 93–102.

Beinart, Peter. "The Failure of the American Jewish Establishment." *New York Review of Books*, June 10, 2010.

Benjamin, Jessica. "The Omnipotent Mother." In *Representations of Motherhood*, ed. Donna Basson, Margaret Honey, and Maryle Mahrer Kaplan, 129–46. New Haven: Yale University Press, 1994.

Benjamin, Walter. "The Task of the Translator." In *Illuminations*, by Benjamin, ed. Hannah Arendt, trans. Harry Zohn, 69–82. New York: Schocken, 2007.

Ben-Yehuda, Nachman. *The Masada Myth: Collective Memory and Mythmaking in Israel*. Madison: University of Wisconsin Press, 1995.

Berger, Alan, and Gloria Cronin. *Jewish American and Holocaust Literature: Representation in the Postmodern World*. Albany: State University of New York Press, 2004.

Berger, John. *About Looking*. New York: Vintage, 1991.

——. *Ways of Seeing*. London: Penguin, 1977.

Buenaventura, Alvin, and Sammy Harkham, eds. *Kramers Ergot #6*. Oakland: Buenaventura, 2006.

Biale, David, Michael Galchinsky, and Susannah Heschel, eds. *Insider/Outsider: American Jews and Multiculturalism*. Berkeley: University of California Press, 1998.

Blanton, Casey. *Travel Writing: The Self and the World*. New York: Routledge, 2002.

Bloom, Lisa E. *Jewish Identities in American Feminist Art: Ghosts of Ethnicity*. New York: Routledge, 2006.

Bloom, Lynn Z. "'I Write for Myself and Strangers': Private Diaries as Public Documents." In *Inscribing the Daily: Critical Essays on Women's Diaries*, ed. Suzanne L. Bunkers and Cynthia A. Huff, 23–27. Amherst: University of Massachusetts Press, 1996.

Blow-Up. Dir. Michelangelo Antonioni. 1966. Metro-Goldwyn-Mayer.

Borden, Sandra. *Journalism as Practice: MacIntyre, Virtue Ethics, and the Press*. New York: Routledge, 2010.

Bourdieu, Pierre. *Photography: A Middle-Brow Art*. Trans. Shaun Whiteside. Stanford: Stanford University Press, 1990.

Brauner, David. "The Turd That Won't Flush: The Comedy of Jewish Self-Hatred in the Work of Corinne Pearlman, Aline Kominsky-Crumb, and Ariel Schrag." In *Graphic Details*, ed. Sarah Lightman, 131–48. Jefferson: McFarland, 2014.

Brodkin, Karen. *How Jews Became White Folks and What That Says About Race in America*. New Brunswick, NJ: Rutgers University Press, 2000.

Brook, Vincent, ed. *You Should See Yourself: Jewish Identity in Postmodern American Culture.* New Brunswick, NJ: Rutgers University Press, 2006.

Brown, Bill, ed. *Things.* Chicago: University of Chicago Press, 2004.

Buhle, Paul, ed. *Jews and American Comics: An Illustrated History of the American Art Form.* New York: New Press, 2008.

Bulkin, Elly. "Hard Ground: Jewish Identity, Racism, and Anti-Semitism." In *Yours in Struggle: Three Feminist Perspectives on Anti-Semitism and Racism,* by Ellen Bulkin, Minnie Bruce Pratt, and Barbara Smith, 91–193. New York: Long Haul, 1984.

Bunkers, Suzanne L. "Introduction." In *Diaries of Girls and Women: A Midwestern American Sampler,* ed. Bunkers, 3–40. Madison: University of Wisconsin Press, 2001.

——. "Whose Diary Is It Anyway? Issues of Agency, Authority, Ownership." *a/b: Auto/Biography Studies* 17, no. 1 (Summer 2002): 11–27.

Bunkers, Suzanne L., and Cynthia A. Huff. "Introduction." In *Inscribing the Daily: Critical Essays on Women's Diaries,* ed. Bunkers and Huff, 1–22. Amherst: University of Massachusetts Press, 1996.

Burstein, Janet Handler. "Recalling 'Home' from Beneath the Shadow of the Holocaust: American Jewish Women Writers of the New Wave." In *You Should See Yourself,* ed. Vincent Brook, 37–54. New Brunswick: Rutgers University Press, 2006.

Cardell, Kylie. *Dear World: Contemporary Uses of the Diary.* Madison: University of Wisconsin Press, 2014.

Cart, Michael. *Young Adult Literature: From Romance to Realism.* Chicago: American Library Association, 2010.

Cassedy, Steven. "A *Bintel brief:* The Russian Émigré Intellectual Meets the American Mass Media." *East European Jewish Affairs* 34, no. 1 (Summer 2004): 104–20.

Cates, Isaac. "The Diary Comic." In *Graphic Subjects: Critical Essays on Autobiography and Graphic Novels,* ed. Michael A. Chaney, 209–26. Madison: University of Wisconsin Press, 2011.

Chabon, Michael. *The Amazing Adventures of Kavalier and Clay.* New York: Picador, 2000.

Charmé, Stuart. "Jewish Identities in Action: An Exploration of Models, Metaphors, and Methods." By Stuart Charmé, Tali Hyman, Jeffrey Kress, and Bethamie Horowitz. *Journal of Jewish Education* 74, no. 2 (2008): 117–23.

Chute, Hillary L. "Comics as Archives: Meta*MetaMaus*." *e-misférica* 9, no. 1/2 (Summer 2012). http://hemisphericinstitute.org/hemi/en/e-misferica-91/chute.

——. *Graphic Women: Life Narrative and Contemporary Comics.* New York: Columbia University Press, 2010.

Chute, Hillary L., and Patrick Jagoda, eds. "Comics and Media." Special issue, *Critical Inquiry* 40, no. 3 (Spring 2014).

Cixous, Hélène. "Coming to Writing." In *Coming to Writing and Other Essays,* ed. Deborah Jenson, trans. Sarah Cornell et al., 1–58. Cambridge: Harvard University Press, 1992.

Clementi, Federica. "The *JAP,* the *Yenta,* and the *Mame* in Aline Kominsky Crumb's Graphic Imagination." *Journal of Graphic Novels and Comics* 4, no. 2 (2012): 1–23.

Corman, Leela. *Unterzakhn*. New York: Schocken, 2012.

Couser, Thomas G. *Vulnerable Subjects: Ethics and Life Writing.* Ithaca: Cornell University Press, 2004.

Crumb, Robert, and Aline Kominsky Crumb. *Drawn Together: The Collected Works of R. and A. Crumb*. New York: Liveright, 2012.

——. "Introduction." In *The Complete Dirty Laundry Comics*, by Kominsky-Crumb, R. Crumb, and Sophie Crumb, 3–5. San Francisco: Last Gasp, 1993.

——. "A Joint Interview with R. Crumb and Aline Kominsky-Crumb." Interview with B. N. Duncan. In *R. Crumb Conversations*, ed. D. K. Holm, 117–32. Jackson: University Press of Mississippi, 2004.

——. "Saving Face." *New Yorker*, November 28, 2005, 164–66.

Culley, Margo. "Introduction." In *A Day at a Time: The Diary Literature of American Women from 1764 to the Present*, ed. Culley, 3–28. New York: Feminist Press at CUNY, 1985.

——. "Preface." In *A Day at a Time: The Diary Literature of American Women from 1764 to the Present*, ed. Culley, xi–xv. New York: Feminist Press at CUNY, 1985.

Davis, Gerald. *Strange Stories: The Photography of Gerald Davis*. Ed. Todd Oldham. Los Angeles: AMMO, 2014.

Davis, Vanessa. "Affectionate yet Arch: An Interview with Vanessa Davis." Interview with Evan Kindley. *Paris Review* blog, February 2, 2015. http://www.theparisreview.org/blog /2015/02/02/affectionate-yet-arch-an-interview-with-vanessa-davis/.

——. "In Search of the Whole Truth: An Interview with Vanessa Davis." Interview with Tahneer Oksman. *Journal of Graphic Novels and Comics* 4, no. 1 (2013): 179–84.

——. "Interview: Vanessa Davis." Interview with Brian Heater. *Daily Cross Hatch*, October 18, 2010 (part 3 of 4). http://thedailycrosshatch.com/2010/10/18/interview-vanessa-davis-pt -3-of-4/.

——. *Make Me a Woman*. Montreal: Drawn and Quarterly, 2010.

——. *Spaniel Rage*. Oakland: Buenaventura, 2005.

——. "Vanessa Davis Keeps It Complicated." Interview with Sasha Watson. *Publisher's Weekly Online*, September 7, 2010. http://www.publishersweekly.com/pw/by-topic/book-news /comics/article/44386-vanessa-davis-keeps-it-complicated.html.

——. "A Womanly Chat with Vanessa Davis." Interview with Chris Mautner. *Robot 6*, July 23, 2010. http://robot6.comicbookresources.com/2010/07/sdcc-10-an-interview-with -vanessa-davis/.

Dayton-Wood, Amy E. "The Limits of Language: Literacy, Morality, and Transformation in Mary Antin's *The Promised Land*." *MELUS* 34, no. 4 (Winter 2009): 81–98.

De Beauvoir, Simone. *The Second Sex*. Trans. Constance Borde and Sheila Malovany-Chevallier. New York: Vintage, 2011.

De Lauretis, Teresa. *Alice Doesn't: Feminism, Semiotics, Cinema*. Bloomington: Indiana University Press, 1984.

Driscoll, Catherine. *Girls: Feminine Adolescence in Popular Culture and Cultural Theory*. New York: Columbia University Press, 2002.

Eakin, Paul John. *Living Autobiographically: How We Create Identity in Narrative*. Ithaca: Cornell University Press, 2008.

Eichler-Levine, Jodi. *Suffer the Little Children: Uses of the Past in Jewish and African-American Children's Literature*. New York: New York University Press, 2013.

Eisner, Will. *Comics and Sequential Art*. Florida: Poorhouse, 1985.

——. "The Walk Through the Rain: Will Eisner and Frank Miller in Conversation." Interview with Frank Miller. In *The Best American Comics Criticism*, ed. Ben Schwartz, 86–92. Seattle: Fantagraphics, 2010.

El Refaie, Elisabeth. *Autobiographical Comics: Life Writing in Pictures*. Jackson: University Press of Mississippi, 2012.

Finck, Liana. *A Bintel Brief: Love and Longing in Old New York*. New York: Ecco, 2014.

Fingeroth, Danny. *Disguised as Clark Kent: Jews, Comics, and the Creation of the Superhero*. London: Continuum, 2008.

Fishman, Sylvia Barack. *Double or Nothing?: Jewish Families and Mixed Marriage*. Waltham: Brandeis University Press, 2004.

——. "'The Girl I Was': The Construction of Memory in Fiction by American Jewish Women." In *Gender, Place and Memory in the Modern Jewish Experience: Re-placing Ourselves*, ed. Judith Tydor Baumel and Tova Cohen, 145–64. London: Vallentine Mitchell, 2003.

Franco, Dean. *Race, Rights, and Recognition: Jewish American Literature Since 1969*. Ithaca: Cornell University Press, 2012.

Freedman, Jonathan. *Klezmer America: Jewishness, Ethnicity, Modernity*. New York: Columbia University Press, 2008.

Friedan, Betty. *Life So Far: A Memoir*. New York: Simon and Schuster, 2000.

Friedman, Susan Stanford. *Mappings: Feminism and the Cultural Geographies of Encounter*. Princeton: Princeton University Press, 1998.

Furman, Andrew. *Israel Through the Jewish-American Imagination*. Albany: State University of New York Press, 1997.

Gallop, Jane. *Living with His Camera*. Durham, NC: Duke University Press, 2003.

Garb, Tamar. "'The human race torn to pieces': The Painted Portraits of Alice Neel." In *Alice Neel: Painted Truths*, ed. Jeremy Lewison and Barry Walker, 16–33. Houston and New Haven: Museum of Fine Arts and Yale University Press, 2010.

Gardner, Jared. "Autobiography's Biography, 1972–2007." *Biography: An Interdisciplinary Quarterly* 31, no. 1 (Winter 2008): 1–26.

——. *Projections: Comics and the History of Twenty-First-Century Storytelling*. Stanford: Stanford University Press, 2012.

Genette, Gérard. *Paratexts: Thresholds of Interpretation*. Trans. Jane E. Lewin. Cambridge: Cambridge University Press, 1997.

Getz, Philip. "The Birthright Challenge." Review of *Ten Days of Birthright Israel*, *Tours That Bind*, *How to Understand Israel in Sixty Days or Less*, and *What We Brought Back*. *Jewish Review of Books* 2, no. 3 (Fall 2011): 24–26.

Gilman, Sander L. *The Jew's Body*. New York: Routledge, 1991.

——. *Making the Body Beautiful: A Cultural History of Aesthetic Surgery*. Princeton: Princeton University Press, 2001.

Gilmore, Leigh. "The Mark of Autobiography: Postmodernism, Autobiography, and Genre." In *Autobiography and Postmodernism*, ed. Kathleen Ashley, Leigh Gilmore, and Gerard Peters, 3–18. Amherst: University of Massachusetts Press, 1994.

Glidden, Sarah. *How to Understand Israel in Sixty Days or Less*. New York: DC Comics, 2010.

——. "An Interview with Sarah Glidden." Interview with Martyn Peddler. *Bookslut*, December 2010. http://www.bookslut.com/features/2010_12_016913.php.

——. "Sarah Glidden on 'How to Understand Israel.'" Interview with Alex Dueben. *Comic Book Resources*, November 3, 2010. http://www.comicbookresources.com/?page=article&id=29216.

Gloeckner, Phoebe. *The Diary of a Teenage Girl: An Account in Words and Pictures*. Berkeley: Frog, 2002.

Gloeckner, Phoebe, Justin Green, Aline Kominsky-Crumb, and Carol Tyler. "Panel: Comics and Autobiography," moderated by Deborah Nelson. In "Comics and Media," ed. Hillary L. Chute and Patrick Jagoda, special issue, *Critical Inquiry* 40, no. 3 (Spring 2014): 86–103.

Gogol, Nikolai. *The Nose*. Trans. Ian Dreiblatt. Brooklyn: Melville House, 2014.

Gooblar, David, ed. "Roth and Women." Special issue, *Philip Roth Studies* 8, no. 1 (Spring 2012).

Gornick, Vivian. *Fierce Attachments: A Memoir*. New York: Farrar, Straus, and Giroux, 2005.

——. "Saul Bellow, Philip Roth, and the End of the Jew as Metaphor. " In *The Men in My Life*, by Gornick, 85–130. Cambridge: MIT, 2008.

——. *The Situation and the Story: The Art of Personal Narrative*. New York: Farrar, Straus and Giroux, 2002.

——. "Why Do These Men Hate Women? American Novelists and Misogyny." *Village Voice*, December 6, 1976, 12–13+.

Gravett, Paul. *Comics Art*. New Haven: Yale University Press, 2014.

Green, Justin. "Binky Brown Meets the Holy Virgin Mary." In *Justin Green's Binky Brown Sampler*, by Green, 9–52. San Francisco: Last Gasp, 1995.

Greenberg, Harvey R., and Rima R. Greenberg. "'A Bintel Brief': The Editor as Compleat Therapist." *Psychiatric Quarterly* 52, no. 3 (1980): 222–30.

Groensteen, Thierry. *The System of Comics*. Trans. Bart Beaty and Nick Nguyen. Jackson: University Press of Mississippi, 2009.

Gubar, Susan. "Eating the Bread of Affliction: Judaism and Feminist Criticism." In *People of the Book*, ed. Jeffrey Rubin-Dorsky and Shelley Fisher Fishkin, 15–36. Madison: University of Wisconsin Press, 1996.

Hajdu, Maya. "Fragmented Memories in the Graphic Novel: Miriam Katin, Bernice Eisenstein, and Miriam Libicki." MA thesis, Concordia University, 2012. http://spectrum.library.concordia.ca/973752/1/Hajdu_MA_S2012_A1b.pdf.

Haraway, Donna. *Simians, Cyborgs, and Women: The Reinvention of Nature*. New York: Routledge, 1991.

Harris, Rachel S., ed. "The Jewish Woman and Her Body." Special issue, *Nashim* 23 (Spring-Fall 2012).

Harvey, Robert C. "How Comics Came to Be." In *A Comics Studies Reader,* ed. Jeet Heer and Kent Worcester, 25–45. Jackson: University Press of Mississippi, 2009.

Hatfield, Charles. *Alternative Comics: An Emerging Literature.* Jackson: University Press of Mississippi, 2005.

——. "Introduction." In "Comics and Childhood," ed. Charles Hatfield and Cathlena Martin, special issue, *ImageTexT* 3, no. 3 (Summer 2007). http://www.english.ufl.edu/imagetext/archives/v3_3/introduction.shtml.

Heilbrun, Carolyn G. *Reinventing Womanhood.* New York: Norton, 1979.

Hirsch, Marianne. *The Generation of Postmemory: Writing and Visual Culture After the Holocaust.* New York: Columbia University Press, 2012.

Hoffman, Eva. *Lost in Translation: A Life in a New Language.* New York: Penguin, 1990.

Hogan, Rebecca. "Engendered Autobiographies: The Diary as a Feminine Form." In "Autobiography and Questions of Gender," ed. Shirley Neuman, special issue, *Prose Studies* 14, no. 2 (September 1991): 95–107.

Hollinger, David. *Postethnic America: Beyond Multiculturalism.* New York: Basic Books, 2000.

Howe, Irving. *World of Our Fathers.* New York: New York University Press, 2005.

Irvine, Janice M. "Cultural Differences and Adolescent Sexualities." In *Sexual Cultures and the Construction of Adolescent Identities,* ed. Janice M. Irvine, 3–28. Philadelphia: Temple University Press, 1994.

Jacobson, Matthew Frye. *Whiteness of a Different Color: European Immigrants and the Alchemy of Race.* Cambridge: Harvard University Press, 1998.

Jervis, Lisa. "My Jewish Nose." In *Body Outlaws: Rewriting the Rules of Beauty and Body Image,* ed. Ophira Edut, 62–67. Emeryville: Seal, 2003.

Jong, Erika. *Fear of Flying: A Novel.* New York: New American Library, 2003.

Kaplan, E. Ann. *Motherhood and Representation: The Mother in Popular Culture and Melodrama.* New York: Routledge, 1992.

Kazin, Alfred. "Introduction." In *Call It Sleep,* by Henry Roth, ix–xx. New York: Picador, 1990.

Kellman, Steven G. "Lost in the Promised Land: Eva Hoffman Revises Mary Antin." *Prooftexts* 18, no. 2 (May 1998): 149–59.

Kleeblatt, Norman L., ed. *Too Jewish?: Challenging Traditional Identities.* New Brunswick, NJ: Rutgers University Press, 1996.

Kominsky Crumb, Aline. "The Aline Kominsky Crumb Interview." Interview with Peter Bagge. *Comics Journal* 139 (December 1990): 50–73.

——. "Drawn Together: R. Crumb's Beloved Aline Kominsky." Interview with Ilana Arazie. *Heeb Magazine* 12 (Spring 2007): 48–51.

——. "Interview with Andrea Juno." In *Dangerous Drawings: Interviews with Comix and Graphic Artists,* ed. Juno, 162–75. New York: Juno, 1997.

——. "Interview with Hillary L. Chute." *Believer* 7, no. 9 (November/December 2009): 57–68.

——. "Interview with Hillary L. Chute." In *Outside the Box*, ed. Chute, 81–98. Chicago: University of Chicago Press, 2014.

——. *Need More Love: A Graphic Memoir*. London: MQ, 2007.

——. "Public Conversation." Interview with Kristen Schilt. In "Comics and Media," ed. Hillary L. Chute and Patrick Jagoda, special issue, *Critical Inquiry* 40, no. 3 (Spring 2014): 118–31.

Kushner, Tony, and Alisa Solomon. "Introduction." In *Wrestling with Zion: Progressive Jewish-American Responses to the Israeli-Palestinian Conflict*, ed. Kushner and Solomon, 1–9. New York: Grove, 2003.

Lasko-Gross, Miss. *Escape from "Special."* Seattle: Fantagraphics, 2006.

——. *Henni*. Z2 Comics, 2015. Z2comics.com.

——. *A Mess of Everything*. Seattle: Fantagraphics, 2009.

——. "'A Portrait of the World Through My Eyes': An Interview with Miss Lasko-Gross." In *Graphic Details*, ed. Sarah Lightman, 176–84. Jefferson, NC: McFarland, 2014.

——. "The Unintentional Rebel." Interview with Hannah Means Shannon. *Bleeding Cool*, December 19, 2014. http://www.bleedingcool.com/2014/12/19/unintentional-rebel-miss -lasko-gross-discusses-new-graphic-novel-henni-plus-process-art/.

Lay, Carol, and Diane Noomin, eds. *Twisted Sisters 2: Drawing the Line*. Northampton, MA: Kitchen Sink, 1995.

Lejeune, Philippe. "The Diary as 'Antifiction.'" In *On Diary*, ed. Jeremy D. Popkin and Julia Rak, trans. Katherine Durnin, 201–11. Honolulu: University of Hawaii Press, 2009.

——. "How Anne Frank Rewrote the Diary of Anne Frank." In *On Diary*, ed. Jeremy D. Popkin and Julia Rak, trans. Katherine Durnin, 237–66. Honolulu: University of Hawaii Press, 2009.

——. "On Today's Date." In *On Diary*, ed. Jeremy D. Popkin and Julia Rak, trans. Katherine Durnin, 79–92. Honolulu: University of Hawaii Press, 2009.

Levinson, Julian. *Exiles on Main Street: Jewish American Writers and American Literary Culture*. Bloomington: Indiana University Press, 2008.

Levitt, Laura. *Jews and Feminism: The Ambivalent Search for Home*. New York: Routledge, 1997.

Lewison, Jeremy. "A Note on *Self-Portrait*." In *Alice Neel: Painted Truths*, ed. Jeremy Lewison and Barry Walker, 252. Houston and New Haven: Museum of Fine Arts and Yale University Press, 2010.

Libicki, Miriam. *Ceasefire*. Vancouver: Real Gone Girl, 2006.

——. "A Conversation with Miriam Libicki." Interview with Ranen Omer-Sherman. In *The Jewish Graphic Novel*, ed. Samantha Baskind and Ranen Omer-Sherman, 244–52. New Brunswick, NJ: Rutgers University Press, 2007.

——. *Fierce Ease: Portraits of Israel August/September 2008*. Vancouver: Real Gone Girl, 2008.

——. "Jewish Memoir Goes Pow! Zap! Oy!" In *The Jewish Graphic Novel: Critical Approaches*, ed. Samantha Baskind and Ranen Omer-Sherman, 253–74. New Brunswick, NJ: Rutgers University Press, 2010.

——. *jobnik! an american girl's adventures in the israeli army*. Vancouver: Real Gone Girl, 2008.

——. *"jobnik* manifesto." Vancouver: Real Gone Girl, 2004.

——. "Miriam Libicki Talks Comics, Art, and Judaism." Interview with Sarah J. *Bust Magazine*, July 21, 2009. http://bust.com/blog/miriam-libicki-talks-comics-art-and-judaismhtml .html.

——. *Strangers.* Vancouver: Real Gone Girl, 2012.

——. *Towards a Hot Jew: The Israeli Soldier as Fetish Object.* Vancouver: Real Gone Girl, 2005.

Lieberman, Rhonda. "Jewish Barbie." In *Too Jewish?: Challenging Traditional Identities,* ed. Norman L. Kleeblat, 108–14. New Brunswick, NJ: Rutgers University Press, 1996.

Lightman, Sarah, ed. *Graphic Details: Jewish Women's Confessional Comics in Essays and Interviews.* Jefferson: McFarland, 2014.

Lipsky, Seth. *The Rise of Abraham Cahan.* New York: Schocken, 2013.

Lipton, Sara. *Dark Mirror: The Medieval Origins of Anti-Jewish Iconography.* New York: Metropolitan, 2014.

——. "The Invention of the Jewish Nose." *New York Review of Books,* November 14, 2014. http://www.nybooks.com/blogs/gallery/2014/nov/14/invention-jewish-nose/.

McCloud, Scott. *Understanding Comics: The Invisible Art.* New York: Harper Collins, 1994.

McDaniel, Nicole. "Self-Reflexive Graphic Narrative: Seriality and Art Spiegelman's *Portrait of the Artist as a Young %@&*!" Studies in Comics* 1, no. 2 (November 2010): 197–211.

McGinity, Keren R. *Still Jewish: A History of Women and Intermarriage in America.* New York: New York University Press, 2009.

McGrath, Charles. "Not Funnies." *New York Times Magazine,* July 11, 2004: 24+.

Magid, Shaul. *American Post-Judaism: Identity and Renewal in a Postethnic Society.* Bloomington: Indiana University Press, 2013.

Mann, Barbara E. *"Bayit."* In *Space and Place in Jewish Studies,* by Mann, 81–97. New Brunswick: Rutgers University Press, 2012.

Marshall, Elizabeth, and Theresa Rogers. "Writing Back: Rereading Adolescent Girlhoods Through Women's Memoir." *ALAN Review* 3, no. 1 (Fall 2005): 17–22.

Martens, Lorna. *The Promise of Memory: Childhood Recollection and Its Objects in Literary Modernism.* Cambridge: Harvard University Press, 2011.

Metzker, Isaac, ed. *A Bintel Brief: Sixty Years of Letters from the Lower East Side to the* Jewish Daily Forward. New York: Schocken, 1971.

Meyers, Helene. *Identity Papers: Contemporary Narratives of American Jewishness.* Albany: State University of New York Press, 2012.

Miami Makeover: (Almost) Anything for Beauty. Starring Aline Kominsky-Crumb and Dominique Sapel. Produced by Ilana Arazie. 2012.

Miller, Frank, et al. *Batman: The Dark Knight Returns.* New York: DC Comics, 1986.

Miller, Nancy K. "The Entangled Self: Genre Bondage in the Age of Memoir." *PMLA* 122, no. 2 (March 2007): 537–48.

——. "Hadassah Arms." In *People of the Book,* ed. Jeffrey Rubin-Dorsky and Shelley Fisher Fishkin, 153–68. Madison: University of Wisconsin Press, 1996.

Mitchell, W. J. T. *Iconology: Image, Text, Ideology.* Chicago: University of Chicago Press, 1987.

Mock, Roberta. *Jewish Women on Stage, Film, and Television*. New York: Palgrave Macmillan, 2007.

Moore, Alan. *Watchmen*. Illustrated by Dave Gibbons and colored by John Higgins. New York: DC Comics, 1986.

Moore, Anne Elizabeth. "The Entire History of Comics Art: On Paul Gravett's Treatise." *Los Angeles Review of Books*, August 28, 2014. http://lareviewofbooks.org/review/entire -history-comics-art-paul-gravetts-treatise.

Moore, Deborah Dash, and S. Ilan Troen. "Introduction." In *Divergent Jewish Cultures: Israel and America*, 1–26. New Haven: Yale University Press, 2001.

Most, Andrea. "Re-Imagining the Jew's Body: From Self-Loathing to 'Grepts.'" In *You Should See Yourself*, ed. Vincent Brook, 19–36. New Brunswick: Rutgers University Press, 2006.

Muñoz, José Esteban. *Disidentifications: Queers of Color and the Performance of Politics*. Minneapolis: University of Minnesota Press, 1999.

Nakhimovsky, Alice. "The Moral Evolution of the Russian-Yiddish-English Writer Abraham Cahan." *East European Jewish Affairs* 38, no. 2 (August 2008): 159–67.

Noomin, Diane. *Glitz-2-Go*. Seattle: Fantagraphics, 2012.

——, ed. *Twisted Sisters: A Collection of Bad Girl Art*. New York: Penguin, 1991.

Oksman, Tahneer. "'Not a word for little girls!': Knowledge, Word, and Image in Leela Corman's *Unterzakhn*." In *Visualizing Jewish Narrative: Essays on Jewish Comics and Graphic Novels*, ed. Derek Parker Royal. New York: Bloomsbury Academic, 2016.

——. "Visualizing the Jewish Body in Aline Kominsky Crumb's *Need More Love*." *Studies in Comics* 1, no. 2 (November 2010): 213–32.

Omer-Sherman, Ranen. *Diaspora and Zionism in Jewish American Literature: Lazarus, Syrkin, Reznikoff, and Roth*. Hanover: Brandeis University Press, 2002.

Paley, Grace. "A Conversation with My Father." In *The Collected Stories*, by Paley, 232–37. New York: Farrar, Straus, and Giroux, 2007.

——. "Faith in a Tree." In *The Collected Stories*, by Paley, 175–94. New York: Farrar, Straus and Giroux, 2007.

Pekar, Harvey. "Introduction." In *Love That Bunch*, by Aline Kominsky Crumb, iii–iv. Seattle: Fantagraphics, 1990.

——. *Not the Israel My Parents Promised Me*. Illustrated by J. T. Waldman. New York: Farrar, Straus and Giroux, 2014.

Pekar, Harvey, and David Buhle, eds. *Yiddishkeit: Jewish Vernacular and the New Land*. New York: Abrams ComicArts, 2011.

Pinsky, Dina. *Jewish Feminists: Complex Identities and Activist Lives*. Champaign: University of Illinois Press, 2009.

Pipher, Mary. *Reviving Ophelia: Saving the Selves of Adolescent Girls*. New York: Ballantine, 1994.

Plaskow, Judith. *Standing Again at Sinai: Judaism from a Feminist Perspective*. New York: HarperOne, 1991.

Pogrebin, Letty Cottin. *Deborah, Golda, and Me*. New York: Anchor, 1991.

Pollock, Griselda. *Vision and Difference: Feminism, Femininity and Histories of Art*. London: Routledge, 1988.

Pratt, Geraldine, and Victoria Rosner. "Introduction." In *The Global and the Intimate: Feminism in Our Time*, ed. Pratt and Rosner, 1–30. New York: Columbia University Press, 2012.

Pratt, Norma Fain. "Culture and Radical Politics: Yiddish Women Writers in America, 1890–1940." In *Women of the Word*, ed. Baskin, 111–35. Detroit: Wayne State University Press, 1994.

Prell, Riv-Ellen. *Fighting to Become Americans: Assimilation and the Trouble Between Jewish Women and Jewish Men*. Boston: Beacon, 1999.

——. "Terrifying Tales of Jewish Womanhood." In *People of the Book*, ed. Jeffrey Rubin-Dorsky and Shelley Fisher Fishkin, 98–116. Madison: University of Wisconsin Press, 1996.

——. "Why Jewish Princesses Don't Sweat: Desire and Consumption in Postwar American Jewish Culture." In *Too Jewish?: Challenging Traditional Identities*, ed. Norman L. Kleeblat, 74–92. New Brunswick, NJ: Rutgers University Press, 1996.

Rand, Erica. *Barbie's Queer Accessories*. Durham, NC: Duke University Press, 1995.

Reid-Walsh, Jacqueline, and Claudia Mitchell. "'Just a doll?': Liberating Accounts of Barbie Play." *Review of Education/Pedagogy/Culture* 22, no. 2 (2000): 175–90.

Rich, Adrienne. "Notes Towards a Politics of Location." In *Blood, Bread, and Poetry: Selected Prose 1979–1985*, by Rich, 210–31. New York: Norton, 1994.

——. "Split at the Root: An Essay on Jewish Identity." In *Blood, Bread, and Poetry: Selected Prose 1979–1985*, by Rich, 100–23. New York: Norton, 1994.

Robbins, Trina. *From Girls to Grrrls: A History of Women's Comics from Teens to Zines*. San Francisco: Chronicle, 1999.

——. *The Great Women Cartoonists*. New York: Watson-Guptill, 2001.

——. *Pretty in Ink: North American Women Cartoonists, 1896–2013*. Seattle: Fantagraphics, 2013.

Roiphe, Anne. "My Jewish Feminism: A Memoir." *Tablet*, October 1, 2014. http://tabletmag.com/jewish-arts-and-culture/books/184822/anne-roiphe-jewish-feminism.

Ronnen, Meir. "Frida Kahlo's Father Wasn't Jewish After All." *Jerusalem Post*, April 20, 2006. http://www.jpost.com/Arts-and-Culture/Books/Frida-Kahlos-father-wasnt-Jewish-after-all.

Roth, Henry. *Call It Sleep*. New York: Picador, 1990.

Roth, Philip. *Portnoy's Complaint*. New York: Vintage, 1994.

Rothman, Julia. "Introduction." In *Drawn In*, ed. Rothman, 12–13. Beverly: Quarry, 2011.

Rothstein, Mervyn. "Danny Thomas Puts His Life and Work on Paper." *New York Times*, January 10, 1991.

Royal, Derek Parker. "Introduction." In "Coloring America: Multi-Ethnic Engagements with Graphic Narrative," ed. Royal, special issue, *MELUS* 32, no. 3 (2007): 7–22.

Rugg, Linda Haverty. *Picturing Ourselves: Photography and Autobiography*. Chicago: University of Chicago Press, 1997.

Russo, Mary. *The Female Grotesque: Risk, Excess and Modernity*. New York: Routledge, 1995.

Sacco, Joe. Preface. In *Journalism*, by Sacco, xi–xiv. New York: Henry Holt, 2012.

Satrapi, Marjane. *Persepolis: The Story of a Childhood*. New York: Pantheon, 2006.

Schjeldahl, Peter. "Words and Pictures: Graphic Novels Come of Age." *New Yorker*, October 17, 2005, 162–68.

Sedgwick, Eve Kosofsky. *Epistemology of the Closet*. Berkeley: University of California Press, 2008.

Sendak, Maurice, and Art Spiegelman. "In the Dumps." *New Yorker*, September 27, 1993, 80–81.

Senderovich, Sasha. "Russian Jewish American Lit Goes Boom!" *Tablet*, June 17, 2014. http://tabletmag.com/jewish-arts-and-culture/books/175906/russian-jewish-am-lit.

Shteyngart, Gary. *The Russian Debutante's Handbook*. New York: Riverhead, 2002.

Silberstein, Laurence J., ed. *Mapping Jewish Identities*. New York: New York University Press, 2000.

Sillin, Sarah. "Heroine, Reformer, Citizen: Novelistic Convention in Antin's *The Promised Land*." *MELUS* 38, no. 3 (Fall 2013): 25–43.

Smith, Sidonie. "Identity's Body." In *Autobiography and Postmodernism*, ed. Kathleen Ashley, Leigh Gilmore, and Gerald Peters, 266–92. Amherst: University of Massachusetts Press, 1994.

Smith, Sidonie, and Julia Watson. *Interfaces: Women, Autobiography, Image, Performance*. Ann Arbor: University of Michigan Press, 2005.

——. *Reading Autobiography: A Guide for Interpreting Life Narratives*, 2d ed. Minneapolis: University of Minnesota Press, 2010.

Sollors, Werner. *Beyond Ethnicity: Consent and Descent in American Culture*. New York: Oxford University Press, 1986.

Sontag, Susan. *On Photography*. New York: Farrar, Straus and Giroux, 1977.

——. *Regarding the Pain of Others*. New York: Picador, 2003.

Spence, Jo. "The Walking Wounded?" In *Jo Spence: Beyond the Perfect Image*, ed. Jorge Ribalta, 314–32. Barcelona: Museu d'Art Contemporani de Barcelona, 2005.

Spiegelman, Art. "Art Spiegelman's *MetaMaus*." Interview with Hillary Chute. 92nd Street Y, New York, October 6, 2011.

——. *Maus I: A Survivor's Tale*. New York: Pantheon, 1986.

——. *Maus II: A Survivor's Tale*. New York: Pantheon, 1991.

——. *MetaMaus: A Look Inside a Modern Classic*. New York: Pantheon, 2011.

Strömberg, Fredrik. *Jewish Images in the Comics: A Visual History*. Seattle: Fantagraphics, 2012.

Tabachnick, Stephen E. *The Quest for Jewish Belief and Identity in the Graphic Novel*. Tuscaloosa: University of Alabama Press, 2014.

Tanenbaum, Leora. *Bad Shoes and the Women Who Love Them*. Illustrated by Vanessa Davis. New York: Seven Stories, 2010.

Tessler, Mark A. *A History of the Israeli-Palestinian Conflict*. Bloomington: Indiana University Press, 1994.

Trites, Roberta Seelinger. *Disturbing the Universe: Power and Repression in Adolescent Literature.* Iowa City: University of Iowa Press, 2000.

Ulinich, Anya. *Lena Finkle's Magic Barrel: A Graphic Novel.* New York: Penguin, 2014.

Weinstein, Lauren. "The Best We Can Hope For" (map). In *The Ganzfeld 7,* ed. Ben Jones and Dan Nadel, 8–9. New York: PictureBox, 2008.

——. "Carriers: A Webcomic on Health, Luck, and Life." *Nautilus,* June 23, 2014. http://nautil.us/blog/carriers-a-webcomic-on-health-luck-and-life.

——. *Girl Stories.* New York: Henry Holt, 2006.

——. *The Goddess of War.* New York: PictureBox, 2008.

——. *Inside Vineyland.* Gainesville: Alternative Comics, 2003.

——. "Interview with Emily Brobow." *Believer,* May 2007, 46–53.

——. "Thinking Panoramically: An Interview with Lauren Weinstein." Interview with Tahneer Oksman. In *Graphic Details,* ed. Sarah Lightman, 176–84. Jefferson: McFarland: 2014.

Weinstein, Simcha. *Up, Up, and Oy Vey: How Jewish History, Culture, and Values Shaped the Comic Book Superhero.* Baltimore: Barricade, 2009.

Wettstein, Howard, ed. "Introduction." In *Diasporas and Exiles: Varieties of Jewish Identity,* ed. Wettstein, 1–17. Berkeley: University of California Press, 2002.

Willis, Deborah, ed. *Picturing Us: African American Identity in Photography.* New York: New Press, 1994.

Willis, Ellen. "Is There Still a Jewish Question? Why I'm an Anti-Anti-Zionist." In *Wrestling with Zion,* ed. Tony Kushner and Alisa Solomon, 226–32. New York: Grove, 2003.

Winnicott, D. W. *Playing and Reality.* New York: Routledge, 1999.

Winter, Margaret Crumpton. "Mary Antin and Assimilation." In *American Narratives,* by Winter, 30–54. Baton Rouge: Louisiana State University Press, 2007.

Wirth-Nesher, Hana. *Call It English: The Languages of Jewish American Literature.* Princeton: Princeton University Press, 2009.

Wolk, Douglas. *Reading Comics: How Graphic Novels Work and What They Mean.* Cambridge: Da Capo, 2007.

Woolf, Virginia. *Three Guineas.* San Diego: Harcourt, 2006.

Wright, Bradford W. *Comic Book Nation: The Transformation of Youth Culture in America.* Baltimore: Johns Hopkins University Press, 2001.

Zeitlin, Irving M. *Jews: The Making of a Disapora People.* Cambridge: Polity, 2012.

Index

Acceptance, 101, *102*

Accountability, 20, 220

Adolescent body, 152–53, *155*, 159–62, *160*; *see also* Puberty

Adolescent girls, 1, 117

Adolescent literature, 19–20, 130, 140

Affiliation, 134–35; *see also* Dis-affiliation; Jewish affiliation

Age, *see* Comics and age

Agency, 145–47

Agenda, 174–75

Airport security, 175–78, *177*, 243*n*10

Alienation, 125, 162; bodies related to, 159–61, *160*; connection and, 152; Diana and, 151–52; differences and, 163

Alixopulos, Trevor, 240*nn*22–23

Amazing Adventures of Kavalier and Clay, The (Chabon), 234*n*21

Ambiguity: of self, 84, 86; from word-image combinations, 28–29

Ambivalence, 98–99

American Jewish women writers: home and, 93–94, 239*n*16; journeys for, 93; memories of, 93

Anonymous portraits, 84, *85*, 86, 239*nn*13–14

Antiessentialism, 7–8

Antin, Mary, 221–22, 244*n*1, 244*n*3

Antler, Joyce, 7, 102

Anxiety, 59; in *Escape from "Special,"* 122–26, *123*, 127, 128–30, *129*, 132, 132–33, *139*; in *Girl Stories*, 146; in *Make Me a Woman*, 90, *91*, 92–93, 106, 239*n*15

Apology, 95, *96*, 100–1

Architecture, 61, *62*

Are You My Mother? (Bechdel), 124

Art, *16*, 16–17

Art comics, 30

Art photography, 34

Assimilation, 241*n*16; in "Euro Dirty Laundry," 55, *55*; Jewish bodies and, 59; postassimilation, 3–4, 231*n*2

Audience: for *Escape from "Special,"* 117; for *Girl Stories*, 116–17; for *Make Me a Woman*, 82; for *Spaniel Rage*, 72–73, 238*nn*6–7

Autobiographical comics, 30, 237*n*12

Aviv, Caryn, 20, 169–70

Barbies, 149–51, *150*

Barry, Lynda, 17, 84

Barthes, Roland, 29–30, 236*n*9

Bat mitzvah: in *Israel*, 176, *177*; in *Make Me a Woman*, 86–89, *87*, 97–98

Bauman, Zygmunt, 17, 69

Bechdel, Alison, 124

Beinart, Peter, 168, 242n2

Bell, Gabrielle, *16*, 16–17

Belonging, 128; in *Girl Stories*, 151, 153–54, 156, 158–59, 161–62; in *Make Me a Woman*, 99

Benjamin, Walter, 230

"Best We Can Hope For, The" (Weinstein), 11, *12*, 234n18; perspective in, 14–15; space in, 13–14

Beyond Ethnicity (Sollors), 44–45

Bias: against Hasidim, 179–80; in *Israel*, 184–85

Bintel Brief, A: Love and Longing in Old New York (Finck), 21; Cahan in, 223–25, *224*, 227–28, 230; dis-affiliation in, 230; dislocation in, 223–25; emotion in, 227, *227*; gaps in, 225–26; grandfather in, 225, *226*; identity in, 222; Jewish identity in, 222–23, 228, 230; name of, 223; photographs in, 228, *229*, 245n7; receptivity in, *227*, 227–28; remembering in, 223–27; sources for, 222–23, 245n6; style of, 222–23, *224*, 245n4; translation in, 223

Birthright, 174, 183, 185; *see also Israel*

Blanton, Casey, 169

Bloom, Lisa E., 232n8, 238n22

Bloom, Lynn Z., 72–73

Bodies, 199; alienation related to, 159–61, *160*; *see also* Adolescent body; Jewish bodies

Borden, Sandra, 243n15

Boundaries: "Euro Dirty Laundry" and, 53–54, 56–57; in "Goldie: A Neurotic Woman," 38, *39*, 44

Bourdieu, Pierre, 34

Boyfriend, 151–57, *155*, *157*; *see also* Non-Jewish boyfriend

Brauner, David, 241n2

Brodkin, Karen, 52, 231n1

Brooklyn, NY, 179, 243n12

Buenaventura Press, 69, 238n3, 239n15

Bunch (semiautobiographical character), 1, 236n7; interdependent word-image combination about, 28; isolation of, *49*, 51; name of, 46–47, 237n6; opposition for, 49, 50–51; past of, *49*, 49–50; pride of, *49*, 51; reorientation of, 48–49, *49*, 61, *62*, *63*; self-representations of, 26–28, 32–34, *33*, 48, 60–61; speculations of, 47, 48–50, *49*

"Bunch Her Baby & Grammaw Blabette, The" (Kominsky Crumb): architecture of, 61, *62*; Jewish mother stereotype in, 60, *62*, 63–64; reorientation in, 61, *62*, *63*; repetition in, 61, *62*

Bunkers, Suzanne, 79

Burstein, Janet Handler, 93

Cahan, Abraham, *224*, 227–28, 230; background of, 223; gaps and, 225; history from, 223–25

Call It Sleep (Roth, H.), 6

Camera Lucida (Barthes), 29–30, 236n9

Cardell, Kylie, 238n6

Cartoonists, 234n19; control by, 161; postassimilation of, 3–4, 231n2; time and space for, 10–11, 233n15; women, 15–18, 234n21

Cartoonists of Color Database, 231n4

Cartoons, 234n19

Cassedy, Steven, 245n7

Categorization, 35

Cates, Isaac, 80, 239n9

Chabon, Michael, 234n21

Charmé, Stuart, 8–9, 89–90

Children, 115–16

Children's literature, 19–20, 130

Chronicling, 75, *76*, 77

Chute, Hillary, 4, 10, 18, 25–26, 84

Cixous, Hélène, 9, 233n14

Index

Clementi, Federica, 235*n*4

Collage, 37

Coloring: in *Girl Stories*, 145–47; in *Israel*, 170, 242*n*5; in *Make Me a Woman*, 81, 89–90, 92, 239*n*15

Comics, 4, 90, 234*n*19; autobiographical, 30, 237*n*12; isolation of, 17–18; as medium, 3, 30; narrative, 67, 238*n*1; underground, 237*n*14

Comics and age, 240*n*4; children in, 115–16; dis-affiliation in, 120; Jewish identity in, 118, 120; marketing for, 115–16; social power and, 130; transitions in, 117–18; *see also Escape from "Special"*; *Girl Stories*

Comics and Sequential Art (Eisner), 234*n*18

Comics Art (Gravett), 4

Comics collaboration: for "Euro Dirty Laundry," 53–56, *55*, 237*n*18; of Kominsky Crumb, 26–27, 51–56, *55*, 236*n*6, 237*nn*18–19; in "Pillowtalk," 240*n*23

Communities: in *Escape from "Special,"* 127, 128, 133–34, 241*n*11; stereotypes and, 103–4

Community, connection to, 180

Complete Dirty Laundry Comics, The, 26–27, 236*n*7

Complications, *189*, 191–93

Confusion, 94–95, 97–99, 101, 240*n*17

Connection, 220, 243*n*13; alienation and, 152; to community, 180; dis-affiliation and, 218; distance and, 218–19; from memories, 223–24, 226–27, *227*

Contradictions, 187–91, *189*

Control, 57; by cartoonists, 161; of stereotypes, 59–60

Corman, Leela, 245*n*7

Counternarrative, 157–58

Couser, Thomas G., 237*n*19

Cover: of *Escape from "Special,"* 117, *119*; of *Girl Stories*, 117, *118*; of *Need More Love*, 35

Critics, 26

Crumb, Robert, 25, 27, 236*n*6; Davis, V., and, 240*n*17; in "Euro Dirty Laundry," 53–56, *55*, 237*n*18; Honeybunch Kaminski from, 46–47; "Saving Face" by, 51–52

Crumb, Sophie, 53–56, 237*n*18

Culley, Margo, 72, 78–79

Davis, Gerald, 239*n*12

Davis, Vanessa, 19, 21; Alixopulos and, 240*n*23; Crumb, R., and, 240*n*17; Kominsky Crumb compared to, 67, 238*n*2; *see also Make Me a Woman*; *Spaniel Rage*

Dear World (Cardell), 238*n*6

Death anniversary (*Yahrzeit*), 244*n*21

de Beauvoir, Simone, 68

Defiance, 161

Degeneration, 42, 44

Diachronic diversity, 8

Diana (semifictitious character): alienation and, 151–52; Barbies and, *150*, *151*; connection to, 154; self-definition and, 158–63, *159*, *160*

Diaries: complications about, 77; fiction and, 79, 239*n*9; journals and, 69–70; structure of, 79–80; *see also Spaniel Rage*

Diary of a Teenage Girl, The (Gloeckner), 161

Diaspora, 20; impotence of, 168; language of, 167

Differences, 2–3; alienation and, 163; in disconnection, 181–82, *182*; in *Israel*, 181–82, *182*, 186–88, 191–92; in Jewish American women's identity, 5; in *jobnik!*, 204–5, *205*, 208; in *Make Me a Woman*, 95–97, *96*, 108–9

Dis-affiliation, 2–3, 20; in *A Bintel Brief*, 230; in comics and age, 120; connection and, 218; ethics and, 169; in *Israel*, 190–94; in *Make Me a Woman*, 106–7

Disconnection, 243*n*13; difference in, 181–82, *182*; isolation as, 180, 182–83; as outsider, 180–81; understanding from, 182, 182–84

Disengagement, 207–8, *209*

Dislocation, 223–25

Disorientation, 175–79

Displacement: in *Escape from "Special,"* 122, 125, 133–35; in *jobnik!*, 197–200, 202, 204–8, 209, 244*n*22; self-fashioning and, 160–61

Distance: connection and, 218–19; in *Girl Stories*, 156, 162–63

Disturbing the Universe (Trites), 130

Divergent Jewish Cultures (Moore and Troen), 107

Doll, 122–24, *123*, 241*n*7

Doubly liminal border case, 231*n*1

Drawings, 196; sketchbooks for, 78

Drawing style: of *Escape from "Special,"* 121; in *Girl Stories*, 146; of *jobnik!*, 197; of Kominsky Crumb, 26–28, 31–32, 236*n*8

Drawn Together (Kominsky Crumb and Crumb), 236*n*6

Dreams, 126, *127*, 128

Driscoll, Catherine, 240*n*4

"Dyspeptic Academic" (Davis, V.), 99–100

Eakin, Paul John, 68, 80

Edits, 71–72

Eisner, Will, 81, 90, 234*n*8

Emotion: in *A Bintel Brief*, 227, *227; see also* Anxiety

Empowerment, 41, 44–45

Engagement, 207–8, *209*; in *Israel*, 182, 182–84, 188–90, *189*; with Kominsky Crumb, 235*n*4

Epistemology of the Closet (Sedgwick), 164

Escape from "Special" (Lasko-Gross), 19–20, 241*n*6; anxiety in, 122–26, *123*, *127*, 128–30, *129*, *132*, 132–33, 139; audience for, 117; communities in, 127, 128, 133–34, 241*n*11; cover of, 117, *119*; displacement in, 122, 125, 133–35; doll in, 122–24, *123*, 241*n*7; drawing style of, 121; fear in, 126, *127*, 128; "The First Mindfuck" in, 131–33, *132*; gap in, 121–22; *Girl Stories* compared to, 140–41, 148; introspection in, 128–30, *129*, 139; isolation in, 131–35, *136*, 137–38, 139; Jewish identity in, 134–35, *136*, 137–38, 140, 164, 166; "Kidnapped" in, 125–26, *127*, 128–30, *129*; memories in, 126, 128–29, *129*; mother in, 122, *123*, 125–26, *127*, 128; rebellion in, 134–35, 137; self-extension in, 122–24; self-representation in, 138, *139*; "special" in, 133–34, 137–38; structure of, 120–21, 125–26; subjectivity in, 129–30; symbols in, 135, *136*, 137; teddy bear in, 124; transitions in, 124, 130–31; truth in, 126, 128–29, *129*

Ethnic heritage, 54–55, *55*, 237*n*20, 238*n*21

"Euro Dirty Laundry" (Kominsky Crumb, Crumb, R., and Crumb, S.): assimilation in, 55, *55*; boundaries and, 53–54, 56–57; comics collaboration for, 53–56, *55*, 237*n*18; ethnic heritage in, 54–55, *55*, 237*n*20, 238*n*21; stereotypes in, *55*, 56–57; styles in, 53–54

Excess, 35–37

Expectations: for Jewish women, 46; in *Make Me a Woman*, 100, 106–7, 109

"Faith in a Tree" (Paley), 14–15

Fantasy, 107–9, *108; see also Bintel Brief, A: Love and Longing in Old New York*

Fashion, 239*n*14

Fear, 126, *127*, 128

Fear of Flying (Jong), 6–7

Female Grotesque, The (Russo), 63

Fiction, 79, 239*n*9

Fierce Ease (Libicki), 215–16, *217*, 218

Finck, Liana, 21, 222; *see also Bintel Brief, A: Love and Longing in Old New York*

"First Mindfuck, The" (Lasko-Gross), 131–33, *132*

Fishman, Sylvia Barack, 93

Frank, Anne, 238*n*4

"Freak," 147, *148*, 151, 160–61

Friedan, Betty, 232*n*5

Friedman, Susan Stanford, 9, 167, 169

"Gallery of Missing Husbands, The," 228, *229*

Gallop, Jane, 34

Ganzfeld, The, 11, *12*, 234*n*17

Gap, 121–22

Garb, Tamar, 239*n*11

Gardner, Jared, 48, 235*n*4

Gender: art and, *16*, 16–17; in *Girl Stories*, 156; Jewish bodies and, 52–53

Genette, Gérard, 71, 238*n*5

Genres, 15–18

Getz, Philip, 174

Gilman, Sander, 23–24, 162, 232*n*7, 235*n*4

Gilroy, Paul, 167

"'Girl I Was, The': The Construction of Memory in Fiction by American, Jewish Women" (Fishman), 93

Girl Stories (Weinstein), 19–20, 241*n*13, 241*n*16; adolescent body in, 152–53, *155*, 159–62, *160*; agency in, 145–47; alienation in, 151–52, 159–63, *160*; anxiety in, 146; audience for, 116–17; Barbies in, *142*, 149–51, *150*; belonging in, 151, 153–54, 156, 158–59, 161–62; boyfriend in, 151–57, *155, 157*; coloring in, 145–47; counternarrative in, 157–58; cover of, 117, *118*; defiance in, 161; Diana in, *150*, 151–52, 154, 158–63, *159, 160*; distance in, 156, 162–63; drawing style in, 146; *Escape from "Special"* compared to, 140–41, 148; "freak" in, 147, *148*, 151, 160–61; gender in, 156; high school in, 151–63, *155, 157*, 159, *160*; introduction of, 141–43, *142*; Jewish identity in, 140–41, 162–64, 166; kissing in, 154–56, *155*; noses in, 159–62, *160*; outcasts in, 147, *148*; parents in, 143, 163; performativity in, 156–58, *157*; physical changes in, 152–53; queerness in, 150–51; quest in, 148–49, 152; school in, 141–43, *142*, 146–47; self-portrayal in, *144, 145*, 147–48, *148*, 160–61; sense of self in, 153–54; sexuality in, 153; structure of, 141, *145*; transformation in, 150–51; urgency in, 143–44, *144*

Glidden, Sarah, 20, 242*n*3; *see also Israel*

Global and the Intimate, The (Pratt and Rosner), 10, 234*n*16

Gloeckner, Phoebe, 161

"Goldie: A Neurotic Woman" (Kominsky Crumb), 18–19, 37; boundaries in, 38, *39*, 44; degeneration in, 42, 44; empowerment in, 41, 44–45; independence in, 44; isolation in, *39*, 40–41, *41*; Jewish identity in, 44–45; movement in, *41*, 44; placement of, 45; profile in, *41*, 42–43; puberty in, *39*, 40–42; sense of self in, 38, *39*, 40; style of, 38; symbols in, 43–44

Gornick, Vivian, 6, 65, 240*n*18

Grandfather, 225, *226*

Graphic Details, 234*n*21

Graphic diary, *see Spaniel Rage*

Graphic memoirs, 19, 30; as sequential art, 10; *see also Need More Love*

Graphic narratives, 10–11, 13–15, 25

Graphic novels, 30

Graphic Women (Chute), 10, 25

Gravett, Paul, 4

Green, Justin, 35, 237*n*12

Gutters, 90, 121

Handwriting, 71

Haraway, Donna, 9

Harvey, Robert C., 234*n*19

Hasidim, 176, 243*n*10; bias against, 179–80;
    in Brooklyn, NY, 179, 243*n*12; in Israel,
    178–80, 243*n*11

Hatfield, Charles, 116, 240*n*3

Hebrew words, 201, 244*n*21; translations of,
    198, 205

Heilbrun, Carolyn, 5

High school, 151–63, *155*, *157*, *159*, *160*

Hirsch, Marianne, 231*n*2

History, 223–25; Jewish Americans in,
    232*n*7

Hoffman, Eva, 221–22

Home, *217*; American Jewish women writers
    and, 93–94, 239*n*16; in *Israel*, 178,
    183, 186, 220; in *Make Me a Woman*,
    90, *91*, 92–95; in *Strangers*, 219–20;
    transnationalism of, 169–70, 218

Homeland, 186, 190–92

Homesickness, 95–97, 101, *102*, 104–5

Honeybunch Kaminski (fictitious character),
    46–47

Howe, Irving, 232*n*7

*How to Understand Israel in Sixty Days or
    Less; see Israel*

Huff, Cynthia A., 79

Hunger, 225–27

Identity, 17; of adolescent girls, 117; affiliation
    and, 134–35; in *A Bintel Brief*, 222; in
    jobnik!, 198–99, 208, *209*, 210–11; from
    memories, 221–22; in "Nose Job," 1–2;
    self compared to, 68; spaces related to,
    169; travel narratives related to, 184–85;
    see also Jewish identity

Identity positions, 24–25

Images, 28, 82, *83*, 101, *102*; in *Need More
    Love*, 26–27, *29*, *31*, 31–35, *33*, *36*, *37*,
    236*n*7; repetition of, 31–32; of *Spaniel
    Rage*, 73, *74*, *75*, 238*n*8

Immigration, 221–22, 231*n*3, 244*n*1

Impotence, 168

Independence, 11

Inner life, 122–23

Insider/outsider, 52, 65, 107

Insider/Outsider, 231*n*1

Inside Vineyland (Weinstein), 164, *165*,
    241*n*14

Interdependent word-image combination,
    28

Interethnicity, 59

Interfaces (Smith and Watson), 26

Intermarriage, 241*n*16

Interviews, 215–16, *217*, 218

Intimacy, 110–12, *112*

Introduction: of *Girl Stories*, 141–43, *142*; to
    Make Me a Woman, 81

Introspection, 128–30, *129*, *139*

Isolation: of Bunch, 49, *51*; of comics, 17–18;
    as disconnection, 180; in *Escape from
    "Special,"* 131–35, *136*, 137–38, *139*; in
    "Goldie: A Neurotic Woman," *39*, 40–41,
    41; in *Israel*, 180–85, *182*

Israel, 215, 242*n*2; Hasidim in, 178–80,
    243*n*11

Israel (Glidden), 20, 169, 242*n*3, 242*n*6;
    aftermath to, 193–95, *194*; agenda in,
    174–75; airport security in, 175–78,
    177, 243*n*10; bat mitzvah in, 176,
    177; biases in, 184–85; coloring in,
    170, 242*n*5; complications in, *189*,
    191–93; contradictions in, 187–91, *189*;
    differences in, 181–82, *182*, 186–88,
    191–92; dis-affiliation in, 190–94;
    disconnection in, 180–83, 243*n*13;
    disorientation in, 175–79; engagement
    in, *182*, 182–84, 188–90, *189*; Hasidim
    and, 176–80, 243*nn*10–12; home in, 178,
    183, 186, 220; homeland of, 186, 190–
    92; isolation in, 180–85, *182*; Jewish
    identity in, 175–80, 185–90; *jobnik!*
    compared to, 195–97, 210; journalism

related to, 184–85, 243nn14–15; maps in, 171–72, *173, 174*; narratives in, 186–88, *187*; propaganda and, 181, *181*, 185; research on, 175, 243n9; secularity in, 178–80; self-portrayal in, *181*, 181–83, *182*; similarities in, 186–88, 190–92; "the situation" in, 181, *181*, 185, 188–89, *189*; spaces in, 171–72, *173*, 174–76, 183; structure of, 170–71, 242n4, 242n7; subjectivity in, 172, 174; time in, 175–76, 183; tribal loyalties in, 192–93; truth in, 176, 178, 181, 188, 190, 192, 194, 215

Israeli men, 103, 107–9, *108*

Israelis: North American Jews compared to, 212, 215–16, 218; Palestinians and, 212, *214*, 215; *see also jobnik! an american girl's adventures in the israeli army; Towards a Hot Jew: The Israeli Soldier as Fetish Object*

Israeli state, 198–200, 244n21

"Is There Still a Jewish Question?" (Willis), 243n16

It Ain't Me Babe: Women's Liberation, 237n14

Jagoda, Patrick, 18

"*JAP*, the *Yenta*, and the *Mame* in Aline Kominsky Crumb's Graphic Imagination, The" (Clementi), 235n4

Jervis, Lisa, 162

Jewish affiliation: choice in, 2; dis-affiliation in, 2–3, 20

Jewish Americans: in history, 232n7; immigration of, 2, 21, 231n3; racial middleness of, 52

Jewish American women, 4

Jewish American women's identity: antiessentialism and, 7–8; differences in, 5; noses and, 232n7; spaces in, 5–10

Jewish bodies, 162, 232n7, 235n4; assimilation and, 59; gender and,

52–53; of Kominsky Crumb, 24, 235n3; stereotypes of, 23, 59, 102–3

Jewish boys, 46

Jewish college students, 242n2

Jewish Daily Forward, 223–27, *224, 227*; "The Gallery of Missing Husbands" in, 228, *229*

Jewish Graphic Novel, The, 234n21

Jewish Identities in American Feminist Art (Bloom, L.), 232n8, 238n22

Jewish identity, 5, 167; in *A Bintel Brief*, 222–23, 228, 230; in comics and age, 118, 120; disavowals in, 20; in *Escape from "Special,"* 134–35, *136,* 137–38, 164, 166; in *Girl Stories,* 140–41, 162–64, 166; in "Goldie: A Neurotic Woman," 44–45; in *Israel,* 175–80, 185–90; in *Make Me a Woman,* 86–89, *87,* 95–114, *102, 108, 112*; in *Mess of Everything, A,* 138, 140, 241n12; noses and, 232n7; past related to, 21; reconceptualization of, 3, 7–8; in travel narratives, 169–70

Jewish Images in the Comics (Strömberg), 234n21

"Jewish Memoir Goes Pow! Zap! Oy!" (Libicki), 243n17

Jewish men, 24, 46, 105–6; Israeli men, 103, 107–9, *108; see also* Non-Jewish men

Jewish mothers, 114

Jewish mother stereotype, 6–7, 113, 232n9; in "The Bunch Her Baby & Grammaw Blabette," 60, *62,* 63–64

Jewish women: as doubly liminal border case, 231n1; expectations for, 46; generalizations about, 57–58; stereotypes of, 57–59, *58,* 102; *see also* American Jewish women writers

Jewish women cartoonists, 234n21; as outsiders, 17–18; sources for, 18

Jews and American Comics, 234n21

Jew's Body, The (Gilman), 232n7

jobnik! an american girl's adventures in the israeli army (Libicki), 244n20, bodies in, 199; difference in, 204–5, 205, 208; disengagement in, 207–8, 209; displacement in, 197–200, 202, 204–8, 209, 244n22; drawing style of, 197; Hebrew words in, 198, 201, 205, 244n21; identity in, 198–99, 208, 209, 210–11; *Israel* compared to, 195–97, 210; Israeli state in, 198–200, 244n21; mother in, 200, 201; perspective in, 196, 198, 244n18; photographs in, 197; psychological diagnosis in, 202, 203, 204; Rabin and, 199–200, 201, 244n21; romance in, 206, 207, 208; sexuality in, 205–7, 207; structure of, 196–97, 210, 244n19; time and space in, 197–200, 210

jobnik manifesto (Libicki), 195

jobnik series (Libicki), 20, 202, 204

Jong, Erica, 6–7

Journalism: interviews in, 215–16, 217, 218; *Israel* related to, 184–85, 243nn14–15; Libicki and, 195–96, 211, 243n17, 244n23; visual subjectivity and, 196

Journalism as Practice (Borden), 243n15

Journals, 69–70

Journeys, 93; *see also* Travel narratives

"Just Think . . . I could've ended up looking like Marlo Thomas instead of Danny! If only I'd had a Nose Job"; *see* "Nose Job"

Kahlo, Frida, 54–55, 146, 237n20

Kahlo, Guillermo, 237n20

Kazin, Alfred, 6

"Kidnapped" (Lasko-Gross), 125–26, 127, 128–30, 129

Kissing, 154–56, 155

Kochalka, James, 239n9

Kominsky Crumb, Aline, 237n16; background of, 24, 31, 45–46; comics collaboration of, 26–27, 51–56, 55, 236n6, 237nn18–19; critics of, 26; Davis, V., compared to, 67, 238n2; drawing style of, 26–28, 31–32, 236n8; engagement with, 235n4; as insider/outsider, 52, 65; Jewish body of, 24, 235n3; *Love that Bunch*, 3; marginalization of, 34–35, 236n11; motherhood and, 57, 63–64; names and, 60, 235n1; negativity about, 37–38; "Nose Job," 1–2, 45, 49, 50–52; perception for, 60; photographs of, 29, 31, 31–32; plastic surgery of, 51–52; real self of, 29, 36, 37; self-control of, 57; self-exploration of, 64; serial related to, 24–25; stereotypes and, 18–19, 23–24; temperament of, 64–66; word-image combination of, 28–29; Yiddishisms from, 23; *see also Need More Love*

Kushner, Tony, 189–90, 192–93

Ladydrawers Comics Collective, 231n4

Language, 23, 167, 230; Yiddish, 223, 224; *see also* Hebrew words

Lasko-Gross, Miss, 19–20, 116; *Mess of Everything, A*, 117, 120–21, 241nn5–6; *see also Escape from "Special"*

Lejeune, Philippe, 69–71, 79

Lena Finkle's Magic Barrel (Ulinich), 231n3

Libicki, Miriam, 20; *Fierce Ease* by, 215–16, 217, 218; journalism and, 195–96, 211, 243n17, 244n23; *Strangers* by, 211, 218–20, 244n23, 244n27; *see also jobnik! an american girl's adventures in the israeli army; Towards a Hot Jew: The Israeli Soldier as Fetish Object*

Life So Far (Friedan), 232n5

Lightman, Sarah, 234n21

Lipsky, Seth, 223

Lipton, Peggy, 49, 50

Living Autobiographically (Eakin), 68

Living with His Camera (Gallop), 34

Lost in Translation (Hoffman), 221–22
"Love, Marriage and Motherhood"
    (Kominsky Crumb), 53
Love that Bunch (Kominsky Crumb), 3
Luntz, Frank, 242*n*2

Madonna, 55, 238*n*21
Make Me a Woman (Davis, V.), 19, 80;
    acceptance in, 101, *102*; ambivalence in,
    98–99; anonymous portraits in, 84,
    85, 86, 239*nn*13–14; anxiety in, 90, *91,*
    92–93, 106, 239*n*15; apology in, 95, *96,*
    100–1; audience for, 82; bat mitzvah
    in, 86–89, *87,* 97–98; belonging in,
    99; coloring in, 81, 89–90, 92, 239*n*15;
    confusion in, 94–95, 97–99, 101,
    240*n*17; difference in, 95–97, *96,* 108–9;
    dis-affiliation in, 106–7; expectations in,
    100, 106–7, 109; fantasy in, 107–9, *108;*
    home in, 90, *91,* 92–95; homesickness
    in, 95–97, 101, *102,* 104–5; intimacy
    in, 110–12, *112;* introduction to, 81–82;
    Israeli men in, 103, 107–9, *108;* Jewish
    affiliation in, 97–99; Jewish identity in,
    86–89, *87,* 95–114, *102, 108, 112;* Jewish
    men in, 105–6; materialism in, 98;
    non-Jewish boyfriend in, 109–12, *112,*
    240*nn*22–23; non-Jewish men in, 105–6,
    109–13, *112,* 240*nn*22–23; opening image
    in, 82, *83,* 101, *102;* perspective in,
    97, 99–100; positions in, *96,* 96–97;
    questioning in, 100, 110; reorientation
    in, 88–89, 113; representation in, 88;
    self-exile in, 101, *102,* 104–5; self in,
    68–69, 114; stereotypes in, 103–6, *112,*
    112–13; structure of, 89–90; time in,
    92–93, 114
Making the Body Beautiful (Gilman), 235*n*4
Mann, Barbara E., 239*n*16
Mappings (Friedman), 167
Maps, 11, *12,* 13; in *Israel,* 171–72, *173, 174*

Marginalization, 34–35, 236*n*11
MariNaomi, 231*n*4
Marketing, 115–16
Marshall, Elizabeth, 156
Martens, Lorna, 121–22, 241*n*7
Materialism, 98
Maus series (Spiegelman), 30, 115
McCloud, Scott, 121, 233*n*15, 234*n*18; on
    sequential art, 11, 13, 234*n*19; on word-
    image combinations, 27–28
McDaniel, Nicole, 25
McGrath, Charles, 116, 240*n*3
Medium, 3, 30
"Meet the Band" (Lasko-Gross), 124
Memoir, 17, 80, 156, 243*n*17; graphic, 10, 19, 30
Memories, 231*n*2; of American Jewish
    women writers, 93; of birth, 126, 128;
    connection from, 223–24, 226–27, *227;*
    in *Escape from "Special,"* 126, 128–29,
    129; hungers from, 225–26; identity
    from, 221–22; notebook and, 225; in
    "Taxoplasmosis," 122–24, *123*
Men, *see* Jewish men; Non-Jewish men
Mess of Everything, A (Lasko-Gross), 117,
    120–21, 241*nn*5–6
MetaMaus (Spiegelman), 233*n*15
Meyers, Helene, 2
"Miami Makeover: (Almost) Anything for
    Beauty," 64
Mitchell, Claudia, 149
Mitchell, W. J. T., 73
"Moo Goo Gaipan" (Kominsky Crumb),
    57–59, *58*
Moore, Anne Elizabeth, 4
Moore, Deborah Dash, 107
Most, Andrea, 235*n*4
Motherhood, 57, 63–64
Mothers: challenge of, 21; in *Escape from
    "Special,"* 122, *123,* 125–26, *127,* 128; in
    jobnik!, 200, *201; see also* Jewish mothers
Movement, 41, 44

Naked Ladies! Naked Ladies! Coloring Book (Barry), 84

Names: of *A Bintel Brief*, 223; of Bunch, 46–47, 237n16; of "Kidnapped," 126, 127; Kominsky Crumb and, 60, 235n1

Narration, 75

Narrative comics, 67, 238n1

Narratives, 157–58; in *Israel*, 186–88, *187*; *see also* Graphic narratives; Travel narratives

Need More Love (Kominsky Crumb), 60–61, *62*, 236n11; categorization of, 35; collage in, 37; cover of, 35; excess in, 35–37; identity positions in, 24–25; images in, 26–27, 29, *31*, 31–35, *33*, *36*, 37, 236n7; photographs in, *31*, 31–36; structure of, 29, 236n7; word-image combination in, 28–29, 35; *see also* "Bunch Her Baby & Grammaw Blabette, The"; "Euro Dirty Laundry"; "Goldie: A Neurotic Woman"; "Moo Goo Gaipan"; "Nose Job"

Neel, Alice, 82, 239n11

Negativity, 37–38

Noah and the flood, 135, *136*, 137

Non-Jewish boyfriend, 109–12, *112*, 240nn22–23

Non-Jewish female (*shiksa*), 235n2

Non-Jewish men, 105–6, 109–13, *112*, 240nn22–23

Noomin, Diane, 236n5

North American Jews, 212, 215–16, 218

"Nose Job" (Kominsky Crumb): identity in, 1–2; placement of, 45; positions in, 49, 50–51; rebellion in, 1–2; "Saving Face" and, 51–52; *see also* Bunch

Noses: in *Girl Stories*, 159–62, *160*; Jewish identity and, 232n7; of Thomas, D., 237n15

Not the Israel My Parents Promised Me (Pekar), 168

Objectivity, 183–84

Objects, 122–24, 241n7

On Photography (Sontag), 29, 236n9

Opening image, 82, *83*, 101, *102*

Opposition, 49, 50–51

Outcasts, 147, *148*

Outsiders: disconnection as, 180–81; Jewish women cartoonists as, 17–18; *see also* Insider/outsider

Palestinians, 188–89, *189*, 195; Israelis and, 212, *214*, 215

Paley, Grace, 14–15

Paratext, 71, 238n5

Parents, 143, 163; *see also* Mothers

Past: of Bunch, 49, 49–50; Jewish identity related to, 21

Pekar, Harvey, 3, 168

Perception, 60

Performativity, 156–58, *157*

Persepolis (Satrapi), 156

Perspective, 14–15; in *jobnik!*, 196, 198, 244n18; in *Make Me a Woman*, 97, 99–100

Photographs, 233n14, 236n9; in *A Bintel Brief*, 228, 229, 245n7; in *jobnik!*, 197; of Kominsky Crumb, 29, *31*, 31–32; in *Need More Love*, *31*, 31–36; response to, 29–30

Photography: A Middle-Brow Art (Bourdieu), 34

Physical changes, 152–53

Picture This (Barry), 17

"Pillowtalk" (Davis, V. and Alixopulos), 240n23

Pipher, Mary, 117, 145

Placement, 45; *see also* Displacement

Plastic surgery, 51–52; *see also* "Nose Job"

Pollock, Griselda, 11

Portnoy's Complaint (Roth, P.), 101, *102*, 104

Positions, 24–25, 76, 77–78; in *Make Me a Woman*, 96, 96–97; in "Nose Job," 49, 50–51

Postassimilation, 3–4, 231n2

Postmemory, 231n2

Pratt, Norma Fain, 10, 234*n*16, 245*n*7

Prell, Riv-Ellen, 59, 101–3

"Preparation Information" (Davis, V.), 98–99

Pride, *49*, 51

Profile, *41*, 42–43

Promised Land, The (Antin), 221–22, 244*n*1, 244*n*3

Promise of Memory, The (Martens), 121–22

Propaganda, 181, *181*, 185

Psychological diagnosis, 202, *203*, 204

Puberty, *39*, 40–42

Punch magazine, 234*n*19

Queerness, 150–51

Quest, 148–49, 152

Quest for Jewish Belief and Identity in the Graphic Novel, The (Tabachnick), 234*n*21

Questioning, 100, 110

Rabin, Yitzhak, 199–200, *201*, 244*n*21

Racial middleness, 52

Racism, 219, 244*n*27

Rand, Erica, 150

Reading Autobiography (Smith and Watson), 134–35

Reading Comics (Wolk), 30

Real self, 29, *36*, 37

Rebellion: in *Escape from "Special,"* 134–35, 137; in "Nose Job," 1–2

"Recalling 'Home' from Beneath the Shadow of the Holocaust: American Jewish Women Writers of the New Wave" (Burstein), 93

Receptivity, *227*, 227–28

Reid-Walsh, Jacqueline, 149

"Re-Imagining the Jew's Body" (Most), 235*n*4

Reinventing Womanhood (Heilbrun), 5

Remembering, 223–27

Reorientation: of Bunch, 48–49, *49*, 61, *62*, 63; in *Make Me a Woman*, 88–89, 113

Repetition: in "The Bunch Her Baby & Grammaw Blabette," 61, *62*; of images, 31–32

Representation, 88; *see also* Self-representations

Research, 175, 243*n*9

Reviving Ophelia (Pipher), 117, 145

Rich, Adrienne, 8–9, 233*n*14

Risk-taking self-representation, 4

Robbins, Trina, 237*n*14

Rogers, Theresa, 156

Roiphe, Anne, 233*n*11

Rolling Blackouts (Glidden), 243*n*14

Romance, 154–56; *in jobnik!*, 206, *207*, 208

Ronnen, Meir, 237*n*20

Rosner, Victoria, 234*n*16

Roth, Henry, 6

Roth, Philip, 101, *102*, 104, 232*n*9

Rothman, Julia, 78

Royal, Derek Parker, 23

Russian Debutante's Handbook, The (Shteyngart), 231*n*3

Russo, Mary, 63

Sabbath, 179, 243*n*12

Sacco, Joe, 184, 196

Said, Edward, 167

Sandler, Adam, 103

Sapel, Dominique, 64

Sartre, Jean-Paul, 89

Satrapi, Marjane, 156

"Saving Face" (Crumb, R. and Kominsky Crumb), 51–52

Schilt, Kristen, 235*n*3

School, 141–43, *142*, 146–47; *see also* High school

Secularity, 178–80

Sedgwick, Eve Kosofsky, 164

Self, 29, *36*, 37; ambiguity of, 84, 86; in *Make Me a Woman*, 68–69, 114; *see also* Sense of self

Self-control, 57

Self-definition, 158–63, *159, 160*

Self-exile, 101, *102,* 104–5

Self-exploration, 64

Self-extension, 122–24

Self-fashioning, 160–61

Self-portrayal: in *Girl Stories,* 144, *145,* 147–48, *148,* 160–61; in *Israel, 181,* 181–83, *182*

"Self-Reflexive Graphic Narrative" (McDaniel), 25

Self-representations, 4; of Bunch, 26–28, 32–34, *33,* 48, 60–61; in *Escape from "Special,"* 138, *139*

"Self Visualization Activity" (Weinstein), 164, *165*

Sendak, Maurice, 115

Senderovich, Sasha, 231n3

Sense of self, 153–54; in "Goldie: A Neurotic Woman," 38, *39,* 40

Serial, 24–25

Sexuality: in *Girl Stories,* 153; in *jobnik!,* 205–7, *207*

Shiksa (non-Jewish female), 24, 235n2

Shneer, David, 20, 169–70

Shteyngart, Gary, 231n3

Similarities, 186–88, 190–92

"Situation, The," 181, *181,* 185, 188–89, *189*

Situation and the Story, The (Gornick), 65

Sketchbooks, 78

Smith, Sidonie, 26, 86, 134–35, 153

Social power, 130

Sollors, Werner, 44–45

Solomon, Alisa, 189–90, 192–93

Sontag, Susan, 29, 236n9

Sources: for *A Bintel Brief,* 222–23, 245n6; for Jewish women cartoonists, 18

Spaces: in "The Best We Can Hope For," 13–14; graphic narratives and, 10–11, 13–15; identity related to, 169; in Israel, 171–72, 173, 174–76, 183; in Jewish

American women's identity, 5–10; *see also* Davis, Vanessa; Time and space

Spaniel Rage (Davis, V.), 19, 68–69, 86, 238n3; audience for, 72–73, 238nn6–7; chronicling in, 75, *76,* 77; edits of, 71–72; images of, 73, *74, 75,* 238n8; juxtaposition within, *76,* 77–78; narration of, 75; structure of, 70–71, 78; unification from, 78–79

"Special," 133–34, 137–38

Speculations, 47, 48–50, *49*

Spiegelman, Art, 30, 90, 115, 233n15, 234n19

Star of David, 43–44

Stereotypes, 3–4, 101; communities and, 103–4; control of, 59–60; in "Euro Dirty Laundry," 55, 56–57; interethnicity in, 59; of Jewish bodies, 23, 59, 102–3; of Jewish mothers, 6–7, 60, *62,* 63–64, 113, 232n9; of Jewish women, 57–59, *58,* 102; Kominsky Crumb and, 18–19, 23–24; in *Make Me a Woman,* 103–6, *112,* 112–13

"Stranger in a Strange Land" (Davis, V.), 95–97, *96*

Strangers: A Long Distance View of Israel (Libicki), 211, 244n23; connection in, 218–20; home in, 219–20; racism in, 219, 244n27

Strömberg, Fredrik, 234n21

Structure: of diaries, 79–80; of *Escape from "Special,"* 120–21, 125–26; of *Girl Stories,* 141, 145; of *Israel,* 170–71, 242n4, 242n7; of *jobnik!,* 196–97, 210, 244n19; of *Make Me a Woman,* 89–90; of *Need More Love,* 29, 236n7; of *Spaniel Rage,* 70–71, 78

Styles: of *A Bintel Brief,* 222–23, 224, 245n4; in "Euro Dirty Laundry," 53–54; of "Goldie: A Neurotic Woman," 38; *see also* Drawing style

Subjectivity, 14–15, 196; in *Escape from "Special,"* 129–30; in *Israel,* 172, 174

"Sunny South of France, The" (Kominsky Crumb), 53
Superhero genre, 17–18
Symbols, 233n14; in *Escape from "Special,"* 135, *136*, 137; in "Goldie: A Neurotic Woman," 43–44
Synchronic diversity, 8, 19

Tabachnick, Stephen E., 234n21
"Talkin' 'bout my Generation" (Davis, V.), 240n17
Talking Back (Antler), 102
Tanenbaum, Leora, 239n4
"Taxoplasmosis: My Earliest Memory" (Lasko-Gross), 122–24, *123*
Teddy bear, 124
Temperament, 64–66
Thomas, Danny, 46, 237n15
Thomas, Marlo, 46, 47, 237n15
Three Guineas (Woolf), 8, 233n14
Time: in *Israel*, 175–76, 183; in *Make Me a Woman*, 92–93, 114
Time and space, 218–19; for cartoonists, 10–11, 233n15; in *jobnik!*, 197–200, 210
Towards a Hot Jew: The Israeli Soldier as Fetish Object (Libicki), 211–12, *213*, *214*, 215, 244nn24–25
Traditions, 5, 110–11; Sabbath, 179, 243n12
Transformation, 150–51
Transitions: in comics and age, 117–18; in *Escape from "Special,"* 124, 130–31
Translations: of Hebrew words, 198, *205*; from Yiddish, 223
Transnationalism: of home, 169–70, 218; of womanhood, 8–9
Travel narratives, 20; identity related to, 184–85; Jewish identity in, 169–70; *see also Israel; jobnik! an american girl's adventures in the israeli army*
Travel Writing (Blanton), 169

Tribal loyalties, 192–93
Trites, Roberta Seelinger, 130, 140
Troen, S. Ilan, 107
Truth: in *Escape from "Special,"* 126, 128–29, *129*; in *Israel*, 176, 178, 181, 188, 190, 192, 194, 215
Twisted Sisters 2: Drawing the Line, 236n5
Twisted Sisters: A Collection of Bad Girl Art, 236n5

Ulinich, Anya, 231n3
Unconsciousness, 122, *123*, 125
Underground comics, 237n12, 237n14
Understanding: from disconnection, *182*, 182–84; objectivity for, 183–84
Understanding Comics (McCloud), 233n15, 234n18
Unification, 78–79
Unterzakhn (Corman), 245n7

Visual subjectivity, 196

Waldman, J. T., 168
Watson, Julia, 26, 86, 134–35
Weinstein, Lauren, 10; "The Best We Can Hope For," 11, *12*, 13–15, 234n18; *Inside Vineyland* by, 164, *165*, 241n14; *see also Girl Stories*
Willis, Ellen, 243n16
Wimmin's Comix, 38, 237n14
Wolk, Douglas, 30
Womanhood, 8–9
Women cartoonists, 15–18, 234n21
Women's autobiographies, 26
Woolf, Virginia, 8, 233n14
Word-image combinations, 35; ambiguity from, 28–29; categories of, 27–28, 236n8
World of Our Fathers (Howe), 232n7

Wrestling with Zion (Kushner and Solomon), 189–90

"Writing Back: Rereading Adolescent Girlhoods Through Women's Memoir" (Marshall and Rogers), 156

Yahrzeit (death anniversary), 244n21
Yezierska, Anzia, 225–26

Yiddish, 223, 224
Yiddishisms, 23
Yiddishkeit, 234n21
You Don't Mess with the Zohan (film), 103

Zionism, 7, 168

GENDER AND CULTURE

A SERIES OF COLUMBIA UNIVERSITY PRESS

Gender and the Politics of History
Joan Wallach Scott

The Dialogic and Difference: "An/Other Woman" in Virginia Woolf and Christa Wolf
Anne Herrmann

Plotting Women: Gender and Representation in Mexico
Jean Franco

Inspiriting Influences: Tradition, Revision, and Afro-American Women's Novels
Michael Awkward

Hamlet's Mother and Other Women
Carolyn G. Heilbrun

Rape and Representation
Edited by Lynn A. Higgins and Brenda R. Silver

Shifting Scenes: Interviews on Women, Writing, and Politics in Post-68 France
Edited by Alice A. Jardine and Anne M. Menke

Tender Geographies: Women and the Origins of the Novel in France
Joan DeJean

Unbecoming Women: British Women Writers and the Novel of Development
Susan Fraiman

The Apparitional Lesbian: Female Homosexuality and Modern Culture
Terry Castle

George Sand and Idealism
Naomi Schor

Becoming a Heroine: Reading About Women in Novels
Rachel M. Brownstein

Nomadic Subjects: Embodiment and Sexual Difference in Contemporary Feminist Theory
Rosi Braidotti

Engaging with Irigaray: Feminist Philosophy and Modern European Thought
Edited by Carolyn Burke, Naomi Schor, and Margaret Whitford

Second Skins: The Body Narratives of Transsexuality
Jay Prosser

A Certain Age: Reflecting on Menopause
Edited by Joanna Goldsworthy

Mothers in Law: Feminist Theory and the Legal Regulation of Motherhood
Edited by Martha Albertson Fineman and Isabelle Karpin

Critical Condition: Feminism at the Turn of the Century
Susan Gubar

Feminist Consequences: Theory for the New Century
Edited by Elisabeth Bronfen and Misha Kavka

Simone de Beauvoir, Philosophy, and Feminism
Nancy Bauer

Pursuing Privacy in Cold War America
Deborah Nelson

But Enough About Me: Why We Read Other People's Lives
Nancy K. Miller

Palatable Poison: Critical Perspectives on The Well of Loneliness
Edited by Laura Doan and Jay Prosser

Cool Men and the Second Sex
Susan Fraiman

Modernism and the Architecture of Private Life
Victoria Rosner

Virginia Woolf and the Bloomsbury Avant-Garde: War, Civilization, Modernity
Christine Froula

The Scandal of Susan Sontag
Edited by Barbara Ching and Jennifer A. Wagner-Lawlor

Mad for Foucault: Rethinking the Foundations of Queer Theory
Lynne Huffer

Graphic Women: Life Narrative and Contemporary Comics
Hillary L. Chute

Gilbert and Sullivan: Gender, Genre, Parody
Carolyn Williams

Nomadic Subjects: Embodiment and Sexual Difference in Contemporary Feminist Theory, 2d ed.
Rosi Braidotti

Rites of Return: Diaspora Poetics and the Politics of Memory
Edited by Marianne Hirsch and Nancy K. Miller

Unlikely Collaboration: Gertrude Stein, Bernard Faÿ, and the Vichy Dilemma
Barbara Will

Nomadic Theory: The Portable Rosi Braidotti
Rosi Braidotti

The Global and the Intimate: Feminism in Our Time
Edited by Geraldine Pratt and Victoria Rosner

Gender and Culture Readers

Modern Feminisms: Political, Literary, Cultural
Edited by Maggie Humm

Feminism and Sexuality: A Reader
Edited by Stevi Jackson and Sue Scott

Writing on the Body: Female Embodiment and Feminist Theory
Edited by Katie Conboy, Nadia Medina, and Sarah Stanbury